POWER, CLASS
AND
FOREIGN CAPITAL
IN
EGYPT

POWER, CLASS
AND
FOREIGN CAPITAL
IN
EGYPT

The Rise of the New Bourgeoisie

Malak Zaalouk

Zed Books Ltd.
London and New Jersey

Power, Class and Foreign Capital in Egypt:
The Rise of the New Bourgeoisie was first published by
Zed Books Ltd., 57 Caledonian Road, London N1 9BU, UK and
171 First Avenue, Atlantic Highlands, New Jersey 07716, USA,
in 1989

Cover designed by Andrew Corbett
Typeset by EMS Photosetters, Rochford, Essex
Printed and bound in the United Kingdom at
The Bath Press, Avon

British Library Cataloguing in Publication Data

Zaalouk, Malak
Power, class and foreign capital in Egypt:
 the rise of the new bourgeoisie.
 1. Middle classes — Egypt — History
 I. Title
 305.5'5'0962   HT690.E3

 ISBN 0-86232-222-7
 ISBN 0-86232-223-5 Pbk

**Library of Congress Cataloging-in-
Publication Data**

Zaalouk, Malak
 Power, class and foreign capital in Egypt: the
 rise of the new bourgeoisie/Malak Zaalouk.
    p.   cm.
 Bibliography: p.
 Includes index.
 ISBN 0-86232-222-7.
 ISBN 0-86232-223-5 (pbk.)
 1. Businessmen–Egypt. 2. Entrepreneurship–
 Egypt. 3. Commercial agents–Egypt. 4.
 Corporations, Foreign–Egypt. 5. Middle
 class–Egypt. 6. Power (Social sciences)
 I. Title
 HC830.Z23 1989.
 305.5'54–dc19.

Contents

Acknowledgements

This book has come into being as a result of research for a doctoral dissertation at the University of Hull. I would, therefore, like to thank the University for giving me this opportunity. I would also like to thank greatly Talal Asad from the University of Hull, for supervising the original work, encouraging me, and giving me a lot of valuable advice. Many thanks also to his wife, Tanya Baker, for moral support.

I would like to single out two people for special thanks for having given me confidence, encouragement and advice and shown interest in my work: David Booth at the University of Hull, Department of Sociology and Social Anthropology, who also read parts of the preliminary draft; Mahmoud Abdel Fadil, Cairo University, who read parts of the later draft and who has been a constant source of encouragement and support at all stages of the present work. His contribution and concern have indeed been invaluable.

I can never thank enough all friends from many parts of the world who have given me so much moral support, encouragement and practical help, and who have made themselves available for discussion, all of which greatly enhanced my work. It would be impossible to mention all their names. I would, however, like to thank Enid Hill and Nader Fergany in this respect for reading and commenting upon parts of the finished thesis during the final rewrite. I would also like to thank Susan Edwards for practical help and encouragement.

Finally, I would like to thank Michael Pallis and Robert Molteno from Zed Books, for taking an interest in the work and giving valuable advice for the final rewrite and ways of making the original work more readable. Working with them has been a pleasure.

Last, but not least, I would like to thank my husband for putting up with my ups and downs and tolerating my moods during the final rewrite.

The imperfections of the work will remain my own responsibility.

Malak Zaalouk

Introduction

Egypt's development: patterns of continuity and change

Egypt's history, like that of many of the Third World countries, has been a long struggle for independent development. The struggle has been an arduous one with many obstacles to overcome. Despite its own specific development Egypt has manifested patterns of continuity within a framework of change. There have been many changes of direction in its internal development and its relations with the outside world, yet a number of trends have persisted since ancient times, and each historical stage of Egypt's political economy has borne the seeds of the following stage.

The struggle for independence has for the most part been a national bourgeois one, with the state taking the leading role. This struggle has not always been completely secular; frequently it has had religious overtones, with certain Islamic groups taking quite an active part.

Some date the beginnings of the national bourgeois movement in Egypt to the late 18th Century at the time of Ali Bey Kebir. Several industries had developed by then and an articulate guild system existed, along with a group of merchant capitalists. However, the influx of large numbers of foreign entrepreneurs and merchants gradually created a new foreign-run sector which pushed the traditional merchant capitalists to the background.[1]

This very embryonic bourgeois development was aborted by internal political instabilities in the period immediately preceding the reign of Mohamed Ali. These instabilities had made savings vulnerable and investment highly hazardous. Thus, when Mohamed Ali came to power, private enterprise could hardly be depended upon. For any economic progress to take place the state would have to take charge of productive activity. This it attempted to do, creating both a landed aristocracy and a bourgeois entrepreneurial class.

Unlike its European counterpart, the bourgeoisie of 19th-Century Egypt was created by the state. Its members consisted of state technocrats, administrators, clerks and army officers. It was mainly a bureaucratic bourgeoisie, state-dominated, largely dependent upon education rather than property, and to some extent patronized by foreign technicians, bankers and merchants. Mohamed Ali had embarked on a nationalist bourgeois movement with the state as its leader. He had aimed to prove to the world that Egypt was not necessarily predestined to remain an agrarian economy providing Western industry with raw materials. He had hoped to turn Egypt into a state-based industrial economy, and he had almost succeeded.[2] A small private sector still existed, run and financed by foreigners, but the major entrepreneur and employer of the nascent working class was the state public sector.

The relative success of the experiment and the promising industrial boom had greatly alarmed the West, while the Ottoman East had felt politically threatened by Mohamed Ali's expanding army. Thus in 1838 England managed to sign an economic treaty with Turkey which established an 'open-door economy' in all its empire, Egypt included. Mohamed Ali's new industries could no longer be protected. This national bourgeois phase finally came to an end when Mohamed Ali's armies were destroyed by the West and Turkey in 1840. The state had become weak and industry was on the decline. Thereafter, foreign technicians, banks and debts were the main features of the new dependent economy.[3]

From the middle of the 19th Century the West succeeded in maintaining Egypt as a dependent export economy. It is only with the 1919 revolution that a nationalist bourgeoisie once again emerged. Through state help, industry was once again protected and some capital was accumulated. The experience culminated in the Nasser regime, which appeared as the natural conclusion to the nationalist bourgeois movement aiming at Egyptianization of the economy.

Nasser's industrial and military ambitions, like those of Mohamed Ali, alarmed the West. His defeat came about militarily, and an open-door policy was internally and externally imposed. His regime was very definitely bourgeois-oriented. Capitalist development was state-directed and the entrepreneurial class was bureaucratic in nature. The regime, like its predecessors, was charismatic rather than democratic, and therefore it lacked a strong basis of popular support. Its working class was co-opted by the state; thus its source of internal political and social support was not sufficiently solid. Remnants of the old bourgeoisie still shared power, a bourgeoisie that had emerged out of the womb of the landed aristocracy and which grew through foreign capital and in very close connection to it.

Although Egypt has shared a number of objective structural conditions with the rest of the Third World, its historical development has maintained its specific character. Like many of the Third World peripheral countries, Egypt was historically an export-based economy which had been enmeshed quite early on in the capitalist world economy. The country was highly dependent upon cotton as a cash crop and the centrality of the state has played an enormous role in creating the various economic phases and interlinks with foreign capital. Egypt moreover is a country with a history of 5,000 years of state centralization. The overdevelopment of the state is thus possibly more pronounced than in most other Third World peripheral countries.[4]

The truly exclusive and specific nature of Egypt's historical development lies in the geopolitics of the country. Egypt is geographically highly strategic. During the traditional colonial phase Egypt was situated at the crossroads of the British Empire's interests in the East. It is often claimed that Egypt was occupied by the British in 1882 in order to safeguard its route to India.[5] Later, during the imperialist phase, Egypt became strategically important for safeguarding American interests in the Middle East. Petrol became a strategic commodity and during the *détente* phase between the East and the West, America's greatest worry became Russian and communist expansion. Egypt was viewed as being vital to the security of American interests.

In a famous speech, Carter's national security adviser Brezezinski analysed the unstable situation in the Middle East as follows:

> An arc of crises stretches along the shores of the Indian Ocean, with fragile social and political structures in a region of vital importance to us threatened with fragmentation. The resulting political chaos could well be filled by elements hostile to our values and sympathetic to our adversaries.

America's remedy for political chaos has been to pump excessive AID (Aid In Development) money into her Third World supporters in order to strengthen their economies, pacify their populations and stifle unrest. Thus, in 1982, Nicholas Veliotes, Assistant Secretary of State, is reported to have justified AID money received by American allies in the following fashion:

> The South-West Asian and Gulf region, a critical source of energy to the free world is simultaneously threatened by the Soviets through Afghanistan and radical forces from within the area. Therefore, our program is directed at supporting our efforts to bolster the security of countries both in the region and en route which are crucial for United States access to and presence in the region in times of crises.

Meanwhile a former Carter White House strategic analyst was quoted as having said:

> We have no alternative to Egypt either in terms of the peace process . . . or strategic position. If we could not get to the Gulf through Egypt, with overflights for example, we would be in very, very serious trouble.[6]

Egypt is strategically important by virtue of its location. It has in addition held a central position in liberation struggles. The 1919 revolution was the precursor of several nationalist independent movements, most significant of which was India's nationalist movement. Moreover the 1952 revolution triggered a number of liberation wars in Africa and the Arab World. During the 1950s and 1960s Nasser became extremely active on the Third World international scene.[7] He supported various independent movements, instigated liberation struggles and helped to establish the non-aligned movement, which still stands as a symbol of liberation and a third force in the world configuration of power.[8]

Egypt has in a sense been forced to play a significant role internationally because of its geographical position. Such has been its destiny. It has extensive borders with several other countries and the buffer zones protecting it from foreign invasion are vulnerable. Syria and Palestine were traditionally important buffer zones. Egypt's independence has depended upon the success of Arab nationalism. During the Nasser period this aspect of independence was greatly emphasized, often at the expense of internal development and internally instigated policies.[9]

All this has succeeded in making Egypt crucial for the imperialist nations. Egypt's energetic foreign policies during the 1950s and 1960s gave it a significant international position while also rendering it the target of the big Western powers. It has suffered some severe setbacks at the hands of foreign powers, especially America and its Middle Eastern ally Israel. Egypt is the key force in the Arab World; thus imperialist powers have been especially harsh on the country and have viciously aimed at destroying its economy when it ceased to serve their interests. Washington always saw Abdel Nasser as its major problem in the area. He had threatened American policies in many parts of the world: in the Yemen, in the Congo and in Vietnam. The American magazine, *The New Republic* (June 3, 1967), stated that the major problem in the area was the presence of Abdel Nasser and that the status quo in the Middle East was threatened, not merely by Arab socialism, but in particular by Nasser's Communist tendencies. It was therefore necessary to get rid of his regime.[10]

The political campaign against Egypt dates back to the Mohamed Ali era, and even slightly before. It now seems like a recurrent pattern. Every time Egypt appears to grow independently strong away from foreign intervention and support, it is given a debilitating blow which renders it very difficult for it to stand on its own two feet again without becoming an ally of the dominant force in the area. A number of significant years stand out as landmarks in the successive defeats faced by national bourgeois attempts to gain independence. The year 1840 marks the end of the Mohamed Ali experience; 1882 marks the end of the Orabi movement; and 1967 marks the end of the Nasserite experience; finally with the Israeli–Egyptian peace in 1977, we have the beginning of a new phase whereby the alliance and collaboration between Egypt and the West become firmly established.

Because of Egypt's special political position and geographical location, the antagonism of the West has been magnified in times of dissent. Western obstructive measures have often prevented the growth of a truly independent economy. Industry was not allowed to flourish and expand, and most productive activities were not allowed to increase. All of this has led to the development of a special kind of political economy.

Egypt's current political economy

In many ways Egypt today presents a typical example of a *rentier* economy. It sustains its economy from sources outside its own productive capacity, being almost totally dependent upon remittances from Egyptians working abroad, the exportation of petroleum, revenues from the Suez Canal, and tourism.[11]

Most productive sectors of the economy are at present stagnating. This is especially true of industry, whilst agricultural production is extremely slow-paced and totally unable to meet the country's food requirements.

The 1970s mark a revolution in the country's economic profile. The symptoms of the country's economic crises are fairly widespread. They range from an acute housing problem, to inflation, price increases, balance of trade and balance of payment deficits, labour shortages, generally low income levels (while the incomes of a minority of the population are disproportionately high), and outmoded and inefficient transport, sewage and sanitation services. Excessive consumerism has become a far reaching socio-economic ill, while government subsidies have become distorted and inefficient, not reaching the rightful recipients. Moreover the country's economy has become almost dual, with a foreign-run modern sector and a traditional one. Discrepancies in incomes generated by both sectors are shockingly large.[12] The public sector, once Egypt's major pillar of planned economic development, still overwhelms the economy in size and magnitude, but its effectiveness is slowly shrinking.[13]

Government planning and supervision also decreased during the 1970s, while corruption and parasitical activity have been gnawing at the economy and society as a whole. The amount and scope of illegal financial activity is alarming. It ranges from drug peddling, to tax evasion, illegal currency transfers, embezzlement and bribery.[14] It has been estimated that the proceeds of this 'black economy' make up between 15 and 30 per cent of the gross national product.[15]

Egypt has indeed become a country ridden with problems, and it is one of the rare Third World countries whose problems and symptoms of under-development are increasing. Foreign intervention and inherited structures have severely distorted the form of development. Even a dependent type of development, like that of Brazil, has become difficult to achieve.

Loans are a major source of capital input in the country's development. Consequently Egypt has become one of the most heavily indebted states in the Third World. Its economy has in fact become totally dependent upon loans. Recent estimates of Egypt's debt have ranged from US$19 to US$31 billion.[16] Even servicing the debt is far more than the economy can afford.

In the new phase which began in the 1970s, Egypt has made a complete U-turn in its political orientation. It has once again turned completely towards the West for assistance, but now it is America instead of Europe who is shoring up the economy. Over the past decade Egypt has become the world's second-largest recipient of United States AID money – the largest being Israel. Moreover America appears as Egypt's largest single creditor. In 1983 Egypt had outstanding debts to the United States of US$8 billion. Debt servicing absorbs about 30–35 per cent of current earnings or about 20 per cent of export receipts.[17] America's concern to pump aid into Egypt is closely related to the country's strategic importance and geopolitics.[18]

AID is also a very significant tool for the reshaping of the country's political economy.[19] The contradiction between the existing modes of production, i.e. the Western-financed and supported free enterprise and planned economic sectors, has allowed for the spread of corruption. It has also encouraged the spread of non-productive parasitical activity, all of which has been highly beneficial for certain classes in society who have succeeded in accumulating huge amounts of wealth. A member of the People's Assembly has estimated that today in Egypt we have about a quarter of a million millionaires, who have made their money through the ownership of large buildings, import and export, transport cars, supermarkets and shoe shops, car dealing, commercial representation and mediation, gold dealings, film, video and cassette production, ownership of casinos, hotels and night clubs, contracting activity in the housing sector, foreign currency exchange, drug peddling, price increases of land and real estate speculation.[20]

Egypt's new social classes

Through loans, the Western nations and America in particular have greatly encouraged and supported the creation of new classes in Egypt with whom they have close ties and shared interests. The new classes are highly parasitical. They serve foreign interests; they are largely unproductive; they indulge in lavish consumerism; they accumulate wealth that is easily transferable abroad; and they have no interest in the country's development – being in fact totally insensitive to its socio-economic problems.[21]

In addition these classes have access to the state apparatus and are exceedingly influential politically. This is particularly true of one group – namely, commercial agents representing foreign firms. In the next few paragraphs a specific case of political decision-making will serve to reveal the new power structure and ruling alliance. It will also serve to show the kinds of secondary social conflict existing in the power structure. Commercial agents are of course not the monopolizers of state power. Members of other classes and class fractions are also represented in the Egyptian state apparatus. They too participate in state power and seek to promote their own interests. The result is the condensation and embodiment of class conflict within the state. Such conflicts are especially acute in transitional phases, when the whole social formation is undergoing fundamental changes. In the case of Egypt, the previously dominant state capitalist mode of production is being gradually replaced by a new mode of production giving rise to new classes and class fractions striving for political dominance.

The political struggle

On March 23, 1977, the public sector Bank Misr requested a permit from the General Investment Authority to set up a complete industrial textile complex for cotton, spinning and weaving, knitting, manufacture of ready-made clothes, the production of synthetic fibres and cloth (both woollen and cotton), the production of synthetic blankets as well as all other synthetic material required for the local clothing industries. Half the project's output would be geared towards local consumption and manufacture. The complex was to produce 115,000 tons of cotton weave, 400 million tons of spun cotton, 100 million tons of knitted wool and blankets, 53,000 tons of synthetic fibres and 14 million units of ready-made clothes, in three stages of production. Total annual output would thus equal a little over half of Egypt's total output in textiles for 1977 and the estimated total national output for the 1978–82 five-year plan in textiles combined.

The total cost of the project was £E530 million, constituting one of the largest, if not *the* largest, such project in the world, at a little over double the size of the sum of local textile complexes. Bank Misr was to be the major source of financing. The bank proposed to provide the project with a loan of US$800 million in foreign currencies and US$300 million in local currency, all repayable in the same currencies and by equal annual instalments starting from the fifth year of production. The project, which was to be located 22 km from Alexandria in Amereya and composed of some 23 factories, proposed to employ between 37,000 and 38,000 workers all of whom could be selected from among the Egyptian youth who had had some degree of formal education and/or technical training.

In addition to £E3.2 million of the founding capital, foreign participation in the project essentially consisted of imported technology, technical know-how, feasibility studies and equipment. Based on the feasibility study prepared by the Swiss 'Jersey' corporation in August 1976, Bank Misr had obtained formal permission from the Ministry of Planning and the General Authority for Investment to go ahead with the project.

Ever since the initial presentation of the project, towards the end of 1976, and the securing of formal permission in 1977, a large opposition campaign, led by the General Industrial Organization, the Misr Company for Synthetic Silk, and the Ministry of Industry, was mounted on the grounds that the establishment of this new textile complex would do considerable damage to the national economy.[22] The project, which had not been included in the 1978/82 five-year plan, would cause an annual deficit of £E26 million. The project was a duplication of already existing and successful textile industrial projects as well as other public sector textile projects which were being renovated. The project would also deprive other, more useful, private sector projects of funds.

The Ministry of Industry in its capacity as the technical authority most knowledgeable and most directly concerned, felt a special responsibility for ensuring that the campaign take on more than verbal dimensions. Thus the Minister of Industry created a special committee for the preparation of a detailed study and report on the project. In June 1978 the very lengthy report was completed and a week later sent to the Minister of Planning along with a letter attached asking that the project be suspended until it was re-evaluated with the help of the accompanying report and studies, as well as discussions involving all the economic sectors concerned with national development and planning. The Ministry of Industry, whose opinion had not been sought before the project had been authorized, condemned it after presenting detailed statistical data and feasibility studies. The complex, according to the Ministry of Industry report, was both unnecessary and harmful to the national economy.[23] The Ministry of Planning as well as officials in the Misr Bank (who supported the project) then prepared reports and studies in reply to the Ministry of Industry's report.[24]

In September 1978 the President of the People's Assembly asked the Planning and Budget Committee, the Economic Committee, and the Industrial Committee and the Mobilization Committee within the Assembly to hold a joint meeting for the investigation of the project with the aim of evaluating its economic feasibility and adequacy. The three committees proceeded to create a specialized committee for the tasks while the latter invited a number of local experts to give their opinion and cooperate in the study. Meanwhile the debate between the ministries, other members of the Assembly and invited experts continued and was the subject of public attention as the proceedings were being regularly reported in the daily press.[25]

During the debate a number of very important facts emerged: the initiators of the project were asked why the decision to undertake such a massive project had been so rapidly made compared to the normal pace of decision-making, and without informing the Ministry of Industry, also why the supply of equipment and technical 'know how' was secured through direct and bilateral unpublished contracts and not through public tendering.

After about eight lengthy meetings, discussions, and the presentation of reports and studies, the specialized committee produced a final report and recommendations regarding the Amereya project. The report, which in the final analysis supported the project, concentrated essentially on its relevance and impact on the national economy and not on matters concerned with the adequacy of its management and administration. In addition the committee produced a number of recommendations regarding the government's rights to supervise such projects, the proper and necessary procedure for the acquisition of permits, and finally the relevance of such projects to Egypt's new economic policies and development plans. The committee's recommendations were to serve as a model for all similar 'open door' investment projects, as well as general government economic planning in the domain of textiles. They also gave valuable guidelines as to the degree of coordination required between the various economic sectors concerned.[26]

Two articles published in the weekly *Rose El Youssef*, one of which was prepared by the administrative board of the Spinning and Weaving Workers' Syndicate, criticize the Amereya committee's account of the methods employed for the purchase of equipment and raw materials. They claim the account was incomplete and that the story of commissions, and of the decision-making process involved in the project, was far more complex than the report and General Assembly meetings revealed. The first article is based on the discovery of an informal report prepared by the Minister of Economy for a 'higher authority'. The author of the article, who had personal access to the document, felt it was a national duty to report its contents. The report was essentially concerned with five commercial agents who had received excessive commissions for the supply of goods to the project. Supposedly, among the five names was that of the son of the project's counsellor and supervisor. He had effectuated six contracts with supplying firms and had received a total of

12,300,000 Swiss francs for four of the contracts and 700,000 Deutschmarks for the remaining two. Another name was that of a former minister and member of the People's Assembly who had received 500,000 United States dollars for a single contract worth 343,400 Kuwaiti dinars. The remaining three names listed had received the following commissions:

1. 3.7 million DM, for a single contract worth 8.2 million DM.
2. 4.10 million Swiss francs for a single contract worth 83.5 million Swiss francs.
3. 400,000 Swiss francs for a single contract worth 7.9 million DM.

According to the article, all the various contracts for the supply of goods had been effected before or shortly after the investment authority studied and allowed the implementation of the project, while the supply of goods, new contracts and payment of the purchases continued even after the investment authority had suspended the project and right through until the completion of the General Assembly discussions and study, which indicates that the contractors and founders of the project were quite confident that the project would be accepted despite all the drawbacks pointed out by national and international experts and in various feasibility studies. Furthermore, members of the project's administration had effected a number of additional contracts for the purchase of equipment and materials that were to go towards the establishment of two of the project's companies which had not yet been founded at the time the report was written.

Meanwhile the public sector Bank Misr, which was the major financer of the project, since the American partner only participated nominally in the original capital, had proceeded to pay for all the imported goods in advance, thus ignoring even the most elementary rules of good banking; namely that it could have employed the funds paid in advance in other investment projects had it obtained credit facilities. It must be remembered that the money disbursed was, after all, public money. Another discovery made by the report was the fact that the American partner had sold material and equipment to the new project at double the price at which these very same goods, produced by the same firms, had been purchased the previous year by the public sector Misr Company for Synthetic Silk.

Despite all this, the investment authority had very hastily accepted the project (within four days) and forged the approval of the director of the General Industrial Organ (as was later discovered during the assembly sessions and report of the Minister of Industry). When all this became public, the investment authority was obliged to revise its report on the Industrial Organ's acceptance and opinion. What the content of the report highlighted, according to the author of the article, was that there was a whole network of politically well-connected receivers of commissions behind the decision to accept the Amereya project and to ignore the criticism and opposition of a number of international experts, financing organizations and world-famous technical firms who had been invited to comment by the Ministry of Industry.[27]

The second article, prepared by the Spinning and Weaving Workers'

Syndicate, essentially moved in the same direction as the first, namely questioning the 'why' and 'how' of the decision to accept the project while highlighting various irregular procedures that had been discovered, such as the fact that the project was included in the five-year plan. According to the Minister of Planning, who made this admission during the preliminary meetings of the Plan and Budget Committee in the General Assembly, the project had not been included in the five-year plan. Meanwhile the Ministry of Industry clearly demonstrated that the five-year plan did not account for the new project. Added to that was the fact that neither the Minister of Industry, the Minister of Planning nor the General Industrial Organ had been advised or consulted about the project despite its size (estimated to be equal to the cost of the High Dam) and its impact on the entire national economy.[28]

Although no clear indictment has been made accusing the officials involved in the final decision-making, the following points clearly emerge:

1. Very serious objections were raised against the project and its impact on local industry and the economy at large.

2. The procedures followed were not in order.

3. The General Assembly committee very clearly limited itself to the discussion of the feasibility of the project.

4. Not all relevant information was discovered during the General Assembly meetings.

5. The General Investment Authority had been very eager to get the project through to the extent of forging official documents and papers.

6. A number of businessmen, among whom were a former minister and the supervisor in charge and counsellor of the project, had, according to the Minister of Economy's report, received large commissions for the erection and supply of equipment. There had been no public tender despite the fact that Bank Misr was the major financer. In addition there had been a number of legal irregularities such as imports under the name of non-existent companies.

Despite all this the General Assembly specialized committee recommended that the project be resumed. The Chamber of Commerce as well as other business associations were directly or indirectly represented in the Committee and were instrumental in the final outcome of decision-making.

The Amereya case reported above was a case of struggle and conflict between:

1. fractions of the modernizing bourgeoisie, composed of Bank Misr, foreign investors and commercial agents, all members of the new power structure and the newly formed alliances between the state sector bureaucrats of Bank Misr, foreign capital and the new parasitical classes;

2. state national industrial capital as represented by the Misr company for synthetic silk, the Ministry of Industry and the general industrial organization in alliance with:

3. private capital as represented by the Federation of Egyptian Industry and private textile entrepreneurs.[29] and finally,

4. workers, as represented by the Spinning and Weaving Workers' Syndicate.

The outcome of the struggle is extremely significant in terms of political power and class dominance. Despite the very serious objections presented by the opposition, the state institutions approved the project, and fractions of the new ascending 'modernizing' bourgeoisie emerged as the victors in the struggle, while the alliance between national industrial capital (both private and public) and workers lost.

The political power enjoyed by such compradorial groups has some very important implications with regard to the 'relative' autonomy of the state, its permeability to foreign influence, and the relationship of the local state to the states in Western capitalism. In the Amereya case, state autonomy was fairly weak and corruption and parasitical activity were correspondingly pervasive.

Parasitical activity, according to a number of observers and economic analysts, is extremely widespread throughout a number of different sectors of the economy. It is, however, important to differentiate between large and influential parasitical groups who dominate the political and economic institutions and serve as the interlink between local and international capital, and those groups who practise various other forms of parasitical activity but are not politically and economically influential.[30]

Commercial agents representing foreign companies have on numerous occasions, whether in alliance with foreign capital or singly, exerted pressure on the government and have succeeded in influencing the outcome of decision-making both regarding legislation and government resource allocation. The access of this group to state power is an important element in the enhancement of foreign Western capitalist interests, both as exporters of commodities and future investors. To enable Egypt to play its role as a strategic asset and a potential economic one, Americans have aligned themselves with and supported the rising classes of the Sadat regime. Both the 'open door' policy launched by Sadat in 1974 and American AID have served to create and strengthen new socio-economically and politically powerful groups. The economic interests of these classes and Western capital are identical. The United States would like to market its goods in Egypt in preparation for further investment whilst the new class of traders and commercial agents are the axis around which such policies can be made possible.[31]

Moreover this group's increasing political power is indicative of the relationship of Western capitalism to the new Egyptian socio-economic structure and has widespread implications for the country's development. After all, 'class formations and the subsequent weighting of different classes will give shape and substance to development as development will, in one form or another, shape the emerging class structure.'[32]

The present work is a detailed study of a group of businessmen in Egypt – namely commercial agents of foreign firms, whose numbers have greatly increased in recent years, and who have been largely associated with Sadat's open door economic policy. The activity of the group under study is of particular importance for two reasons. First, it is one of the major activities that has been allowed the private sector under the Presidential Decree number 1906 (1974), which stipulated that foreign companies wishing to export their products to the

Egyptian market could only do so through the mediation of Egyptian private sector agents. Secondly, during the early stages of the open door economic policy, the activity was numerically the largest and most significant of all private sector business enterprises.[33]

Based on in-depth interviews and case studies of owners of the leading commercial agency firms, this book presents an analysis of the emergence, continuity and consolidation of commercial agents as a dominant class fraction within a newly ascending bourgeoisie in contemporary Egypt, their position in the new socio-economic structure and their role in the country's development. The book will address itself to a number of significant questions, such as: the social origins of the new class fraction; how and why the new class fraction came to power; how the transformation from a proclaimed radical socialist regime to a conservative one responding to the interests of private capital occurred and, finally, why a form of associated dependent development, let alone an independent form of development, did not take place under the Sadat regime.

Although no definitive answers will be provided, this book is a modest attempt at reaching a clearer understanding of the Egyptian social formation and the predominant mode of production. In order to obtain a more holistic and complete picture many more detailed studies of the same nature and on different classes and class fractions need to be carried out.

The book is divided into two major parts. The first part is basically historical, since it is this author's very strong belief that it is well-nigh impossible to comprehend Egypt's current crisis situation without a clear understanding of the evolution of its political economy. Moreover the periodization of the historical parts of the book will be made according to structural transformation rather than changes in leadership. The second part deals with the contemporary situation.

Notes

1. Samir Amin, 'Some Thoughts on the Nature of Capitalism in Egypt' in *Al Taliah*, June 1985, pp. 96–118, and Louis Awad, *The History of Egyptian Thought: From the Period of Ismail till the 1919 Revolution*, Part 1, pp. 338–64.
2. Ibid.
3. Awad, p. 345.
4. Ismail Sabri Abdallah, 'The Round Table Discussion on the Nature of Power in Egypt', *Qadaya Fikriya*, July 1985, p. 187.
5. Awad, p. 288.
6. Joost Hiltermann, 'Egypt and America, an Uneasy Embrace', *The Middle East*, no. 131, September 1985, pp. 49, 50.
7. Gamal Hamdan, *The Strategy of Imperialism and Liberation*, pp. 234–5, 343–72.
8. Ibid., and Ali El Din Hilal, 'National Independence as Strategic Premiss for the 1952 Revolution', pp. 16–33, in Ali El Din Hilal (ed.), *National Independence* (Cairo 1982).
9. Ahmed Youssef Ahmed, 'The Arab Policy of the July Revolution and the Formula of Priority Setting: Independence versus Social Revolution', pp. 110–30.

10. Mostafa Al Alwi, 'International Behaviour from the Viewpoint of National Independence', pp. 198–219.

11. Mahmoud Abdel Fadil, *Reflections upon the Economic Matter in Egypt*, pp. 48–58.

12. Adel Hussein, *The Egyptian Economy from Independence to Dependency, 1974–1979*, Part 1, p. 310.

13. Abdel Fadil, pp. 94–6.

14. Mahmoud Abdel Fadil, 'Mesures et composants de "l'économie cachée" et mouvements des capitaux noirs dans l'économie Égyptienne, 1974–84, dans le cadre d'un système développé de comptabilization nationale', pp. 133–68, in *L'Egypte Contemporaine*, April 1985.

15. Ibid., p. 166.

16. Gamal Hamdan, *Egypt's Personality: A Study in the Genius of its Location*, p. 56, and Midhat Hassanein, 'Our Foreign Debt – What is the Reality?', in *Al Ahram al-Iqtissadi*, no. 870, September 1985, pp. 15–17.

17. Hiltermann, p. 52.

18. Ibid., pp. 49, 50.

19. Ibid.

20. Gamal Sharqawi, 'A Preliminary Investigation on the Issue of Millionaires', *Qadaya Fikriya* no. 1, July 1985, pp. 89–92.

21. For a discussion of the concept of parasitical activity and parasitical classes, see Mahmoud Abdel Fadil, 'Critical Comments around the Concept of a Parasitical Capitalist Class in the Egyptian Context', *Al-Taliah* January–March 1985, no. 1, pp. 115–20, and Ibrahim Saad El Din, 'Parasitical Capitalism – is it the Essence of the Economic System in the Analyses of the Left in Egypt?', *Ibid.*, pp. 127–7.

22. Engineer Ibrahim Mahmoud Sharkas (Vice-President of the General Industrial Organization), 'The Amereya Project and the Dangerous Effects upon the Egyptian Economy', pp. 6–11. The report was published with the permission and cooperation of the author and was the same study presented to the committee concerned within the People's Assembly during the public debate from September 1978 to March 1979.

23. *Al Ahram al Iqtissadi*, no. 557, November 1, 1978, 'What is Happening in Al Amereya?' The *Ahram Iqtissadi* presents a complete file on the case, pp. 4–16.

24. Ibid.

25. See *Al Akhbar*: September 2, 1978, p. 3; October 15, 1978, p. 3; October 21, 1978, pp. 3, 5; October 22, 1978, pp. 3, 4; October 24, 1978, p. 4; October 29, 1978, p. 4. See also *Al Ahram*: October 16, 1978, p. 6; October 22, 1978, p. 6; October 23, 1978, p. 6; October 24, 1978, p. 6.

26. *Al Ahram al Iqtissadi*, no. 564, February 15, 1979, 'The Amereya Battle in the People's Assembly, a Full Report of the Specialised Committee's Report', pp. 8–14.

27. Shafiq Ahmed Ali, 'Top Secret, Those who Received Commissions for al-Amereya', *Rose El Youssef* no. 2641, January 22, 1949, pp. 20–3.

28. The Administrative Board of the General Spinning and Weaving Workers' Syndicate, 'The Truth and Scandals behind the 1,300 Million Dollar Project', pp. 12–15.

29. Although the views of the syndicate and private textile entrepreneurs were not specially referred to in the above example, through an interview with the general director of the federation of the Egyptian industries on 2 January,

1981 it was discovered that the syndicate had been represented in the People's Assembly committee and had vehemently opposed the Amereya project.

30. Ibrahim Saad El Din, p. 124.

31. Hiltermann, p. 50.

32. James Petras, 'Class and Politics in the Periphery and the Transition to Socialism', *Review of Radical Political Economies*, 8 (2), p. 21.

33. According to the Ministry of Trade Department of Companies and Statistical Supervision, the total number of registered private sector companies up to the end of 1977 was 335. These include companies involved in trade, industry, agriculture, contracting, pharmaceuticals. For that same year companies registered as commercial agents were in the order of 764.

Part 1
A Historical Sketch of Socio-economic Changes

1 The Egyptianization of the Economy: The Emergence of a Local Bourgeoisie from the World War Two Period to the Early Nasser Phase (1937–56)

For the purpose of the present work, which is concerned with the study of one section of the bourgeoisie, namely the foreign company commercial agents in their contemporary setting and the historical antecedents that gave rise to them, the 1930s appear to be a suitable historical point of departure for several reasons. It is during this period that Egypt witnessed the accelerated development of its national, industrial, financial, commercial and business bourgeoisie. Several factors, both national and international, had combined together to give Egyptian industrialists and businessmen a real impetus. It was also during the 1930s, with increased industrialization and government involvement in development plans, that local agents of foreign companies emerged, although commercial representation was still mostly carried out by foreign nationals.[1]

On the international scene the outbreak of the war had temporarily interrupted the flow of foreign imports into Egypt, thus encouraging it to launch its own industrial campaign in order to provide substitutes for the missing commodities. Hence from the late 1930s up until 1952 industrial development scored quite impressive figures.[2]

On the national level, other developments in the form of general commercial policies were being introduced in order to protect the nascent national industries. Thus the first tariff protective law since Mohamed Ali's time was promulgated in 1930 in order to control the traditional free trade policy. Duties ranging from 15 per cent to 20 per cent were imposed on consumer goods that competed with local products. The tariff charges continued to increase progressively throughout the decade beginning with 1930, and were thus able to protect and enhance local industries. By 1947 the protection afforded to local industry was, according to Dr El Gritly, as quoted by O'Brien, prohibitive to foreign competitors.[3]

The Egyptian entrepreneur was also being encouraged to develop industrially by the various political policies adopted by the state to Egyptianize the economy generally, and joint stock companies in particular. In 1937 an important step was taken in that direction when on 8 May the capitulations were abolished.[4] The call for the formation of a national bourgeoisie was of course a much earlier development.[5]

In 1920 after a long formative history Bank Misr was established. This constituted a landmark for the emergence of a small and still undeveloped local bourgeoisie.[6] The *raison d'être* of the bank and its major policy lines had been the Egyptianization of the economy. The bank, with its policies designed to create a national bourgeoisie, was frowned upon by the British authorities as well as other foreign elements and their local allies who had a vested interest in obstructing such a development.[7]

The bank had pioneered the call for Egyptianizing joint stock companies. It encouraged nationals to step into the economic institutions of their country: to establish chambers of commerce, syndicates, and industrial and commercial companies. In the report of the administrative board to the General Assembly a month and a half after the establishment of the bank, there was a very strong appeal to the Egyptian legislator to issue laws that would effectively nationalize the economy by Egyptianizing existing companies.[8] The nationalistic movement born out of the 1919 revolution and the Harb experience later constituted a very real pressure upon the government to Egyptianize economic institutions. This lengthy process culminated with the nationalization of the Suez Canal.

Highly indicative of the impact of this general movement towards Egyptianization is that in 1948 the percentage of share and bond capital subscribed to by Egyptians had increased to 39 per cent of the total as opposed to nine per cent in 1933. In the years that followed the post-war period, a substantial amount of share and bond capital originally subscribed to by foreigners had in addition changed hands to Egyptians.[9] Furthermore, between 1946 and 1948, 84 per cent of the companies were founded by Egyptians.[10]

Despite all these developments in economic nationalism, and despite the fact that foreign economic monopoly was indeed curtailed, particularly in the field of industry, one must not jump to the conclusion that foreign influence had totally disappeared. Issawi points out that foreign control was still widespread during that period. However, the term 'foreigners', as used by Issawi, not only designated the European community proper, but also the Jewish, Armenian and Levantine communities, whose members constituted 37 per cent of the company directors in 1951, over and above the 30 per cent European directors.[11]

Berque also points out that a proper evaluation of foreign capital's retreat is rather complicated, since foreign capital thrived in the hands of local agencies. The true nationality of such companies as the Khedival Line directed by Abboud had been brought into question in 1938. Nevertheless the fact remains that due to the 1930 protective legislation there was an increase in Egyptian capital as well as an increase in the number of Egyptian employees in the various companies; 75 per cent of the employers and 90 per cent of the workers were Egyptian, in addition to a progressive increase in the number of administrators and directors.[12] This last fact alone no doubt greatly enhanced the rise of a national bourgeoisie, who were now able to acquire the expertise and managerial skills required. In fact Egyptian entrepreneurs were being introduced to areas of economic activity which had been unknown to them.

The traditional pattern of investment had been in land and real estate.[13]

This then brings us to another set of factors further enhancing the rise of a national bourgeoisie. During the World War Two period, traditional outlets of investment had been partly abandoned. This was not totally a matter of choice. Although it is true that Egyptian entrepreneurs were becoming increasingly conscious of profits made by foreigners through business and were therefore willing to follow their example, two factors played a key role in this shift of interest: during the inter-war period and up until the 1930s, at the time of the Great Depression, international demand for primary exports shrank greatly, causing a marked slump in prices of raw cotton, Egypt's major cash crop. It therefore became clear to Egyptian landowners (some of whom were policy-makers) that agriculture was no longer very remunerative, and that they would have to diversify their investment.[14] Meanwhile, during the same period, the government had issued several restrictions on the prices of food and agricultural commodities. The prices of industrial goods were, however, totally unrestricted.[15] Secondly, some restrictions were also imposed on housing, the second traditional outlet for capital investment. During the war period a ceiling had been set upon the rent of apartment houses.[16] It is also likely that the decrease in foreign residents at the time[17] may have caused a shortage of demand for high-rent accommodation. Wealthy Egyptians were here again encouraged to step into different areas of economic activity. The available statistics on patterns of investment at the time show that the position of land and real estate was declining.[18]

A final point should be made in relation to investment, namely that due to the war a marked decline in consumption had occurred which gave rise to what most economists have called a situation of forced saving. Issawi points out that according to Anis, savings had increased from £E8 million, or just under five per cent of the national income, in 1939, to £E76 million, or 23 per cent, in 1942, and reached a peak of £E132 million, or 29 per cent, in 1944.[19] It is therefore clear that on the eve of World War Two, and during the subsequent years, several important factors had combined to give the emerging national bourgeoisie a real boost: the interruption of foreign imports; the protection of national industries through trade regulations; the Egyptianization policies adopted by the state; the decline in consumption thus giving rise to a situation of forced saving; and the declining value and attraction of the traditional outlets of investment such as agriculture and housing.

Parallel to the emergence of a national bourgeoisie, Egypt witnessed its industrial revolution during the inter-war and post-war periods, so that one had both a relative increase in local bourgeois activity as well as an absolute increase in total industrial and commercial output, both of which gradually expanded the scope of activity for commercial representation. At first the activity was exclusively conducted by foreigners; later, however, it was gradually undertaken by Egyptians. Meanwhile the overall socio-economic structure appeared to be unchanging, with both the foreign capitalists and their local counterparts taking on a leading role.

Economic developments

Salient features of Egyptian industry: 1937–1956

The war period and the first years immediately following were prosperous times for industry even though some signs of decline had begun to emerge by 1943. During the Korean War (1950–1), when Egyptian cotton prices increased, accompanied by an increase in internal purchasing power and a diminution in foreign competition, local industries prospered once again.[20] What has been called the 'Korean Boom' was, however, short-lived. By 1952–3 there were important signs of decline in output growth and investment activity. The decline has been explained as a function of the deep political crisis at the time, which included labour and student unrest. Furthermore, it appears that while the Korean boom had increased purchasing power, industrial investment did not benefit to a corresponding extent. Landowners and merchants had increased their investments in land and middle-class houses, while import and consumption of foreign goods also increased markedly.[21] It was only in 1954 that signs of output growth emerged once again. In 1955 a United Nations study confirmed the progress made by Egyptian industry and testified that a number of vital industries, such as fertilizers, cement and food-processing had advanced sufficiently to be able to dispense with tariff protection.[22] It should be mentioned that the year 1954 was a turning point for industrial output, due to the fact that during the preceding years there had been substantial re-equipment and modernization of the industrial sector.[23] Post-war industrial expansion had been accompanied by an important rise in investment which according to Mabro and Radwan equipped the country with significant productive capacity.[24] By 1954, most of the key industrial projects were based on modern and efficient production techniques.[25]

A survey of the establishments developed during the post-war period points to the fact that most were in light industries, the majority of which were producing consumer goods. In a situation of free market enterprise with very little government intervention and guidance, it is only natural that entrepreneurial activity should have become geared towards projects yielding rapid rates of profit. Egyptian light industry was in fact highly profitable at the time. Declared net profits averaged 13 per cent of shares in the pre-war period and over 20 per cent in the war and post-war period.[26] Light industries not only had captive markets, but they required little investment and fairly modest technology.

Intermediate industries were not developing at the same pace. Most intermediate engineering activity was concentrated in repair shops, while heavier types of industries, such as fuel, power and petroleum, mining, quarrying and metallurgy, were far less developed.[27] After 1954, although the textile industry continued to dominate the economic scene, some innovative steps were taken in the iron and steel, fertilizer, paper and mineral industries.[28] Direct government investment in industry had begun in 1954.[29] The government acted as the partner of private enterprise, but only with regard to basic and heavy industry, such as iron and steel, fertilizers and cement, military factories, electrical cables, rubber tyres, transport and railway equipment. The remaining industrial enterprises were completely left to the private sector entrepreneurs.[30]

In the post-war years Egyptian industry operated in a *laissez-faire* context which was in fact more of a free market system than Western capitalist systems.[31] Government intervention and participation were minimal. The only large state-owned enterprises were: oil refinery in Suez[32]; the government press; a few military factories; and some workshops belonging to various ministries.[33] The government assisted industry directly through tariff protection.[34]

Most industrial enterprises were in the form of joint stock companies, which is reflective of the limited numbers of promoters, who aimed at retaining control and constituted an oligopoly.[35] Furthermore, the growth of projects, with the exception of the Misr group, was auto-financed, investments being extracted from retained earnings and profits. Most banks were extremely reluctant to lend to industrialists, particularly owners of small and medium-sized firms (the former constituted the majority). It was not until 1949 that the government founded the industrial bank to meet their needs.[36] Prior to that date, it should be mentioned that foreign authorities had also financed industry directly. Thus the Middle East Supply Centre had set up a few modern industries. The Centre was founded by the British Army and aimed at meeting the demands of its troops.

The industries established were mainly metallic and chemical factories.[37] Also during the post-war years, some British and American capital had participated in industrial projects. The US Government had also provided Egypt with grants and loans. Between 1945 and 1952, grants amounted to US$50,000, and loans were in the order of US$18 million.[38]

During the period under study, industrial development was largely an attempt at import substitution, which had obvious and immediate repercussions on patterns of foreign trade, as well as its volume. Meanwhile the country was becoming extremely dependent on foreign imports.

Foreign trade

The major characteristics of foreign trade were the diversification of imports and the country's great dependence upon Western goods, coupled with very limited exports. Since the age of Mohamed Ali, Egypt had largely depended upon cotton as its major exportable good. Although there were periods of decline, cotton occupied the most important position throughout the period under study. After the war period certain goods were added to the list of exports.[39]

As a result of Egypt's specific pattern of trade, along with some political considerations, the country's major problem gradually became one of a serious balance of trade deficit which reached the alarming total of £E95.7 million during the 1940s and by the early 1950s the deficit was in the order of £E500 million.[40] The trend towards an increasing deficit was persistent during the 1950s, with the exception of 1953–4, when small surpluses were obtained. From

1955 onwards, the deficit was expanding rapidly.[41]

With regard to the nationality of the trading enterprises, prior to the end of the capitulations period in 1937, production units in commerce were almost totally managed by foreigners.[42] The latter had concentrated their efforts in commercial agencies for export and import,[43] while Egyptians controlled some sectors of internal trade.[44] With the nationalist movement towards Egyptianization during the post-war years, and the tremendous increase in imports, some Egyptians had stepped into the business of commercial representation and import/export activity. A notorious example of an Egyptian agent representing the interests of British firms at the time is Abboud Pasha.[45]

According to the experience and knowledge of a key informant who had been in charge of inspection and the application of subsequent laws for commercial representation, up until 1957, almost all such agencies were run by (in order of importance) Jews, Levantines and other foreigners, while Egyptians were employed in some of the larger offices. Several of these establishments, however, had been nothing more than a small room in town, owned, directed and staffed by a single person, and mostly importing tools, workshop machinery, equipment and car spare parts.[46]

An accurate estimate of the proportion of Egyptians involved in foreign trade is not possible since business was, during the period under study, chaotic; no registers were kept for commercial agencies, nor was there any law organizing the activity, save for the licence policies generally applicable to all importers and exporters. Although there had appeared to be greater opportunities for commercial representation, the nationality of the trading enterprise continued to be foreign, despite the fact that Egyptians may have increasingly stepped into the activity. Up until 1956 foreign capital re-invested in the various joint stock companies represented 50 per cent of the total capital of enterprises operating in Egypt, notwithstanding the large number of liaison and commercial representative offices of foreign companies which continued to play a very important role in the Egyptian economy. Issa suggests that on the eve of the Suez crisis the Egyptian economy was still largely dominated by foreign capital.[47] The first attempt to regulate and Egyptianize commercial representative activity was made in 1957.[48] These regulations included the establishment of registries and the promulgation of various disciplinary and administrative legislation concerning the activity, such as the right to a commission, the amount of payable taxes, etc.

The Egyptian bourgeoisie: its origins, nature, pattern of development and relationship to the power structure

The first point to make about the origins of the national bourgeoisie is that it emerged in the colonial situation. Furthermore, the first generation of industrial capitalists were the Egyptianized foreign settlers. The fact that they succeeded in making substantial profits helped to generate an industrial consciousness among large, landed proprietors.[49]

The second point to make about the origins of the Egyptian bourgeoisie is their agrarian nature. Since landowners were the only indigenous economic force that survived after the colonial penetration, they alone were in possession of sufficient capital to join the Egyptianized foreign capitalists. It is indeed the large landowners or the landed aristocracy who, during the inter-war and post-war period, became bourgeois and invested in industry. H. Riad calls the large Egyptian bourgeoisie of the time *une aristocratie embourgeoisée*.[50]

Other members of the Egyptian industrial bourgeoisie had emerged from the state bureaucracy. They were high-ranking government officials who, by virtue of their position, had acquired land and real estate, the revenues of which they reinvested in industry. Meanwhile some of the Egyptian aristocracy had owned real estate in the cities, and this had generated enough capital for industrial investment.[51]

The Egyptian aristocracy, which was small in number and in whose hands the country's wealth was concentrated, was rapidly becoming Westernized and emerged as the national counterpart of the foreign bourgeoisie, imitating its lifestyle and pattern of investment.[52] Like the foreign capitalists, the national bourgeoisie had been very narrowly based regarding both its capital and locality, and had developed large monopolies and cartels – examples of which were the Abboud and Rabat groups.[53] And like their foreign counterparts, the bourgeoisie had stepped into those industrial fields yielding the highest profits, as well as those having a rapid turnover – especially light and consumer goods industry in which the national bourgeoisie simply replaced foreign capital when the latter withdrew during various international crises.[54]

The relationship of the bourgeoisie to the power structure

For the period under study and before, it was essentially the large landowning aristocracy who controlled government. During certain phases certain members of the aristocratic bourgeoisie split their capital between agrarian and industrial investment, but one cannot make a class distinction based on the two types of investment.[55]

Some of the most prominent members of the aristocratic bourgeoisie involved in industrial investment, such as Ismail Sidki, Hafez Afifi, Hussein Sirri, Ahmad Ziwar, Ali Maher and Hafez Ramadan, occupied high-ranking government and ministerial positions and had been instrumental in promoting the interests of both foreign and local industrialists. These high-ranking officials were also participating in foreign-owned enterprises.[56] One cannot think of them as a nationalist bourgeoisie – given their strong links to foreign capital. Yet one can at least understand why the pressure of nationalism, together with a desire to serve their own interests, induced such industrialists to use their positions to promote the Egyptianization movement. However, industrialists were not consistent in power, nor did they seek to promote an autonomous nationalist industrialist movement. Government policies appeared rather ambiguous. On the one hand an Egyptianization movement was necessary to expand local industry, and thus both the Sidki and Nokrashi governments promoted the 1930 tariff protection law and the 1947 company law; on the other hand the government had been active in obstructing the Egyptian nationalist movement led by Talaat Harb, which had seriously threatened foreign interests.

This then constituted the nature and origins of the bourgeoisie which continued to play an important role in Egypt's political economy even after the change of regimes in 1952. It was a bourgeoisie which was not born out of a bourgeois revolution like that which had occurred in the West. Democracy was not a strong component of the new development. Rather it was a bourgeoisie which emerged largely through state intervention, under foreign rule, and with agrarian capital. All these factors did nothing to promote the positive cultural and social characteristics that often accompany bourgeois development, such as the growth of democratic institutions, national sovereignty and independence, and a working-class movement. Could this be remedied in Egypt through the kind of bourgeois nationalism that did exist? Was there any room for democracy? Was there a genuine and mature working-class movement rooted in a sufficiently well-developed industrial structure? A close look at the Nasser period of Egyptian development will partly help answer the above.

The early Nasser period: 1952–1956
Upon accession to power as a group, the Free Officers had not very much to offer in terms of a political platform or a comprehensive programme of socio-economic change, nor were they equipped with ideological sophistication, reflective of a real consciousness. Nor indeed were they endowed with special analytical skills or the farsightedness which might have spared them the various miscalculations on both the national and international scene which ultimately led to the emergence of conflict within their ranks, the transformation of their nature, and the incapacity to achieve their goals, most important of which had been political and economic independence.

Nasser, a young officer of very modest background, had flirted with most of the existing ideological and political currents of the 1940s. He had, however, only focused on the element closest to his emotional and intellectual orientation: namely, bourgeois national liberation. Nasser was not particularly keen on the issue of democracy, nor was he keen to allow a working-class movement to develop. This was only too clear when Shuhdi Atteya, a working-class political activist, was murdered in prison during the early years of Nasser's rule. Atteya had been a defender of working-class democratic rights. Moreover Nasser had, since the early stages of his rule, developed a very strong aversion to Communist groups as well as religious fundamentalist groups. He had in fact proceeded, quite undemocratically, to impose serious restrictions on their right of political expression. It was fairly clear that a false dilemma had been created between national independence and democracy. Nasser had very early on claimed that, at that stage of the country's development, democracy could not be afforded. Totally mesmerized by the existing political power, the Egyptian masses rallied against democracy and in full support of Nasser, as though independence and democracy were mutually incompatible.

The Free Officers can be defined as a nationalist military group of petty bourgeois origin. They had primarily been concerned with the whole issue of independence. In power, they recognized the need for industrialization, for the construction of a strong army, and for the restitution of national pride, and were sensitive to the plight of the poor dispossessed. Yet they lacked a clearly thought out programme for change. Thus it was natural for the forces of continuity to overpower the forces of change and for the initial years of the Nasser regime to become an extension of the post-war period with only minor alterations, most important of which was increased government intervention in economic planning. Riad goes as far as to maintain that during the first few years of the new regime, the Free Officers in fact did only what the old bourgeoisie might have done, had it dethroned Farouk and turned nationalist.[57]

On the international scene, during the first three years of the regime, the focal theme of all Nasser's speeches centred around the struggle against imperialism. However, it appears that at this initial stage the struggle was directly aimed at the old colonial forces, with the purpose of ending the oppressive system they had imposed and their military protection and tutelage, which they claimed Egypt still needed. The complexities of imperialist penetration had not been grasped by the military regime. Hence, during its initial years the regime invited foreign capital to invest and lend a hand in their development plans, whether in the form of aid, capital investment or technical assistance. The government's eagerness to attract both foreign and local capital was so great that, through law 430 (1953), it exempted newly founded joint stock companies from the payment of tax on commercial and industrial profits for a period of seven years.[58]

The Free Officers had in their own minds made a false distinction between the large landowners – the holders of political power – and the bourgeois capitalists, who were thought to hold only economic power. They had perhaps not fully grasped the fact that both were fractions of one and the same class; nor had they apparently understood that economic power was not entirely separate from political power. With regard to the first point, i.e. the distinction between large landowners and capitalists, the Free Officers believed that by curtailing the political and economic power of the former and encouraging the latter to produce, they might win the collaboration of the old industrial bourgeoisie, who would automatically adhere to their nationalist plans. Most capitalists at the time were panic-stricken. Many emigrated abroad. Most did not abide by the state's plans; instead they continued to do business and to accumulate and consolidate their own wealth and economic power.[59]

With regard to the second distinction made, namely between economic and political power, the Free Officers believed that a politically dominant position would be sufficient for them to guide the country into a nationalist, independent capitalism, i.e. one that essentially depended on the country's own resources, particularly in the field of industrial expansion. However, by allowing the old bourgeoisie to retain its position of economic dominance, the regime had in fact enabled it to become politically influential as well, and to penetrate the various political and economic organisms set up by the state.

Politically the military regime was determined to become dominant. Two major steps were taken in order to curtail the power of the large landowners who were identified as the former ruling class. The first step was the agrarian reform which, among other goals, aimed at depriving the old aristocracy of its source of power and wealth.[60]

Not many people would quarrel with the claim that the land reform did indeed fulfil its purpose; i.e. it undermined the political power of large landowners. Business circles and industrialists were optimistic about the reform; however, it did not seem to change their investment patterns.

The land reform had in large part resulted in the creation and consolidation of a stratum of politically powerful rich peasants. Thus while the old large landowners were being undermined, there emerged a new class of medium-sized farmers each owning between 20 and 50 feddans of lands.[61]

The land reform had not succeeded much in alleviating the condition of the 'landless' and 'poor peasants'. It had, however, released almost a million feddans for redistribution and improved life for some 342,000 families, namely tenant families and permanent wage labourers. Still the reform was essentially 'liberal' and not terribly socialist in spirit and orientation, all of which was reflected in the continued hardship of the landless labourers. Moreover the new class of rich and averagely wealthy peasants was soon in a position to obstruct the implementation and extension of the agrarian policies in the countryside, and to become a new power bloc.

The second step taken by the regime to undermine the old ruling class was to deprive them of the political organs which had been their stronghold and repository of power. Thus in January 1953 the regime had legally dissolved the old parties and prohibited the creation of new ones. Three days later the Free Officers announced the birth of a new political organ, the 'liberation rally' that would bring about all the diverse elements of the society under one common organization.[62]

The liberation rally lasted till 1956 when it was replaced by the National Union. The Free Officers had underestimated the influence which business and capitalist circles could have within the rally. Thus by 1955/56, the rally greatly resembled the Wafd of the 1930s and 1940s. The leading officers were won over to the capitalist ranks with the aim of accumulating wealth and the rally soon began to serve their interests.[63]

Although the old bourgeois capitalists and businessmen had indeed penetrated the liberation rally and become influential, they were not in direct control of the state apparatus, nor were they able to directly obstruct nationalist development policies. If they were able to do so at times it was essentially through corruption and venality, and through the intermediation of those military men whom they were able to win over to their side. It was a period of struggle between the forces that desired a return to the complete *laissez-faire* system of capitalist development that had existed in the post-war years, and those adhering to the nationalist government's desire for change and guided economic and industrial development. The conflict was, however, submerged and controlled through the coalescence existing between the industrial bourgeoisie and the new regime, as well as the autonomy the state apparatus appeared to enjoy as arbitrator between both, and as the surveyor of nationalist economic development.

During the period under study no significant efforts to abolish private property were made. Both the Misr group and the Federation of Egyptian Industries devised their own economic strategies. It had always been the Federation's desire to encourage foreign investors to step into the economy in order to enhance economic development. After the revolution the Federation continued to make its voice heard, and its advice was indeed fully heeded by the new regime.[64]

Although private property was not threatened in any direct way, there were, however, signs of increased government intervention and economic planning. In 1952, law no. 213 instituted for the first time in Egypt a permanent council for the development of national production. The majority of the members were former businessmen.[65]

Despite all the encouragements, the anticipated increase in investment and national growth was not forthcoming. The local capitalists had shown a marked preference for large and quick profits resulting from short-term investments, monopolistic enterprise and tariff protection, i.e. the old system.[66] With the loss of political power their apprehension had grown even greater than during the post-war period, when political instability was already a factor in the industrialists' anxiety and reluctance to invest.[67] Meanwhile foreign investors had also been extremely hesitant to step in, particularly in the areas desired by the new regime. These investors took the role of observers until they could have a clearer comprehension of the new situation and what it had to offer. The new regime would be reinforced by American capital investment only in its capacity of policeman in the area against the Eastern bloc and internal mass upheavals. Some industrial development would be tolerated, or indeed encouraged, in the areas which enhanced American dominance and Egypt's capacity to purchase United States arms and agricultural surplus.[68]

The Free Officers' initial naive and simplistic conception of national liberation soon acquired more complex and sophisticated dimensions. The regime acquired a clearer view of the changing global context: namely the Cold War, and the change in strategy it entailed. A series of events had provoked this new consciousness in the minds of the new regime, Nasser's in particular. Immediately following the evacuation of British troops both America and Britain had expressed their desire to see the creation of a Middle Eastern counterpart to the NATO defence organization, with Egypt featuring as an important member. British Prime Minister Eden had visited Cairo to persuade Nasser to join a collective defence military alliance with the West, known as the Baghdad Pact. Nasser had refused and from then on a chain of pressures were exerted with the hope of forcing the new leader back into the fold.

The US-promised military and economic loans were withdrawn; this included the IMF's withdrawal from the High Dam project. The series of pressures on the part of the West and resistance on Nasser's part, culminated in the Suez Crisis of 1956, which constituted a turning point in Nasser's internal and foreign policies.

Notes

1. Robert Tignor, 'Nationalism, Economic Planning and Development Projects in Interwar Egypt', *International Journal of Middle East Studies*, 8 (1977), pp. 185–208.

2. Mohamed Roushdy, *Economic Development in Egypt*, vol. 2, p. 186.

3. Patrick O'Brien, *The Revolution in Egypt's Economic System, from Private Enterprise to Socialism, 1952–1962*, pp. 13, 56.

4. J. H. D. Anderson, 'Law Reform in Egypt: 1850–1950', in P. M. Holt (ed.), *Political and Social Change in Modern Egypt*, p. 226.

5. Charles Issawi, 'The Entrepreneur Class', in S. N. Fisher (ed.), *Social Forces in the Middle East*, New York, Cornell U.P., 1956, pp. 124, 125.

6. Ibid., p. 126.

7. For a discussion on the relationship between Bank Misr and foreign capitalism see Robert Tignor, 'Bank Misr and Foreign Capitalism', pp. 161–81.

8. Roushdy, pp. 16–20.

9. Issawi, op cit., p. 127.

10. Rashed El Barawy, *Economic Development in the UAR (Egypt)*, p. 40.

11. Issawi, 1968, p. 63.

12. Berque, Jacques, *L'Égypte, Impérialisme et Révolution*, Paris: Editions Gallimard, 1967, pp. 624, 626 and 628.

13. O'Brien, p. 25.

14. Robert Mabro and Samir Radwan, *The Industrialisation of Egypt, 1939–1973*, p. 26.

15. Wahib Messiha, 'The Evolution of Egyptian Industry within the Past Fifty Years', p. 475.

16. Ibid.

17. Roushdy, pp. 171, 172.

18. Messiha, pp. 472, 475.

19. Issawi, 1968, pp. 90.

20. Ibid., p. 124.

21. Mabro and Radwan, p. 83.

22. D. C. Mead, *Growth and Structural Change in the Egyptian Economy*, pp. 103, 105.

23. Ibid., p. 114.

24. Mabro and Radwan, p. 83.

25. Mead, p. 114.

26. Issawi, 1968, pp. 161, 162.

27. Ibid., pp. 143–8.

28. O'Brien, pp. 72, 73.

29. Mabro and Radwan, p. 87.

30. O'Brien, pp. 72, 73.

31. Roushdy, pp. 139, 140.

32. Issawi, 1968, p. 169.

33. Mabro and Radwan, p. 96.

34. Issawi, 1968, p. 169.

35. Ibid., p. 159.

36. O'Brien, p. 150.

37. Mabro and Radwan, pp. 81, 82.

38. Issawi, 1968, p. 207.

39. Abdel Moneim Kaissouny, 'Some Aspects of Foreign Trade in the Southern Region within Half a Century', Studies in Honour of the Fiftieth Anniversary of the Egyptian Society for Political Economy, Statistics and Legislation (Cairo, 1960), p. 135.

40. Ibid., p. 132.

41. Bent Hansen and Girgis Marzouk, *Development and Economic Policy in the UAR (Egypt)*, p. 188.

42. O'Brien, p. 64.

43. Roushdy, p. 210.

44. Issawi, 1968, p. 63.

45. Tignor, p. 201.

46. Interview with former Inspector-General for the Application of the Commercial Law Prohibiting Agencies no. 107 (1961), on Wednesday, January 25, 1978.

47. Issawi, p. 150.

48. Law no. 24 (1957) regulating commercial activity obtained from the Ministry of Trade legal publications.

49. Anouar Abdel Malek, *Egypt Military Society*, p. 11.

50. Hassan Riad, *L'Egypte Nassérienne*, p. 202.

51. Mahmoud Mitwalli, *The Historical Origins of Egyptian Capitalism and its Development*, pp. 340, 341.

52. Riad, 75.

53. Abdel Malek, p. 14.

54. Mitwalli, pp. 130–72, 248–9, 257.

55. This thesis on the unity of the agrarian and industrial fractions of the bourgeoisie was originally presented by Hassan Riad and later was supported by various other researchers, such as 'Assem al Disuqi; also see Patrick Clawson, 'Egypt's Industrialisation: a Critique of Dependency Theory', p. 21.

56. Mitwalli, p. 245.

57. Riad, p. 220.

58. Rashed El Barawy, *Economic Development in the UAR (Egypt)*, pp. 56–8.

59. Abdel Malek, p. 99.

60. Mahmoud Abdel Fadil, *Development, Income Distribution and Social Change in Rural Egypt (1952–1970): A Study in the Political Economy of Agrarian Transition*, p. 8.

61. Ibid., pp. 22–5, 49, 116–17, 121, 126.

62. Imam, Abdallah, *Al Nasseriya* (Beirut: The Arab Nation, 1977).

63. Madame El Kosheiry Mahfouz, *Socialisme et pouvoire en Egypte*, p. 82.

64. Abdel Malek, pp. 88, 89.

65. Barawy, 1972, p. 51, and Ismail Sabri Abdallah, *The Organisation of the Public Sector: Theoretical Bases and Major Political Problems*.

66. Abdallah, p. 260.

67. O'Brien, p. 71.

68. Imam, pp. 82–98.

2 Dominant State Sector 'Socialism': From the Suez Crisis to the Suez War (1956–67)

Towards the latter part of the 1950s due to a series of national and international developments, the nature of the coalescence between the old bourgeoisie and the Nasser regime was changing, as the latter was preparing the ground to become the owner of the means of production, as well as the holder of political power. However, during the period under study, part of the old bourgeoisie had already been able to consolidate its economic power and penetrate more deeply the state apparatus and new political organs. Thus while the genesis of a public sector was being created and the old bourgeoisie was being threatened and dismantled as a 'class' towards the end of the period, some of its members had managed to survive and help give rise to a new class within the state ruling class, i.e., a 'state bourgeoisie'.

Private enterprise was being systematically attacked and undermined. On February 13, 1960, Bank Misr became public property. In June of the same year all Egyptian newspapers became state-owned. Cairo bus services were soon municipalized, while both internal and external trade in tea and pharmaceutical products was removed from private hands in July.

Towards the end of June 1961 the entire cotton trade passed into government hands. Moreover four firms which pressed and baled raw cotton were nationalized. In July the Khedival shipping line was nationalized. Later the state proceeded to nationalize large sections of Egypt's industrial and commercial property. Banks and insurance companies were nationalized. By 1964 all large companies in every field of economic activity had been nationalized. Only some land remained privately owned. A ceiling was, however, placed on large landholdings, allowing for some redistribution of land.

The old bourgeoisie had quickly learnt to adapt to the new situation and very soon financiers, promoters, merchants and industrialists were managing to extract large profits from the state. This of course was made possible by the various networks of relationships established between members of the new regime, finally resulting in a new set of alliances.[1]

International developments

Two important international developments were to have a major impact on the new regime's economic policies, political power and position *vis-à-vis* the old bourgeoisie. The first of these two developments had been the tripartite aggression of 1956 which was in effect the reaction of the old colonial powers against Nasser's decision to nationalize the Suez Canal. Following the aggression, Nasser had nationalized a large number of companies. The second development had been the Soviet Union's increased presence in the area.

With regard to the first development, a combination of war and international negotiations had finally resulted in a ceasefire and a containment of the colonialists' attack on Egypt, whereby the latter emerged as the political victor, particularly in the eyes of the Egyptian and Arab people. In the course of the war with the three colonial forces, England, France and Israel, Egypt had discovered a good friend in the Soviet Union, which had not only been highly supportive and eager to condemn the aggressors, but had also provided Egypt with arms.[2] Meanwhile, the United States had not been prepared to go along with the colonial forces and thus, under the presidency of Eisenhower, the White House had exerted substantial pressure on the three powers to end its military action,[3] which left the new Egyptian regime in a very powerful position, both politically and economically. On the political front the Free Officers had acquired immense popularity amongst the masses and the nation at large as the heroes and defenders of national sovereignty.[4] Meanwhile amidst massive popular enthusiasm and patriotic fervour, the Nasser regime had proceeded to nationalize all other remaining foreign interests and pushed the Egyptianization movement to its extreme.

Preceded by the sequestration of Anglo-French property, in 1957 a series of laws were promulgated to end the most direct forms of foreign control. Law no. 22 required that all banking business be carried on only by Egyptian joint stock companies, managed and directed by Egyptians, with nominative shares owned by Egyptian subjects. The banks were given a five-year grace period to effect the changes. The same provisions applied to insurance companies by law no. 23.[5] With regard to commercial agents of import and export companies, law no. 24 of that same year stipulated that commercial representation, both in the form of import–export companies and individuals, must be Egyptian.[6]

The Egyptianization movement had really taken place through two processes; the first process included the sequestration of British and French companies, and the second process was nationalization, which primarily meant government ownership. With regard to the sequestrated companies, a number of them had been purchased by already existing Egyptian companies[7] or by Egyptian individuals, such as the many foreign commercial and trading representative companies.[8] Although the government was emerging as an important shareholder of economic enterprise and was gradually possessing most industrial projects as well as agricultural irrigation, transport and power supplies, the private sector continued to dominate the construction trade and commercial services. The government could at most guide the flow of imports and exports through the system of premiums, but the business was to a large extent run by private individuals.[9]

The second process in the Egyptianization movement, following the initial sequestration, was the government nationalization of foreign interests, which had in fact included the majority of overall sequestrated companies. The Economic Agency was created one day before the promulgation of the Egyptianization laws, and can be regarded as the foundation stone of the public state sector.

Although the major goals and functions of the Agency were legally defined in terms of promoting the national economy, its more immediate and practical aim had been to fulfil the government's desire to set up a centralized institution capable of assuming the control of the numerous sequestrated companies soon to be nationalized.[10]

The government was no longer merely encouraging industry but actively involved, and by 1958 the state was in control of a large part of the economy and was in a 'position go' plan.[11] The agency was responsible for a complex of industrial property extending to steel, minerals, chemicals and textiles. With the exclusion of small-scale manufacturing not amenable to centralized authority, companies that were affiliated to the Economic Agency constituted a fairly important share of total industrial output – roughly a third of aggregate output, employing 20 per cent of the labour force.[12]

The agency also had supervisory functions over various companies. In the cases where 25 per cent or more of the shares were government-owned the organization could appoint a majority of directors to its board, as well as the managing director, and influence policy-making. The agency could furthermore finance its own affiliated companies in addition to the establishment and formation of companies without any outside participation.[13]

The second major international development which further strengthened the new regime politically and thus encouraged it to take bolder steps towards state planning and ownership of the means of production, and to persist in its industrialization plans, was the beginning of Soviet strategic aspirations and presence in the area.

The period following Bandung and Suez witnessed the emergence of the Soviet State as a major power. This development allowed for a change in the balance of forces between the old traditional bourgeoisie and the new regime, in favour of the latter. The new regime now had strong Soviet support for its development plans. Furthermore it provided the Nasser regime with manoeuvring space with respect to the West. The Russians now offered to provide technical assistance, modern equipment for the army, financial assistance for the purchase of machinery, steel products and all necessary industrial materials on relatively easy terms. Most important of all, it offered to finance and assist the construction of the long-desired High Dam. Furthermore the Soviet state would become the new primary purchaser of Egypt's cotton exports.[14] Meanwhile, the United States continued to compete with the Soviets and was still determined to fill the power gap that had been left behind by the old colonial powers defeated in 1956.[15]

The Egyptian nationalist regime was unable to exploit to the full the potential this situation was to offer for the achievement of independent economic development. It was not a 'public' sector under populism that was going to launch this development, but a 'state' sector, one that had not emerged out of a radical socialist transformation, but 'was growing within the framework that had existed in the past – the political and economic apparatus created by the imperialists and traditional bourgeoisie'.[16]

Internal political and economic developments

The conflict between the new regime and old bourgeoisie became more acute following the Bandung and Suez period. Parallel to the Egyptianization drive, the government gradually extended its control over the private sector. The government not only controlled the flow of investable funds through the various banks and economic organizations, but it now determined the industrial projects that would be accepted as promoting the national interest.[17] Not only was the government eager to regulate industry with regard to size and quality of output, but it also stepped into the domain of company law and attempted to regulate the internal administration of companies.[18]

The old bourgeoisie's anxieties and apprehensions were not totally unjustified. The changes the Nasser regime was about to make were now becoming clearer. A state sector had been formed and already, on the levels of economic, political and managerial responsibility, a different calibre of men had begun to appear on the scene. In the past, responsibility in these areas had been in the hands of ministers, business executives and politicians who had been trained in law, often with a French orientation. But now they were being increasingly replaced by a new group – a 'technocratic' one, formed largely of economists, engineers or administrators trained in Europe and America.[19]

Even more indicative of the fate that awaited the traditional bourgeoisie, was the regime's change in ideological orientation and overtones during the period under study. Towards the end of 1957 Nasser declared before the Third Co-operative Congress that the new socialist co-operative Egyptian democratic society no longer had room for an exploitative minority but that the state must supervise capitalist activity. Shortly following this declaration, on the eve of the union with Syria, Nasser, during a press conference, talked about controlled capitalism.[20]

From 1957 to 1961 the regime launched a campaign against the 'compradorial' elements within the Egyptian capitalists. In the regime's view these elements had proved untrustworthy during the 1956 war and lacked nationalist solidarity. Their organic ties with the West were very strong, and they had only supported the government's Egyptianization measures because of their opportunistic quest for power and their hope of inheriting sequestrated property.[21] The press had introduced new concepts to the Egyptian public; slogans such as the 'Men of Trust' emerged as opposed to the 'Men of Knowledge'.[22] In 1956 the Liberation Rally was dissolved and replaced by the National Union. The Union began operation in 1957 with the change of a few of the previous political leaders, leaving its structure unchanged.

The National Union brought in the term 'socialism' for the first time as part of the official ideology, and declared its intention to build Egypt as a 'socialist co-operative democratic' society. The Union's labour programmes were also more advanced than those of the 'Rally'.[23]

Although the government was undertaking about 74 per cent of gross capital formation by 1959–60, certain domains were still completely controlled by private entrepreneurs, such as construction, the provision of motorized and marine transport, storage facilities for small-scale manufacture and the assets required for financial, commercial and trading services.[24] Meanwhile the regime continued to encourage the private sector despite its failings and the growing strength of the state sector.[25]

In January 1957 a second national planning committee was formed in order to draft a national comprehensive plan for social and economic development. The committee drafted two quinquennial programmes for industry and agriculture. The plan aimed at doubling the national income. Regarding industry, during the first five-year plan, the estimated share in value added of the total national income was 25.4. Most capital formation and investment planned for the years 1960–65 was to be the responsibility of the state sector. The private sector was, however, encouraged through tax exemptions and other financial incentives to participate in a specifically defined role. Four-fifths of all new investment during the first two years of the plan was to be undertaken by the public sector. Yet in certain areas the private sector would be dominant. For example, in building and construction 60 per cent of total investment would be met by private entrepreneurs. The latter was also allowed to play a role in the creation of fixed assets required for trade and commercial services. During the first two years of the plan, almost a quarter of net industrial investments was left to private individuals. The co-operation between state and private sectors was already evident in the establishment of mixed committees to draft the plan.[26]

Following Egyptianization, the old bourgeoisie had become wealthier in absolute terms. According to reports from the National Bank of Egypt, private entrepreneurs had made large profits during that period. The capital of the Misr Bank alone, which continued to be the nerve centre of all sectors of the bourgeoisie till its final nationalization in 1960, had increased from £E1 million in 1950 to 2 million by 1960, and its net profits had increased from £E788,000 to £E1,135,000.[27] Alongside the bank and the Misr complex, the Abboud complex had also made enormous profits; 'this whole world of finance, industry and business prospered as never before in the shadow of a strong authority concerned with order and economic progress.'[28]

Not only had the massive Egyptianization of foreign firms provided the old bourgeoisie with opportunities of rapid enrichment, particularly with regard to trade and commercial representation, but also during the period under study Egypt had united with Syria. Nasser had at first resisted this step, but pressurized by the business circles (Bank Misr and Bank of Cairo) and the economic agency, the President had agreed to the union. The creation of the United Arab Republic in 1958 had provided grounds for a coalescence between the old bourgeoisie and the new regime at a time when the latter was once again making overtures to the West, having strained relations with the Soviets, and was eager to suppress the Communist movement at home. This coalescence presented the old bourgeoisie with new Arab markets, and openings for business investments and exports.[29]

Meanwhile, the replacement of the Rally by the National Union had not prevented businessmen from being represented and the first council created after the constitution in 1957 had included a large number of prosperous businessmen.[30] The council had in fact succeeded in obstructing the regime's attempt to increase land taxes by law.[31] In the field of planning, as mentioned previously, the private sector business entrepreneurs had been jointly appointed on the state's planning committees and participated in drawing up the plan.

Following the dissolution of the union with Syria, the traditional bourgeoisie, as a 'class', no longer had the political influence it had enjoyed during the 1952–8 period. After the break with Syria in 1961, Nasser spoke of internal reactionary forces and opportunism as the new form of imperialist penetration. The old bourgeoisie could no longer survive as a 'class', i.e. private capital and entrepreneurial activity was greatly restrained by the July 1961 measures through which the most important banking, financial, commercial and industrial enterprises passed into state hands. The agents of the old class would have to find individual means of integrating and surviving. The path that offered the most secure, inconspicuous shelter was the whole area of trade, particularly since the regime was about to launch its first five-year industrial plan, which would require very large amounts of imports. Thus prior to the nationalization laws of 1961, the number of trade representative officers established abroad by large Egyptian companies had quintupled, and so as Abdel Malek puts it,

> several thousand people waiting for the chance to get rich had finally found the means to do so under the banner of nationalism and revolution, thanks to the combination of nationalisation and Egyptianisation. In this way public socialist disbursements were contributing to an increase in the number of millionaires.[32]

The stage was set for the emergence of that new class which Mahmoud Hussein refers to as the 'state bourgeoisie'.[33]

The concept of a state bourgeoisie is useful in the case of Nasser's Egypt provided we observe two conditions. First we must make a distinction between the state bourgeoisie and the private bourgeoisie proper. Secondly, we must clarify the interlinkages and alliances between the state bourgeoisie and private capitalists. The first group, that of the state bourgeoisie, comprises the upper stratum of the bureaucratic and managerial élites, high-ranking civil servants, army officers and directors, and managers of public sector companies. The second group, that of private capitalists, is made up of wholesale traders, contractors, exporters and other capitalist entrepreneurs.

It is very difficult to draw a demarcating line between these two groups, State and private. There were significant overlaps and alliances between both, i.e.

some members of the state bourgeoisie were also engaged in private enterprise, while alliances, interlinkages and interdependencies existed between the two groups – some by virtue of mutual business interests, others by virtue of kinship or the social background of the top managerial élite, 15 per cent of whose fathers had been businessmen.[34]

The creation of the state sector (1961–1967)

By the end of the 1950s, as mentioned before, the Nasser regime had acquired a different outlook on development; an outlook with new ideological overtones. At the beginning of the new decade Nasser had clearly discussed the 'necessity of the socialist solution' for Egypt's independent development in both the national charter and in his book *The Philosophy of the Revolution*. This solution required a number of socio-economic and political transformations. In the regime's own view, such a transformation essentially signified full state control and ownership of the means of production. This trend found its roots and beginnings in the preceding period. However, it now dawned upon the Nasser regime that development required not only partial state control and indiscriminate accelerated industrialization, but a specific form of carefully planned co-ordinated and centralized industrial development. Moreover it had also become quite clear to the regime that the state would have to rely first and foremost upon its own resources and that it (the regime) would have to consolidate its political power over the state apparatus, as well as its economic power, if the desired development was to be achieved. Meanwhile collaboration with the old capitalist bourgeoisie was no longer feasible and dependence upon foreign assistance would have to be minimized.[35]

Two major policy lines characterized the period under study as attempts by the regime to bring about the desired economic development: first the nationalization laws, and second the five-year plan, both representing increased centralized state control.

It was in the summer of 1961 that the government began its massive nationalization policies. By July the Nasser regime was determined to take over all the country's major productive enterprises. As a starting point the cotton trade had passed into government hands in the form of joint stock companies where the government withheld a minimum of 35 per cent of the shares. In addition some four firms baling raw cotton were nationalized. Furthermore all export–import houses were compelled to exchange 25 per cent of their share capital for an equivalent amount in public bonds with a 40 per cent interest. With the aim of strengthening government control over foreign exchange, all the firms engaged in external trade were placed under the jurisdiction of the Ministry of the Economy.[36] Finally by 1963 all imports were to be carried out by the public sector, whilst the private sector was allowed to contribute to 25 per cent of the country's exports. Import quotas were to be allocated by each ministry to be subsequently approved and co-ordinated by a central authority.[37]

Another crucial set of measures were taken by the state during the summer of 1961. Law no. 117 provided for the nationalization of all banks and insurance companies still in private hands. Meanwhile law no. 118 compelled some 77 enterprises listed by presidential decree to become joint stock companies wherein government enterprises would participate with about 50 per cent of the shares. Such enterprises were mainly concentrated in light and intermediary industries as well as public works. An equally crucial measure was effected under law no. 110 whereby no individual or corporate body could own more than £E10,000 worth of shares in some 147 companies listed by law. Shares in excess of that amount would become state-owned.[38]

In 1962 the national charter was promulgated, clearly defining the limits of each of the two sectors. The public sector was to include the infrastructure generally, heavy and medium industry and the institutions and companies responsible for foreign trade and financial operations; the private sector was limited to the ownership of land, buildings, construction and contracting, light industry, 25 per cent of the national exports, and internal trade under state guidance. Land ownership had of course been limited through the various land reform laws and private ownership was being controlled through the co-operative system. With regard to internal trade, the private sector did not have a totally free hand since the public sector would, over the years, take over at least 25 per cent of internal trade. The private ownership of buildings was allowed but their rents were controlled and taxed.[39]

During the years following the promulgation of the charter, i.e. 1963–64, the government had totally nationalized all the companies it had partly owned. By the end of 1964 all the large companies where private individuals had still withheld shares, were becoming totally government-owned.

The plan

The idea of a plan had emerged and materialized during the late 1950s; however, it was only in the early 1960s that the plan began to be implemented. Broadly speaking the objectives of the plan had been the following:

1. To double national income over a period of ten years, which involved an annual growth rate of 7.2 per cent. The plan, which had been divided into two periods, hoped to achieve a 40 per cent increase in national income during the first five-year plan.
2. To expand employment opportunities, and
3. To achieve a greater equality of opportunity, as well as more even distribution of income.[40]

There seems to be a consensus amongst economists writing about the period, that among the most serious failures of the plan, was the increasing balance of trade and balance of payment deficits which ultimately led to a deceleration and decrease in output.[41]

The rise in Egypt's imports in the first half of the 1960s 'was made possible by foreign aid', which enabled the country to run for a while a large current deficit, namely because the deficit was associated with an increase in the investment ratio. When in 1965, United States aid was withdrawn, accompanied by stagnant exports and increasing military requirements, the country's import and consequently investment coefficients greatly decreased, which could only result in a 'situation detrimental to economic growth'.[42]

The success of the plan was dependent on tight state control over the economy, which was not possible at the time due to a number of factors on both the national and international scenes.

National developments

The first point that needs to be clarified if one is to gain a clear understanding of the various internal developments and class formations at the time, is the nature of the public sector and ownership that existed. In other words, how and by whom was the plan carried out?

The legal structure

The formal beginnings of a public sector can be traced back to the creation of the Economic Agency in January 1957, to manage property acquired by the state through the Egyptianization laws. Following that date four laws were promulgated to organize the public sector. The first, law no. 32 of 1957, was primarily concerned with the regulation of the public enterprise. This law was followed by law no. 265 in 1960, specifically regulating public enterprises having economic activities. In 1963 the law was amended, and finally in 1966 it included for the first time a bill concerned with the regulation of public sector firms.

All the above-mentioned laws operated within the framework of a capitalist economic system, since the various firms continued to abide by the shareholding model. Thus the participation and intervention of the public enterprise (or the Economic Agency) in the various firms under its supervision resembled the intervention of the major shareholder. The only difference between an ordinary shareholding company and the Economic Agency was the fact that the latter was legally allowed to own all the shares in a given firm, i.e. it could found its own firm.

Although the Egyptian economy had undergone radical transformations between 1961 and 1964, the old company laws continued to operate. It was only in 1966 that for the first time a law was promulgated to bring about a total reorganization of public sector firms. According to this law the public sector falling under the supervision of the government (the Economic Agency) was divided into three forms of productive unit: public sector firms; co-operatives; and 'establishments'.

Our major concern here will be with the public sector firms. The law of 1966 was only really innovative with regard to public firms or companies; the other two forms of productive units were somewhat neglected. Co-operatives still operated under the 1956 law, while 'establishments', in their capacity as productive units, were very vaguely defined in the law. In the absence of any legal regulation an 'establishment' was left to the jurisdiction and supervision of the Economic Agency, without any further clarification as to the manner in which it would be administered. In a very general sense an 'establishment', typically a factory, was any technical unit which was part of a larger productive unit enjoying a legal existence and the rights to decision-making.

The co-operatives were simply a form of collectivizing and organizing small-scale production with governmental supervision and subsidy with the purpose of improving and facilitating production. Ownership in this case is not public but collective, hence the role of the government was primarily an organizational and supervisory one based on the political power enjoyed by the state rather than on its economic power, i.e. the cooperative was the property of its members rather than the state. The cooperatives were normally placed under the regular supervisory organs, most important of which were the Central Accounting Agency and the fiscal agency through the Cooperative Bank. Finally, as previously mentioned, the administrative regulations of the cooperatives still followed the 1956 law. Thus the only unit that could truly be regarded as an autonomous productive one under the new legislation was the public company.

The 1966 law defined public sector companies in the following manner: the public company is the central unit of the public sector. It is composed of a group of employees who have at their disposal public or state money which they are to utilize for production in accordance with the national plan. The activities of such legal entities will spread over various fields of agriculture, industry, commerce, transport and telecommunications, construction, business and fiscal activities. The law also made provisions for the company's budget, labour and employment, planning, investment and the required and necessary procedures for the dissolution or merger of various companies.[43]

The formation and establishment of the public sector had not been without problems. We have seen in the previous sector how it was built upon the nationalization of the various companies that had existed within the liberal capitalist system. One of the major problems it confronted was the inherited structural constraints. Despite some reorganization and the partial change of names, the division of labour between the various production units was not fundamentally changed to fit in with the economic plan or even with basic technical and administrative requirements. The field of foreign trade presents a perfect example. Export was distributed among two firms or establishments: the trading company and the cotton company. Meanwhile some other public sector firms continued to export independently. The majority of imports on the other hand were the responsibility of the government trading establishment and the twelve public companies operating under it.[44] Specialization in the various fields of import was again absent.[45]

The question of ownership appeared to be one of the most important and controversial issues at the time, which very directly reflected the broader issue of whether Egypt's public sector truly represented a genuine phase of socialist transformation. Was the public sector really public ownership? Were the interests of the working class properly represented and were the workers really participating in the administration as partners and partial owners of the enterprises?

According to a debate conducted by *Al Taliah* in 1965, to which several progressive public sector directors and administrators were invited, it appeared that workers were not adequately and sufficiently represented in the administrative boards. This the contributors attributed to the fact that factories were normally run on a three-shift basis which left very little time, if any, for workers to attend political consciousness-raising and technical administrative training sessions – the result being that elections were carried out very much as before.[46]

Although government control seemed to be quite strong and centralized at first, since it allocated the budget, controlled some of the prices and subsidized the production of various commodities, each of the enterprises continued to operate as an autonomous entity resembling the old competitive capitalist companies, and profit continued to be the measure of success in most cases. As Ali Sabri points out, there was a general lack of coordination, which he considered to be one of the main problems confronting planning.[47]

Another major problem faced by the public sector upon its inception was the dearth of technically qualified personnel. Thus there was no core of qualified persons with nationalist progressive tendencies capable of assuming managerial responsibilities in the various companies. The state was faced with two options, either (a) postpone the creation of a public sector until such time as it had trained and created a public-spirited managerial stratum, which also meant that the private sector would meanwhile continue to dominate economic production; or (b) establish a public sector with the available managerial and human resources in the hope of future improvement.[48]

With the idea of enhancing economic development and the five-year plan, the latter solution was adopted.[49] Thus the managerial élite which was to lead the country in its drive for development was initially recruited from the old private sector companies. A large number of the pre-1952 businessmen were recruited by the state to become administrators and civil servants, such as Mohamed Roushdy, the director of the Bank Misr. Very soon a whole network of family ties and friendship relations were established between this old bourgeoisie and members of the new regime's bureaucratic apparatus. Moreover, most members of the old traditional bourgeoisie who had been barred from joining state enterprises were not eliminated as a class (i.e. totally sequestrated and blacklisted) as the Levantines, Syrians and Jews had been.[50]

Other members of the managerial élite were recruited from the civil service, while a smaller number at first came from the army and the universities.[51] However at a somewhat later stage of the public sector's development there was an influx of new elements within the managerial élite as well as a proliferation of high government and managerial positions. Nasser's efforts to train a group of technocrats was by 1963/4 yielding results. In 1961 a military technical faculty had been set up to train career officers and civilian engineers to become managers of various enterprises. Moreover this was the epoch when holders of Ph.D. degrees sprang up in increasing numbers out of the ranks of the officers.[52] Engineers, chemists and managers were also being trained abroad in increasing numbers. A new class was being shaped.

In the initial stage the new class emerged, as a result of the manner in which the 1952 revolution was conducted, in a 'bloodless' non-radical fashion: the old structures were being inherited. At a later stage, the rise of a technocracy, with engineers occupying the first position, gave a different shape to this new class and its relationship to the power structure. In 1964 the majority of the ministers and members of the ministerial cabinet were engineers, as were 70 of the deputy ministers who were actively participating in development conferences. Furthermore between 1962/63 and 1966/67 the number of high government and managerial positions occupied by such technocrats had increased from 967 to 1,544, constituting a 61 per cent increase. The income of this group had doubled within the same period. This was partly because of their government salaries and the various privileges enjoyed by high government officials and managers, but even more important were the various economic activities they were privately engaged in or helped others to perform through the power they enjoyed in economic decision-making.[53]

Although Nasser may have set out with the idea of creating a public enterprise under populism, and later proposed a socialist transformation, and although a small amount of the surplus was redistributed (in the form of medical care, pensions, labour salaries and education), the Egyptian public sector did not, however, essentially serve the state as the guardian of national independence; nor did it essentially serve the interests of the working classes. Instead it gave rise to a 'state bourgeoisie' that was later able to consolidate politically and to pressurize the state to serve its own interests.

Within this new state sector, corruption, infiltration, exploitation and ultimately destruction of the Nasserist experiment were unavoidable. The success of the plan and economic development had after all depended on strict government control over consumption and investment patterns as well as price controls, none of which was possible given the growing influence of a 'state bourgeoisie' pursuing its private economic interests. The increases of income in the managerial strata became instrumental in encouraging added consumption, and members of the new state bourgeoisie and their protégés became actively involved in the smuggling of such goods as tobacco, apples, tea seeds, car spare parts and various machines and electrical appliances. Ghazza soon became Egypt's 'Oxford Street'.[54]

Gradually dreams of Egypt emerging as a 'great power' in the Middle East were disappearing. As the country's public deficit, military and security expenditure grew, and its national wealth was wasted by individuals, the country became increasingly reliant on foreign aid. Just before the 1967 Arab–Israeli war the debt was of the order of £E500 million, with no signs of rapid repayment, since the whole productive system was in a situation of total anarchy.[55]

Let us now take a look at some of the activities of private profiteers who were able to prosper during the Nasserite experiment.

There were two essential means through which the private sector was able to do rather well through its connections during the five-year plan.[56] The first of these was internal trade, whereby merchants in a price-controlled economy created artificial shortages of merchandise by hoarding goods for some time and then reselling them at inflated prices. Such mechanisms were successful because of the very limited supervision and organization the public sector offered. The second was contracting: because the public sector had not completed its organs in the various economic spheres due to a shortage in personnel and trained managerial staff, private sector contractors were allowed to exist.[57] Quite a number of business deals in that domain were given to the private sector through subcontracting. Thus the latter were able to make large profits by requiring exorbitant fees for the various operations they undertook even when these were acquired through public tendering. This was possible through price-fixing by private sector contractors. They charged inflated prices for buildings and contracting projects which absorbed about 40–50 per cent of investments in the total plan. By the third year of the plan the cost of construction projects had shot up by 25 per cent, most of which represented profits made by contractors.[58] According to Adel Ghoneim, if we take into consideration the various infiltrations and subcontracting strategies the private sector contractors employed, it appears that during the first five-year plan the private sector had taken up about 70 per cent of the contracts, whilst the public sector dealt with the remaining 30 per cent. Subcontractors from the private sector were receiving a five per cent commission plus 22 per cent of the profit towards administrative expenses. The private contracting sector had managed to accumulate capital through the profits it made on informal loans to merchants, often at 30 per cent interest rates. They had not, however, tied up their capital, i.e. it had not been invested in factories or buildings. Quite a number of the subcontractors were able to acquire key administrative positions in the public sector and exploited that privilege.[59] Both afore-mentioned forms of infiltration were of course 'parasitical', since the profits made did not result from an actual participation in the productive sectors.[60]

A third form of infiltration occurred during the period. Its effects, however, appeared much later. This form of activity, although extremely detrimental since it attacked one of the economy's most crucial sectors, was not given much weight, nor barely mentioned in the press and literature at the time. Yet those responsible formed what was in all likelihood the strongest amongst the various economic groups operating from both within and without the public sector. The form of parasitical economic activity in question occurred in the field of foreign trade, imports in particular. Although the state had in theory total control over imports through its public sector companies, the private sector commercial agents actually continued to do quite well.[61]

The conflict between the old traditional bourgeoisie and the new regime had been replaced by an internal conflict within the ruling class between the state bourgeoisie, i.e. the managers of the public state sector, and the government administrative and executive organs, which continued for a time to be the stronghold of Nasser and his close associates. Four ideological currents prevailed within the ruling class.

The first trend was adopted by a pressure group who believed that only science and technology could save the country from economic and cultural underdevelopment. This group did not have faith in the role of the masses, dismissed the role of a revolutionary political leadership and believed that only the technocratic and bureaucratic élite could lead the country into development. Nationalization was necessary while democracy was a deterring factor in the drive for development. Socialism was not to be regarded as an end, but a practical solution to technological and industrial development. This ideological trend was espoused by the technocratic élites who had occupied leading administrative positions in the state sector.

A second group within the ruling class also believed that democracy was unnecessary and that the state administration was perfectly capable of leading the country into industrialization. However, although this group believed that nationalization had been necessary at a given time, they were not keen to see the public sector expand any further and hoped the private sector could resume an important position in the economy. The system aspired to by this group was a bureaucratic state capitalism that would also enhance the development of private capital. This trend was reflective of the new bureaucracies within the public sector who now had aspirations of private accumulation and investment.

A third group believed in scientific socialism, the socialist revolution and the active participation of the masses in policy-making. This group was, however, a small minority and mostly represented the views of medium administrators and civil servants who had believed in Nasser's proclaimed ideology, particularly during the latter's most radical phase.

The fourth and last tendency represented the continuing ideology of the traditional bourgeoisie and conservative bureaucracy who were completely opposed to any form of 'socialist application', who did not believe in Egypt's new friendship with the Eastern Bloc, and believed in a free enterprise road to capitalist development, with the West, and the United States in particular, as their model. This group, which continued to rely on the political and economic support of the West, pressurized the state to normalize relations with the Western technically advanced countries and to gradually dismantle the public sector.[62]

With the exception of the third tendency, there appeared to be a general aversion to democracy and active mass participation. The third group, as mentioned, constituted a negligible minority and became involved in the conflict only in those times when the Nasserite ideology tilted more towards the left and appealed to the masses. This ideological current perhaps became more pronounced when it became necessary to balance the growing influence of the 'state bourgeoisie' and in order to retain relative autonomy of the 'state power' in face of the growing pressure groups within the ruling class. Moreover, as the influence of the state bourgeoisie proliferated, the threat of an acute conflict and confrontation between the ruling class and the dispossessed masses increased, and the regime's popularity appeared to decrease as the state bourgeoisie's shameful consumption and lavish spending could only alienate and anger the hungry masses.[63]

During the period under study, up until shortly before the 1967 war, the relationship between the state bourgeoisie and the state power structure was such that the latter still enjoyed a certain amount of control. Nasser, whose influence over the state apparatus continued to be strong, did not wish the state to become a 'representative' of ruling class interests once again. Moreover, he also wished to avoid acute conflict between the masses and ruling class. Nasser therefore attempted to restrain the new bourgeoisie's appetite for rapid enrichment.

The problems of corruption in the state sector were quite numerous, yet there appears to have been a constant re-evaluation of the experiment as it was being implemented. The problems existed but they were consciously perceived by the press and responsible officials, and in the process of this constructive self-criticism, some solutions and methods of control were being suggested. In the contracting sector, a number of regulatory measures had been created.[64] Meanwhile each year there were a number of cases of smuggling involving charges against members of the state bourgeoisie.[65] In addition, some purges were carried out in an effort to end corruption. After the 'committee to end feudalism' had settled some of its investigations and inquiries against large landowners who had circumvented the law, it launched several inquiries in the public sector against officials who were heavily involved in or compromised by corruption, black market activities and embezzlement.[66]

However, by the end of the Yemen War in 1964/65 and at the close of the five-year plan, a second stage was characterized by the relationship between the 'state bourgeoisie' and state power whereby the latter was losing its relative autonomy, while the former was increasingly spreading its hegemony over the ruling class. By virtue of their command and control positions in the various state sectors, the new bourgeoisie could use any means of getting richer and acquiring the greatest share of surplus. This was not only true of the state economic sector but also of the army.

The years 1965/66 mark a total unleashing of the state bourgeoisie's appetite. Nasser's increased dependence on, and protection by, Russia had created some anxiety amongst its members. Having lost hope in a return to capitalist investment, they concentrated on rapid enrichment and investment in luxurious houses, increased smuggling of their capital abroad, coupled with unrestrained consumption of illicitly imported luxury goods.[67] The state bourgeoisie had by then extended its networks to the highest levels of state power and the repressive apparatuses, where most of the leaders were beginning to derive personal benefits from the protection they were able to provide the state bourgeoisie. The whole productive system was in a situation of chaos, and industrial output and national income were on the decline.[68]

These then were the internal conditions that prevailed on the eve of the third Arab–Israeli War. Astonishingly enough the system was not crumbling and Nasser continued to manoeuvre for the support of the masses, who had exhibited signs of unrest, and continued to enjoy the support of the Soviet Union, which was eager to suppress the Western-oriented state bourgeoisie, for it realized that if the latter acceded to power, it would threaten Russian interests in the area. The Nasser regime had even spoken of a new five-year plan. But the plan became non-functional with the outbreak of the June war with Israel in 1967.[69]

International developments
By the mid-1960s Egypt had very definitely entered the Soviet orbit. In 1965 following a substantial arms delivery to Egypt, the Russian fleet now permanently resided in the Mediterranean Sea[70] and Russian technicians constituted a very real foreign community within the country's major cities. Trade relations were increasingly bilateral and loans increased along with the development of a unilateral dependence on Russia for the completion of such projects as the High Dam. In other words, the USSR could by then literally stifle the country's economy. With regard to army supplies the Eastern countries laid the foundations of a military apparatus which could only function and develop along Soviet lines. Meanwhile in the area of industrial production the key sectors such as the High Dam, the chemical complex (KIMA), iron and steel, and other heavy industrial materials, gradually became Soviet Bloc strongholds. Between 1961 and 1967 the Soviet Union's role in civilian goods (both industrial and agricultural) became crucial, particularly regarding wheat supply. Furthermore, Egypt depended almost totally on the Soviet Union for the sale of its cotton crop. On top of all this, there was the country's total technical dependence on the Soviet Union.[71]

Nasser, who resented the new situation had, however, continued to make some weak attempts at regaining state autonomy. His proclaimed international ideology and policy continued to be 'non-alignment'. It had not been his intention to replace British colonialism by Russian imperialism. Within the international context of a cold war, Nasser's Egypt had been able to utilize its double dependence on the two major powers to its benefit and had thus maintained relative independence and manoeuvring space. However, the situation was now different. Egypt's increased dependence on the Soviet state had been preceded by a *détente* between the two major powers, whereby each at least respected the other's sphere of influence in order to avoid direct confrontation. Thus whilst the United States had not totally lost hope for its renewed influence in Egypt and had continued to foster its inner contradictions by supporting certain groups of the state bourgeoisie, it had by the mid-1960s come to depend on other states for the safeguarding of its interests and strategies in the area. A new network of solid bases of support was established in the Middle East, mainly in Saudi Arabia, Tunisia, Morocco, and most important of all, Israel.[72]

The period under study is characterized by Egypt's increased involvement in Arab politics, its striving for Arab unity under its leadership as the defender of progressive Arab forces. This new role inevitably revived the Cold War in the Arab Middle-Eastern context between so-called conservative and revolutionary forces, and hence the competition between the two major international blocs. Examples of Egypt's new role and increased involvement in Arab affairs include the regime's intervention and active support of the South Yemen revolt against the Saudi-supported royalists, the severing of ties with Federal

Germany when it delivered arms to Israel, and the closing of the Tiran Straits after Israel's threats against Syria.[73] Nasser presented Arab unity as an essential tool for the struggle against Western imperialism in general, and Israeli colonialism in particular.

Egypt's new role as defender of anti-reactionary forces extended beyond the Arab Middle East. The notion of a Third World united struggle against imperialism was developed as an important theme in Nasser's politics. Egypt's involvement in African politics increased in the way of supporting revolutionary forces and the territorial claims of independent African states, for instance in the Congo, Somalia, South Africa and Rhodesia. Another form of Egyptian involvement in African politics was the spread of the Islamic faith.[74]

All these new developments became a source of great concern for American interests in the area, and for Israel, America's closest ally. It was no longer a question of waiting until the regime crumbled from its contradictions; nor of waiting until the situation led to direct confrontation between the United States and the Eastern bloc. A military defeat appeared to be the ideal solution. Not only would it destroy the regime, its military and economy, but it would impose a change of foreign policy, largely capitulating to the West and would also indirectly strike a double blow against the Soviets since (a) their credibility and. popularity as Egypt's friends would weaken if their arms and support proved ineffective, and (b) it would remind the Soviets of Western military supremacy once again as well as reshuffling areas of influence in favour of the United States. The time was indeed ripe for a third Arab–Israeli war, and while Nasser continued to give little credence to the possibility of its outbreak the scenario was being set.[75] The time was ripe for the enforcement of internal liberalization and capitulation to the West.[76] Nasser's regime had been weakened and had not managed to build up its own inner resistance, nor had it nurtured sufficient popular and political support.

Notes

1. Anouar Abdel Malek, *Egypt Military Society*, p. 55.
2. Russell Bradon, *Suez, the Splitting of a Nation*, p. 70.
3. Abdel Malek, p. 107.
4. Mahmoud Hussein, Class Conflict in Egypt, *1945–1971* (New York, 1979), pp. 146–7.
5. Issawi, *Egypt in Revolution: An Economic Analysis*, p. 57.
6. Hossam Issa, *Capitalisme et sociétés anonymes en Egypte*, p. 219.
7. Ibid., pp. 215–16.
8. To be discussed in greater detail in a subsequent chapter.
9. Patrick O'Brien, *The Revolution in Egypt's Economic System*, p. 109.
10. Issa, p. 216.
11. O'Brien, p. 96.
12. Barawy, *Economic Development in the UAR (Egypt)*, p. 69.
13. Ibid., pp. 66–9.

14. Mahmoud Hussein, pp. 134, 142, 143.
15. Ibid., p. 140.
16. Ibid., p. 52.
17. O'Brien, p. 89.
18. Issa, p. 420.
19. Abdel Malek, pp. 100, 101.
20. O'Brien, pp. 101, 102.
21. Kosheiry, p. 84.
22. Ibid., pp. 84, 85.
23. Ibid., p. 89.
24. O'Brien, pp. 101, 102.
25. Abdel Malek, p. 133 and O'Brien, pp. 101 and 102.
26. O'Brien, pp. 109, 111, 115, 122.
27. Abdel Malek, pp. 112, 113.
28. Ibid., pp. 114, 115.
29. Ibid., pp. 123, 136, 137.
30. Ibid., p. 118.
31. Abdel Malek, p. 161.
32. Ibid., p. 155.
33. For a discussion of the emergence of the 'state bourgeoisie' see Hussein, pp. 134–59.
34. Mahmoud Abdel Fadil, *The Political Economy of Nasserism: A Study in Employment and Income Distribution in Urban Egypt, 1952–72*, p. 102. Abdel Fadil also implies the existing interlinkages through kinship between sections of the bourgeoisie.
35. Immam, p. 163.
36. O'Brien, p. 130.
37. Mabro and Radwan, p. 73.
38. Issa, pp. 484, 485.
39. O'Brien, pp. 131–6.
40. Bent Hansen and Girgis Marzouk, *Development and Economic Policy in the UAR (Egypt)*, p. 295.
41. Essam Montasser, 'The Housing Sector as a Component in Egypt's Development Planning', p. 5 and Mabro and Radwan, pp. 192, 193.
42. Mabro and Radwan, pp. 192, 193.
43. Ismail Sabri Abdallah, pp. 273–306.
44. Hansen and Marzouk, p. 292.
45. Ismail S. Abdallah, *The Organisation of the Public Sector: Theoretical Bases and Major Political Problems*, p. 306. Also according to two interviews conducted with both the chairman and the director of the general and chemical trading company, on Tuesday April 4, 1978, and Sunday April 9, 1978, the company's internal organization has remained virtually unchanged since the days when it was the British ICI. The present chairman, of Levantine origins, had been working with the company since 1940, when it was established.
46. 'A Debate: The Public Sector from Within', *Al Taliah*, 1965, no. 8, pp. 40–78.
47. Ali Sabri, *The Years of Socialist Transformation and the Evolution of the Five Year Plan*, pp. 85–111.
48. Ibid., p. 100.
49. O'Brien, p. 245.

50. Hassan Riad, *L'Egypte Nassérienne* pp. 86, 87.

51. O'Brien, p. 245.

52. Abdel Malek, p. 177.

53. Adel Ghoneim, 'Around the Issue of the New Class in Egypt', pp. 82–93.

54. Adel Ghoneim, 'Some Light on the Tendencies of Nationalist Capitalism', pp. 96–104.

55. Mahmoud Hussein, pp. 222, 223.

56. Ali Sabri, pp. 100, 111, 118.

57. See *Rose El Youssef*, no. 2646, February 22, 1979, pp. 6–8, in an interview conducted with Othman Ahmed Othman, one of Egypt's largest contractors, in fact the largest in both Egypt and some Middle Eastern countries, who is also a leading business figure in various fields, the founder of countless private sector companies in contemporary Egypt and known to be one of the wealthiest capitalists in the country, is reported to have worked and prospered greatly during the Nasser era and more specifically during the plan years.

58. Ali Sabri, pp. 101, 102.

59. Adel Ghoneim, 'Some Light', pp. 96–104.

60. See ibid., and Ali Sabri and Abdel Razik Hassan, 'The National Economic Map – between the Public Sector and Private Sector'. Hassan, on p. 74 of his article in *Al Taliah*, 1966, no. 6, states that some of the major areas where the private sector was able to develop its parasitical activities have been in housing, the internal trade of spare parts (some of which were being acquired through the public sector at cheap prices and then resold to the consumer as well as the public sector at elevated prices), fruit and vegetables, milk products and their manufacture, and transport by trucks or lorries. All these are areas where the public sector was still weak. See also the debate conducted by *Al Taliah*, August 1965, no. 8, entitled 'The Public Sector from Within', where several public sector directors were invited to discuss and evaluate the inner workings of the system, its past heritage and some of the problems confronting it.

61. More specific details of their activity will be discussed in a subsequent chapter.

62. Adel Ghoneim, 'Around the Issue of the New Class in Egypt', pp. 22–93.

63. Hussein, pp. 191–3.

64. The Arab Centre for Political and Economic Studies, *The Problems and Bases for the Establishment of the Contracting Sector: Preliminary Studies*, pp. 4, 5.

65. Adel Ghoneim, 'Some Light on the Téndencies of Nationalist Capitalism', p. 103.

66. Hussein, p. 236.

67. Ibid., p. 202.

68. Ibid., pp. 195, 196, 197.

69. Barawy, *Economic Development in the UAR (Egypt)*, pp. 308–12.

70. Olivier Carrée, 'Pouvoir et idéologie dans L'Egypte de Nasser et de Sadate (1952–1975)', *L'Egypte d'Aujourd'hui, permanence et changements 1805–1976*, pp. 254–8.

71. Hussein, pp. 202–16.

72. Ibid., p. 209.

73. Carrée, pp. 254–8; and P. J. Vatikiotis, 'Some Political Consequences of the 1952 Revolution in Egypt', p. 382.

74. Ibid.

75. Most of these views on the interpretation of the war are also shared by Mahmoud Hussein, as well as a number of commentators writing on the event. See also V. Ernst, *Impérialisme au Moyen-Orient*.

76. Samih Farsoun and Walter F. Carroll, 'State Capitalism and Counter-revolution in the Middle East: A Thesis', pp. 157–3.

3 The Aftermath of the Sinai War: From Liberalization to the 'Open Door' Policy (1968–73)

The Six-Day War had struck the final blow to the Nasserite regime, not only militarily, but ideologically, politically and economically as well. Besides, Israeli aggression did not stop with the end of the June 1967 war, but continued for another two years in the form of a war of attrition which brought widespread destruction to Egypt and which ended only when Egypt accepted the Rogers Plan.

Ideology, politics and the economy after the Six-Day War

On the *ideological* level the period was characterized by general confusion. The power structure no longer had a constructive, positive ideology to present, as in the preceding period. Instead a defensive ideology prevailed which purported to pursue national independence and socialism, a concept which had by now become a mere slogan, void of much of the fervour and content it had had during the brief alliance between the power élite (state power) and the Left. Even amongst intellectual circles not much was being elaborated in terms of socialist theories. Fouad Morsi, writing on the problematic of the socialist transformation a year before the war, had observed a growing tendency amongst Egyptian intellectuals to distort the true essence and significance of socialism and to regard capitalist development as progressive because it constituted an advance over feudalism and a possible solution to Egypt's economic problems.[1]

Despite the fact that in 1969 the land ceiling had been further reduced to 50 feddans, it was by now obvious that the ideological emphasis was no longer upon social justice and the dissolution of class differences, but upon 'national unity' in order to confront the external enemy and regain lost territory and national pride. Ideological debates in the press in favour of an 'Arab application of socialism' as opposed to 'Arab socialism', with its Islamic and nationalist connotations, had now disappeared. 'Nasserism' was gradually weakening and attempts at socialist radicalization which had characterized the mid-1960s had come to an end leaving behind an ideological vacuum which was gradually being filled by a rightist pragmatic tendency.[2] A new candidate from within the regime was in fact selected by the state bourgeoisie to represent the new pragmatic trends and replace Nasser. Zakariya Mohieddin was chosen as the regime's pro-Western spokesman and representative of the state bourgeois group which advocated (a) stronger repressive measures against the masses instead of Nasser's proposed concessions, and (b) opening up to the West and resuming friendly relations with the United States.[3]

The matter had been slightly complicated by the masses' support of Nasser following the latter's resignation – a support that had been dictated by their rising political consciousness and a clear understanding of what a Mohieddin government would signify with regard to their own interests and exploited position. This was a historical moment indeed in mass participation and political power.[4] The people would not accept the presidency of Mohieddin and capitulation to the West; the defeat would have to be avenged, and short of any other visible, prominent, influential leader who enjoyed Nasser's background and history of nationalist heroism, the latter was selected to represent their opposition to the state bourgeoisie's solution. The masses had very clearly now come onto the scene as strong participants in Egypt's internal ideological and class conflict.

Having accepted the resumption of his presidential responsibilities, Nasser was faced with a situation of conflict within the ruling class, of a weakened state apparatus, of continued Israeli aggression and of pressures from the masses (namely student and workers' demonstrations) to resume war or launch a popular battle, and of a certain reluctance on the part of the Soviet state to encourage such a tendency. Although Nasser continued to rely heavily on Soviet support, firmer overtures were made to the United States, the masses were being increasingly repressed, signs of economic liberalism appeared, and by the end of this period the dialogue with the United States was openly resumed, Nasser accepting the Rogers ceasefire plan in 1970.[5]

Politically, as mentioned previously, state control had weakened, and the regime's credibility had decreased as a result of the defeat. Internal contradictions became acute both within the ruling class and between the latter and the mass of the population.[6] The Nasser regime had admitted partial responsibility for the defeat and was now forced to promise democratization of the political organs with the masses' genuine participation. In a gesture of solidarity with the masses, and as an effort to concede to their demands, the March declaration was promulgated and was ratified by a popular referendum. Although the new manifesto aimed at a revision of the existing political institutions in favour of a more democratic participation by the masses, the effort had been circumvented by the despotic actions of the secret organization in the heart of the Arab Socialist Union. The organization had been led by Ali Sabri, Sami Sharraf and Charawi Gomaa.[7] The situation was thus aggravated and the years following the war marked the spread of student and workers' revolts, the most important of which occurred in February 1968.[8]

With regard to the contradictions within the ranks of the ruling class, severe strife had occurred between Nasser and the armed forces under the leadership of Field-Marshal Amer.[9] The weakening of the state apparatus and Nasser's authority allowed the pressure group calling for a decentralized economy and a strengthened private sector to gain particular importance and influence. Thus after 1967, the private sector's investment in housing reached the high level it had attained in the 1950s.[10] Furthermore, in the field of exports, the state apparatus had shown signs of liberalization which enabled the private sector to flourish.[11]

In the field of imports, certain public enterprises were allowed to purchase their equipment directly from abroad without having to go through the foreign trade companies, the central authority for foreign trade, and ministries, for permits.[12] Added to all that was the mass exodus of some 350,000 Egyptians following the 1967 war. Prior to that period travel had been tightly controlled. With the weakening of state control, a considerable number of Egyptians took the opportunity to travel abroad. Emigrants were mainly skilled labourers and qualified technocrats.[13] The opportunity to travel, notably to rich oil-producing Arab countries, enabled the private sector entrepreneurs to consolidate their economic power abroad. During the period under study one gets the feeling, both from the contemporary press and from personal recollections of the time, that parasitical activity, corruption and the smuggling of imported goods from neighbouring Arab countries were all becoming very pronounced.[14] Smuggling was increasingly becoming geared towards the purchase of durable and luxury consumer goods, while bribery had become institutionalized. Abd al Samad, when describing the internal strife that ensued after the defeat, also describes some of the corruption that was occurring at the time among military men and members of the National Assembly. According to his account, a large number were active in export/import business, or more specifically involved in various forms of corruption. The author recounts how one of his colleagues, a Member of Parliament, had even been involved in the sale of Egyptian petrol to Poland against a very large commission. The role of the colleague in question was simply to introduce his Polish client to the right Egyptian channels, one of whom was Abd al Samad, who would in turn introduce both his colleague and the Polish businessman to a fourth person. The author expresses his surprise at the existence of this new activity amongst his colleagues, and indicates that such practices became quite widespread at this time and emerged as a visible phenomenon.[15] Meanwhile there is evidence to show that members of the regime had already started a series of contacts with America to re-establish friendly ties.[16]

Economically prospects of investment and development had suffered greatly after the outbreak of the war. The war had not only meant an interruption to state planning and investment, but had also caused serious material losses both directly and indirectly. With regard to direct losses, any estimate translated into Egyptian pounds would have to take into consideration not only the cost of destroyed constant capital, i.e. buildings and equipment, but also the value of productive output potential lost as measured against the average output during the five-year plan. Such a loss in output is likely to spread over a number of years. Some have estimated the loss over 15 to 20 years,[17] whilst others have calculated the losses till 1974.[18] The productive sectors suffering most were the extractive and mineral enterprises situated in Sinai and the Canal Zone.

According to El Gritly, the estimated loss for the metal companies in Sinai, El Nasr company for fertilizers, and El Nasr for petrol up until 1974, was £E20 million.[19] Another estimate of losses in key sectors is presented by Yusuf Ahmed, who maintains that the interruption of revenues from the Suez Canal, petrol in Sinai and tourism, all together caused a loss of US$30 million per month.[20] Another sector that was deeply affected was that of transport, particularly in the Canal Zone, since income obtained from the passage of ships and cargoes in the waterway had constituted a very important source of revenue to the country.[21] This is quite apart from the great losses in human resources.

The indirect losses caused to the economy were those occurring as a result of political instability in the area, as well as the mobilization of the various productive sectors for a war economy plan ranging from the immediate requirements of war to the requirements of its aftermath, such as a government subsidy for consumer goods. With respect to the relation of the country to the outside world, revenues from telecommunications (airmail) and aviation were greatly reduced. The estimated loss for the Misr aviation company alone was £E81 million. The postal enterprises sustained an estimated loss of £E6 million. In the field of agriculture an estimated £E44 million loss was attributed to the agricultural insurance company's exclusion of interest on loans as well as the sale of insecticides and fertilizers at less than factory cost. Moreover the meat, poultry and fishing enterprises lost £E5 million, since they were included in state-subsidized consumer goods. Finally, the vast expansion in mass media expenditure during the war amounted to £E10 million. Thus, according to El Gritly's calculations, the losses resulting from the war and its aftermath at 1974 prices totalled £E210 million.[22] According to the calculations made by Dr Issawi and Dr Nasser, who extend the period of estimated damages caused by the war over 15–20 years, and who have a much broader vision of the war's effects than El Gritly, losses caused by the military debacle were in the region of £E20–24 billion at 1975 prices.[23]

Taking into consideration all the above estimated losses, let us now look at the chain effects provoked by the war, resulting in a great deterioration of the country's balance of payments. During the war and after, the percentage of national income devoted to defence had greatly increased. This increase led to a great deterioration of national savings and investment. While savings constituted 13 per cent of gross domestic production in 1967, in the years that followed the war they constituted only six per cent. The decrease in savings also meant a decrease in investment and the inability to complete projects which were crucial to the economy, such as land reclamation, and the projects connected to the High Dam, i.e. irrigation and the generation of electricity necessary for the various chemical industrial projects. All these factors led to the swelling of the balance of payments deficit following the war. Thus, while from 1960–66 the deficit constituted 3.35 per cent of gross domestic production, in the period following the war it increased to 6.62 per cent. A major cause of the decline had been the great increases in imports after the war, which had been met by a negligible and unsustained increase in exports.[24] There was no way Egypt could continue to invest, pursue economic development, repay some of its already accumulated debt, or import foodstuffs in order to meet the increasing demands of a rising population. The situation was temporarily saved through Arab aid totalling £E125 million by 1969. Military indebtedness, however, continued to weigh heavily on the economy.[25]

The increased conflicts and contradictions between Nasser's radical policies and the dominant bourgeois fractions of the regime's social base contributed largely to the weakening of the regime. The development of state capitalism had in its process allowed for the consolidation and enrichment of a new capitalist class. Entrepreneurs became wealthy through wholesale trade, blackmarket activity and contracting mediating activity. Moreover, in the countryside middle-sized landowners coalesced with the remaining large landowners to accumulate power. They obstructed the regime's land reform. In sum the private bourgeoisie became a latent interest group which exerted pressure for more openings to the West and widened opportunities for a market economy.

A new 'state bourgeoisie' which had acquired power and control over national wealth, had become firmly established within the regime. This new bourgeoisie had been largely recruited from families whose ideology, economic interests, opportunities and lifestyle were at best confused with regard to Nasser's development policies of the 1960s. Many of the Free Officers married into these families and gradually became 'bourgeois' themselves. This new bourgeois constituency within the ruling ranks was in contradiction to the Nasserite ideology. Not only was its ideological orientation different to the regime in power, but it was on the whole insecure, since it did not own the means of production but simply controlled them and therefore very much desired the expansion of a market economy to secure its position.

> By the mid-sixties, the twin ills of embourgeoisement and patrimonialization were undermining Nasser's policies and shifting the balance of social forces against them. These threats could probably have been contained; but ultimately they were not, chiefly because Nasser failed to create the political instruments to mobilize and organize those social forces which favoured or benefited from Nasserism.[26]

Thus while Nasser's policies were being systematically attacked, there was little resistance to the attack. Meanwhile the 1967 defeat firmly reinforced the profound crises which the country was already undergoing. The forces calling for change and the opening up of the economy were gaining ground. The war had seriously shaken the country's economy.[27]

Thus the Nasser regime had not only been confronted by a bitter internal battle, but an external one as well, which had destroyed it on many levels. The regime had failed to resolve its own internal contradictions within the ruling class, hence capitalist accumulation and a national capitalist development along Japanese lines was precluded; meanwhile, ideologically, it had not sufficiently matured to rid itself of all residual conservatism, nor had its repressive policies succeeded in mobilizing the masses, so an independent socialist development like that of China was also blocked. In sum, the shackles of dependency were never fully broken; the 'bolts' had simply been loosened for a while only to be tightened again. As Farsoun and Carroll describe the Arab periphery:

> State capitalism emerged as a mode of production of the 'intermediary strata' which was the means for resolving the crisis of dependent capitalism . . . However the state–capitalist project triggers its own internal contradictions and is unable to resolve either the national or class questions. The state–capitalist ruling strata, in alliance with a new parasitical bourgeoisie and the resurgent old bourgeoisie fears displacement or destruction at the hands of mass-based revolutionary movements. They must seek salvation in a counter-revolution and integration into imperialism.[28]

The 'open door' policy (*infitah*)

Under Nasser's successor, the trend towards the liberalization of the economy accelerated and, following the fourth Arab–Israeli War in 1973, an 'open door' policy was officially declared which entailed an opening to the West and the promotion of a mixed economy comprising a State capitalist sector and a substantial free enterprise sector. Although the various policy changes occurred under the same political regime and one can trace a logic of interlinked continuous events leading to the final declaration of the new policy, for organizational purposes it is more accurate to look at the period in two phases. The first phase beginning with the Sadat political regime in 1970, represents the preparatory phase of *infitah*, while the second phase commencing with the October working paper in 1973, immediately followed by Investment law no. 43 of 1974, represents the operational phase. The latter phase is distinguished from the former in as much as the economy was now being legally liberalized, i.e. the official policy was being translated into economic legislation to change and legitimize the new relationship with Western capitalism and to encourage the private sector. Furthermore, the second phase of *infitah* is indistinguishable from the first by virtue of the fact that economic liberalization was not only moving faster, but was also particularly directed at internal conditions. During the first phase the new policy had concentrated on the attraction of foreign capital and investment. In this section I will briefly outline the preparatory phase; the second phase will be more closely examined in subsequent chapters.

The period from 1970 until the outbreak of the fourth Arab–Israeli War in 1973 was, to a large extent, a continuation of the war economy period which followed the 1967 debacle, in as much as the economy continued to face serious obstacles to its development. The various difficulties in economic development were once again being reflected in the increasingly alarming balance of payments and trade deficits which pushed the country into increased dependence on foreign loans. The second five-year plan had still not been launched and the economy came to a standstill. Imports, in the form of both arms purchases and consumer goods, continued to increase greatly, while exports remained stagnant in comparison. Thus in 1970 the trade deficit was in the order of £E160 million and by 1972 the figure had increased to £E260 million.[29] The only means of survival in this emergency situation appeared to be the recourse to foreign loans which came from a variety of sources, namely international organizations such as the World Bank, and the International Monetary Fund, as well as Arab aid and deposits made to the Central Bank. In addition, both military and non-military loans came from the Soviet Union and other socialist countries. The structure of foreign loans and the means of servicing the debt became a source of great concern to the Egyptian Government. Egypt's total foreign debt by the end of December 1973 was estimated at a little above US$3.5 billion. The government had temporarily managed to reschedule some of the deadlines for debt servicing, but the situation on the whole looked bleak.[30]

Foreign loans, particularly from Western and international sources, were being accompanied by suggested solutions to Egypt's endemic problems and deteriorating economy. The International Monetary Fund had in the past already made some suggestions to Egyptian economists under the Nasser regime, when Egypt was importing a large amount of basic food grain from the United States. The IMF would secure the inflow of foreign exchange from Western sources to Egypt, if the latter were to adopt its proposed 'stabilization' plan. The plan entailed a re-allocation of investment outlays, the adoption of an exchange rate for the pound which would promote exports and attract foreign investment, a cut-down on government subsidies, and a campaign to increase public sector efficiency. Although not fully accepting the direction in which the IMF hoped to push the Egyptian economy, some minor concessions had been made in 1962: the Egyptian pound was devalued by 20 per cent, and as a result of political conflict between the USA and Egypt over the former's role in the Congo, the US interrupted its shipment of wheat under its PL 480 Aid programme. Egypt's response was to intensify its trade relations with the socialist bloc and to resist the pressures for the acceptance of a stabilization plan.[31]

When Sadat came to power, as previously mentioned, the economy had reached a watershed and the contradictions between development aspirations and the 'no-war/no-peace' situation emerged very strongly. Furthermore, it appeared to the regime in power that the solution to Egypt's disastrous position lay, in large part, in the hands of the United States. Any improvements over the Rogers plan and in the Arab–Israeli conflict would necessitate US collaboration, which was of course conditional. The lines along which the US hoped to see Egyptian policy move were summarized in the statement made by the American Secretary of State, Henry Kissinger, in St Clement in 1970. He declared that the United States was trying 'to get a Middle East settlement in such a way that the moderate regimes are strengthened and not the radical regimes'. 'The US', he went on to say, was 'trying to expel the Soviet military presence.'[32]

In order to achieve the desired peace settlement and ensuing economic development, it became obvious that Egypt's political ideology needed some visible modifications. Sadat's personal ideological orientations were not incompatible with those of the US. It was not long after his accession to power that drastic purges had been carried out within the ranks of the ruling élite in May 1971. The purges had been directly aimed at those figures in the regime who had not only attempted a take-over of power, but were also known to be the most pro-Soviet elements of the regime and who had fostered the relations between their Soviet protectors and Egypt.[33] In July of that same year Egypt's willingness to reinforce moderate regimes and fight radical pro-Soviet ones was signalled when Sadat helped restore the Numeiri government in Sudan after a brief take-over by the Sudanese Marxists.[34] Another indication of good faith towards the Western powers was given in July of the following year, when the Soviet military mission was expelled from Egypt.[35]

Internally the Egyptian economy was now beginning to acquire a new look. Although a fully fledged stabilization plan was not yet being applied, there were signs of its acceptance and some serious efforts were being made to attract foreign investment, enhance the private sector, and reorganize the public sector. As early as January 1971 the Egyptian Federation of Industries was already discussing the establishment of a new plan that would encourage the participation of the private sector in industry.[36] The following month another gesture was made to the private sector, when 800 proprietors, whose land had been sequestrated, had their land restored, whilst compensation was paid to the 5,000 landowners who had been affected by the 1969 agrarian reform.[37] In an attempt to reorganize the public sector, law no. 64 of 1971 was promulgated to restrain the general organization from interfering in the administration of the companies and to encourage company directors to become more independent in their decision-making.[38] Furthermore public sector employees were now divided into four categories instead of nineteen, and a new system of incentives was introduced whereby promotions were based on aptitude.[39]

With regard to encouragement of foreign investment, during the preparatory phase of *infitah*, some steps were already under way. As a gesture of good faith to foreign investors, an old grudge was being settled by the payment of £E2 million as financial compensation for European subjects who had suffered from past agrarian reforms and sequestration measures following the 1956 Suez War. This measure was to settle finally the debt owed to British sequestrated proprietors.[40] In May 1971 a committee had been set up to study the extension of foreign investment in Egypt, which had hitherto been restricted to the oil industry. In September of the same year, law no. 65 was promulgated through a presidential decree to encourage Arab investment in Egypt and the establishment of free zones. The law provided the Arab investor with guarantees against sequestration and nationalization while also granting prospective investors certain facilities and privileges such as tax exemptions. The law also allowed foreign non-Arab investment and gave it equal privileges provided the projects met with the approval of the Council of Ministers and the President of the Republic. Meanwhile the Egyptian International Bank for

Trade and Development was established. The function of the bank was to attract Arab capital and rechannel the funds into investment programmes. The bank dealt only in foreign convertible currency and enjoyed a number of privileges.[41]

In October 1971 yet another step towards 'opening' was being made when Egypt signed an accord with the International Bank for Reconstruction and Development for the settlement and arbitration of foreign investment disputes. The agreement also provided for tax exemptions for a grace period of five years, as well as for the establishment of free zones. Most important of all it allowed joint ventures with the Egyptian public sector to be treated as autonomous units. By the end of this first preparatory phase a total of 250 projects with a capital of £E171 million had been presented for approval. Fifty of the listed projects had been accepted. Immediately preceding the October war, in the spring and summer of 1973, the 'open door' policy had acquired official recognition, and despite the ongoing debate around the subject in the press and Assembly, policy-makers were already acting according to the new guidelines.[42] It must here be mentioned that during the preparatory phase the major emphasis had been upon external opening to the West and the attraction of foreign investment and capital. Higazi, who had been appointed Minister of Finance in 1968, had been the architect, organizer and executor of the new economic order. Internal liberalization and opening had only received minor attention in terms of legislative innovation. It was only on the eve of the war that the public sector's efficiency became the subject of debate and criticism in the press.[43] It was also one month before the October war that the parallel market was established with the aim of attracting the hard currency savings of Egyptians abroad by devaluing the Egyptian pound to half its official price.[44]

Bolder steps towards liberalization were made immediately following the fourth Arab–Israeli War in 1973. The war had succeeded in breaking the military stalemate in the Middle East, and had a favourable impact upon the willingness of Arab states to participate in Egypt's economic efforts. During the war period Algeria had purchased emergency shipments of arms from the Soviet Union. Shortly after, oil rich countries, Saudi Arabia at the forefront, poured loans and gifts into the Egyptian economy in order to enable the country to import necessary foodstuffs and raw materials. Despite the help obtained, Egypt's economy continued to deteriorate after the war.[45] According to Morsi, the crisis in Egypt's balance of payments had reached unprecedented proportions by 1974. The deficit during that year was in the order of £E500 million, and rapidly increased to £E1,300 million in 1975. Meanwhile, shortages in Egypt's raw materials and the need for imports intensified, coupled with tremendous price increases, with which export revenues could not keep pace.[46] The balance of trade deficit increased from £E260 million in 1972 to the alarming figure of £E680 in 1974, and £E1,000 in 1975. Imports from the West increased from 62 per cent of Egypt's foreign trade in 1973 to 74 per cent in 1974. Meanwhile Egypt's exports to the Western bloc manifested a negligible increase of three per cent between 1973 and 1974. The percentage of Egyptian exports to the West was 33 per cent and 35 per cent for the two respective years.[47] Egypt's foreign exchange reserves could only suffer from such conditions, especially since military expenditure continued to weigh quite heavily on the economy, all leading to the obstruction of economic development. Once again Egypt was depending heavily on foreign loans as an emergency measure. In 1974 Egypt was forced to borrow £E940 million from abroad at the disadvantageous interest rate of 19 per cent.[48] US aid alone had increased from $8.5 million in the following fiscal year.[49] Continued heavy indebtedness was not the only problem, for along with heavy borrowing Egypt was far behind schedule in the servicing of previous short-term loans, which could only jeopardize its chances for future loans,[50] and could also be viewed as a reflection of economic stagnation.

Although the war did not salvage the Egyptian economy in any real sense, it certainly resulted in deeper US involvement in the peace settlement and its acceleration, which was regarded as a cornerstone of Egypt's new road to development by the Sadat regime. With peace it was hoped that a number of Egypt's economic sectors would once again yield impressive revenues. The Canal would be reopened, tourists would pour into the country again and the oilfields in Sinai would be restituted. The most important hoped-for effect of a final peace settlement was the inflow of foreign capital;[51] in other words reaping the fruits of the 'open door' preparatory phase which had preceded the war.

The liberalization of the Egyptian economy came about naturally and gradually as the outcome of the defeat of the Nasserite regime. Although the regime had had its own internal problems and contradictions, by the mid-1960s, it was the war situation, rather than internal class conflict, which gave the regime its final blow. Meanwhile, within the ranks of the regime's ruling class, those who had called for a *rapprochement* with the West as a solution due to Nasser's weakness had won, and Nasser himself had begun to capitulate to Western pressures by accepting the Rogers Plan. This constituted the beginning of a long-lasting dialogue with the West, accompanied by a gradual restructuring of Egypt's political economy.

Notes

1. Fouad Morsi, 'Specific Socialism and Scientific Socialism', p. 73.
2. Madame El Kosheiry Mahrouz, *Socialisme et pouvoir en Egypte*, p. 272.
3. Mahmoud Hussein, pp. 234, 302.
4. Ibid., pp. 259–69. This view on the political position of the masses after Nasser's resignation is not Hussein's original contribution, but was a widely held view amongst intellectuals, journalists and observers who witnessed events in Egypt at the time.
5. Mahfouz, pp. 273, 274.
6. Kamal Rifaat, 'The Internal Front is the Key to the Situation', pp. 61–4, and *Al Taliah* editorial board, 'Glances at the Critical Internal Situation', pp. 10–17.

7. Mahfouz, p. 271.

8. Mahmoud Hussein, pp. 283–97.

9. For a detailed account of the conflict that ensued, see Abdel Samad, *The Field Marshal's Last Supper*.

10. Robert Mabro and Samir Radwan, *The Industrialization of Egypt, 1939–1973*, p. 162.

11. Ceres Wissa Wassef, 'Problèmes économiques et sociaux'.

12. Ibid.

13. Ibrahim El Issawy and Mohamed Nasser, 'Some Indicators of the War Costs'.

14. For a discussion of the above developments see *Al Taliah*, February 1967, no. 11, pp. 20–75, the section entitled 'The Black Market', a series of reports and researches.

15. Abdel Samad, p. 156.

16. Hassanein Haykal, *The Autumn of Fury* (in Arabic), p. 164.

17. Ibrahim El Issawy and Mohamed Nasser, pp. 7, 8.

18. Ali El Gritly, *Twenty-Five Years: An Analytical Study of Economic Policies in Egypt*, p. 216.

19. Ibid.

20. Youssef J. Ahmed, *La Capacité d'absorption de l'Economie Egyptienne: une analyse des problèmes et perspective*, p. 38.

21. El Gritly, p. 216.

22. Ibid.

23. Issawy and Nasser, pp. 16–23.

24. Ibid., p. 12.

25. Ahmed, pp. 38, 39.

26. Raymond Hinnebusch Jr., *Egyptian Politics under Sadat, The Post-populist Development of an Authoritarian–Modernizing State*, pp. 29–33, 34, 35.

27. Ibid.

28. Samih Farsoun and Walter Carroll, 'State Capitalism and Counter-Revolution in the Middle East: A Thesis', p. 153.

29. El Gritly, p. 147.

30. Ahmed, p. 34.

31. John Waterbury, 'Egypt 1976', p. 3.

32. Ibid., p. 4.

33. Waterbury, 'The Opening: Part I: Egypt's Economic New Look', p. 7.

34. Waterbury, 'Egypt 1976', p. 5.

35. Waterbury, 'The Opening: Part I', p. 7.

36. Fouad Morsi, *This Economic Opening*, p. 8.

37. Wassef, p. 289.

38. Waterbury, 'Public versus Private in the Egyptian Economy', p. 21.

39. Wassef, p. 287.

40. Ibid., p. 291.

41. Morsi, p. 9.

42. Waterbury, 'The Opening: Part II: Luring Foreign Capital', p. 6.

43. Morsi, p. 11.

44. Waterbury, 'Luring Foreign Capital', p. 10.

45. Waterbury, 'Egypt's Economic New Look', p. 6.

46. Morsi, p. 219.

47. El Gritly, pp. 147, 148.

48. Morsi, p. 219.
49. El Gritly, p. 153.
50. Waterbury, 'Egypt 1976', p. 6.
51. Ibid., p. 5.

4 The Commercial Agents: A Historical Background

During the inter-war period and into the early 1950s, commercial activity in foreign trade had been largely carried out by foreigners. As previously mentioned, the nascent Egyptian bourgeoisie had concentrated its efforts upon industrial activity, whilst commercial enterprise was largely left to foreigners. According to the experience and knowledge of a key informant who had been in charge of inspection and the application of subsequent laws relevant to commercial agencies, up until 1975 almost all such agencies were run by Jews, Levantines and other foreign nationals, while Egyptians were employed in some of the offices. Several of these establishments were run from a small room in town, owned, directed and staffed by a single person and mostly importing tools, workshop machinery, equipment and car spare parts.[1] One of the contemporary agents interviewed had begun his career in the business as early as 1948. However he had acted only as a local dealer to a foreign commercial agency in Cairo, since at the time, import/export activity was totally monopolized by foreigners. The informant also explained that Egyptians were not yet experienced enough, nor had they the contacts or means to step into that field.[2] This does not, however, signify that there were no exceptions. A famous example of a successful businessman who was also politically well-connected was Abboud Pasha. This pasha closely collaborated with the British and represented their interests on the local market.[3] A few Egyptian commercial agents were employed by foreign companies when political influence and intrigue were required. Berque writes that during the war and post-war years, when practically all the economic sectors in the society were being rehabilitated, public tenders for foreign goods were in abundance. British and French firms divided amongst themselves certain fields of specialization; the British considered the railways their domain, while the French concentrated on the Suez Canal Authority. From a report in the Alexandria British Chamber of Commerce Review describing a particular adjudication or tender for water pipes, it appears that one firm had an Egyptian agent who was in charge of all the intrigue and deviant practices relating to the local administration.[4] Owing to the existence of projects in those domains run by the Government during the post-war years when imports once again met the demands of local projects after the interruption during the war period, some Egyptians, although very few in number, collaborated closely with foreign commercial attachés in embassies to obtain tenders and adjudications by corrupt means.[5]

These then are the rare indications in the literature which seem to suggest that some Egyptians had become involved in the business as agents. However an accurate estimate of the proportion of Egyptians involved in foreign trade as agents is not possible, since the business was at the time chaotic, no registries were kept for commercial agencies, nor was there any law organizing the activity. The first attempt to regulate the activity was made at a much later date – in 1957.

In the period immediately following the Suez Crisis, when foreign interests were being sequestrated, Egyptian commercial agents clearly emerged as a distinctive group and prospered. Law no. 24 (1957) stipulated that commercial agency activity, in the form of both import–export companies and individuals, would have to be Egyptian. The first article of the law stipulated that commercial agents would not be allowed to practise their activity, unless their names were enrolled in the appropriate registry under the supervision of the Ministry of Trade. The second article of the same law allowed only Egyptian subjects or Egyptian joint stock companies to enrol their names in the registry.[6] By August 1959, 532 Egyptian commercial agents or companies had registered.[7] Many of the foreign-owned companies had been purchased by Egyptian businessmen, some of whom had been employed in the foreign company offices.

According to several commercial agents who started their business slightly before or during the Egyptianization process, it was during the late 1950s that Egyptian businessmen became increasingly involved in foreign trade and commercial agency. This was also the period when they made the greatest profits. One such businessman, the son of a pasha and large landowner, and one of the most prominent commercial agents at the time of writing, remarked that he was greatly indebted to Nasser for his present prosperity and the great success of his business, since it was thanks to Nasser that the Egyptianization process took place and so allowed him to take the place of previously foreign-owned companies and set up his own business. He added that those who had begun business during this epoch had been able to build on an extremely strong basis, which meant that they could continue their business and in time dominate the market – as they do to this day.[8]

According to the key informant who had been in charge, first of registration and later of inspections during the early 1960s, the figure of registered agents between 1957 and 1961 was in the order of 1,284 Egyptians, not counting another thousand who had not registered and whom the informant maintained were in all probability Egyptianized subjects of Levantine origin. Amongst the Egyptians registered the informant recalls such names as Serag El Din and Younes who were large landowners.[9] The fact that large landowners moved into the commercial sector during this period is not surprising, given that following the agrarian reform they had been deprived of their estates, and industrial investment appeared precarious due to the government's greater involvement and regulation. The industrialists had growing suspicions about their future under a regime which was acquiring increasing political and economic power. The commercial sector thus appeared to be a feasible alternative for private enterprise, where their capital and personal contacts, both in Egypt and abroad, gave them an advantage.

Egyptian private commercial companies and individuals took over not only most of the sequestrated British and French companies, but also other foreign commercial representation firms, whose owners were becoming increasingly nervous about their future security in the country and who were therefore very eager to sell out to their Egyptian managers and employees, some of whom made subtle agreements to share a given amount of profit and continue collaboration with the former company. A Swedish firm, for example, sold all its shares to its Egyptian manager, who became the owner of the trading company while continuing to represent the firm's interests.[10] A similar arrangement was made by a Spanish business group and the new Egyptian owner.[11] Likewise an Italian liaison office which feared sequestration continued to operate clandestinely in Egypt, protected by the fact that its formal owners were Egyptian.[12] The same arrangement was also made by several small-scale British commercial firms.[13] The larger enterprises, such as the British ICI, were purchased by the government and later became the General Trading and Chemical Company, one of the twelve public sector firms working in foreign trade.[14]

During the late 1950s the Egyptianization process gave a great boost to Egyptian commercial agents, but other objective conditions seem also to have strengthened their position and increased their numbers. It is during this period that the government became extremely active in creating industrial projects which not only called for more imports and public adjudications involving commercial agents, but also inhibited private industrial entrepreneurs from expanding their activity. It is not unlikely that as industrialists turned away from manufacturing and looked for less risky and more profitable activity, they may have joined the group involved in commercial activity. It is also during this particular period that Egypt's union with Syria occurred, which undoubtedly widened the scope for Egyptian commercial activity.

The second major law issued to regulate and control commercial agency activity was passed in 1961. Law no. 107 (1961) issued by presidential decree annulled the previous law no. 24 (1957) and stipulated that no company or individual could be enrolled in the commercial agency registry at the Ministry of Trade, save for government companies and those companies attached to a public establishment in which the government owned a minimum of 25 per cent of the capital.[15] Thus the business was quite clearly nationalized. At a later stage Nasser spoke publicly about this particular group, the commercial agents, in a speech delivered in November 1961 during the inauguration of the preparatory committee for the national conference; Nasser mentioned the names of some of the businessmen working in the field of imports who were able to make huge profits by illegal methods. He warned that unnecessarily expensive equipment was being brought into the country by bribing state officials, and that managers of state enterprises were similarly being bribed to tilt adjudications in favour of such corrupt businessmen, and that in this way the country was wasting its limited foreign exchange.[16]

Dr Hassan, a leading leftist economist working during the mid-1960s on the private and public sectors in the national economy, suggests that one of the factors leading to the strengthening of the public sector was its total control over foreign trade.[17] Yet, although in theory the state had complete control over imports through its twelve commercial public sector companies, in practice it seems that the private sector commercial agents continued to operate.

A very strong campaign was launched by the government in 1961 to prevent any of the former private sector commercial agents from interfering in imports or continuing their activities generally. An inspector was to visit the offices which had not been nationalized and which had in the past registered as agents, in order to carry out investigations into the nature of the work they were involved in and what their present source of livelihood was. The offices were obviously still working for productive foreign firms, which was legally accepted provided they were registered with the Ministry of the Interior as anything other than commercial agents, and were receiving a regular salary and not a commission. The latter form of remuneration or payment was absolutely prohibited. The government could not control tax payment or social justice and income distribution as part of the socialist ethos if commissions were allowed. The government would have no way of knowing how much commission was being paid to commercial agents abroad, and hence no control over that source of revenue.

From 1957 to 1961, a total of 1,284 Egyptian commercial agents were registered as delegate, consultant, technical adviser, propagandist, etc. (all legally accepted categories to the Ministry of Interior provided the contracts did not mention payment by commission or representation of foreign firms). Subsequently about 700 of the offices previously inspected registered as consultants or technical advisers, although basically doing the same job as before. The remaining ex-agents either joined the public sector or went abroad.[18]

Intermediary activity had certainly not been taken away completely from the private sector. Former commercial agents continued to survive by registering as consultants, while essentially performing the same functions as before through the newly founded public sector organs.

Many of today's most prominent and successful commercial agents were among those able to continue their business during the period from 1961 to 1971. They employed various mechanisms to avoid nationalization and continue business. The capital of those commercial agents was not tied up or invested in projects save when the agent was also a manufacturer, which was not very common. Normally agents only kept in the country enough capital to keep their offices going. The purchase of apartment houses, rooms or offices in town was perhaps the only concrete manifestation of their capital. In order to distract the government's attention and avoid nationalization, most agents who were now registered as consultants greatly reduced the number of employees working for them. In fact one such businessman, who was also involved in contracting, dropped the activity as it required too many employees. According to this individual, as well as others who lived through the socialist period, the only criterion the government could employ to determine the size of the business was the number of employees, since profit and capital remained unknown and very hard to discover.

Within the group of founding fathers of Egyptian commercial agency activity, a large number registered as delegates or consultants during the 1960s following the nationalization laws. In fact a businessman who is today one of the most famous in the market and concentrates essentially on industrial projects and the erection of whole industrial plants, maintained that business had never been as great as during the early 1960s. In his words,

> Our business prospered very much during the early 'sixties, our office did not have much competition. . . . For some reason (?) the government did not nationalize our business . . . although we did not expect it, we were left alone . . . our turnover was very high, however we had no liquid capital available that the government could have laid hands on . . . so they were not interested.[19]

Another interesting example is that of a commercial agent specializing in trading transactions carried out through clearing accounts or barter trading agreements. His major trading partner had been Japan, to which he exported cotton and rice in exchange for a variety of commodities. By 1958 his business was extremely prosperous, while he acquired great expertise in financial transactions and the mechanisms of trade agreements. In 1962 the agent and his father, who had been a wealthy jeweller and large landowner, were sequestrated. A month later this same agent had borrowed money from friends, re-established his contacts with foreign firms abroad, and registered as their local 'delegate', working through the public sector. Between 1962 and 1964 the agent had become the 'consultant' of the Swiss Andrée Lauzanne Corporation, which specialized in grain. He became active in agricultural trade, dealing in commodities such as cotton prior to the nationalization of its trade, as well as the sale of wheatflour and maize to the Ministry of Supply through a public sector firm, on behalf of the Swiss Andrée Lauzanne Company which he represented.[20]

According to the general manager and director of one of the public sector trading firms specializing in chemicals – a man who worked for the firm for some thirty years – during the 1960s there was quite a lot of 'collaboration' with private sector 'consultants'. According to this director the company had always cooperated with private sector trading offices. The general manager, himself one of the old 'cadres' of employees in this initially foreign company, later inherited by the public sector during the Egyptianization process, stated that he had never believed in making a distinction between the private and public sectors. 'We are all Egyptians', he declared. He admitted that he had not been averse to collaborating with the private sector and personally encouraged it:

In the beginning, during the sixties, we needed the advice and cooperation of

the private sector consultants who had their contacts abroad. They helped our company with the allocation of suppliers and they got their share of the commission abroad. We never interfered, or asked them for any account as long as we did our business, the private sector agent was free to get whatever he pleased.[21]

Those businessmen or commercial agents who survived the middle Nasser period employed other mechanisms for legal circumvention whilst still continuing their original activity. Some of the agents were recruited by the public sector during the early 1960s, and a number of these had resigned by 1965/66 to go into business on their own again. Some also went abroad during this period and represented foreign companies for the whole of the Middle East. Although their main offices were transferred to Beirut or Athens, the agents continued to make business deals with Egypt. One of the agents following this pattern lived in Germany and succeeded in penetrating the Egyptian market through old colleagues at university and at work who now occupied influential positions in the public sector.[22]

Other surviving commercial agents had been involved in different economic activities. A few had been industrialists in such fields as textiles, paints, fire extinguishing pumps and food industries. During the early 1960s, those originally in industries whose foreign trading enterprises had been nationalized survived by turning their efforts to manufacturing and continued their import activity on a more limited scale. A few other survivors were involved in exports, a perfectly legitimate activity for the private sector since they were legally allowed to participate in 25 per cent of the country's exports. They therefore had a good cover for any importing activity they may have had. Finally there were of course some who had been completely nationalized and whose activities had been paralysed. Most of the agents nationalized had, however, been in possession of enough stored goods to keep them going for quite a while. In the process of liquidating their goods such agents often became involved in internal trade, another legitimate activity, while maintaining their contacts abroad until such time as they could resume their former activity.

The above account simply indicates a few of the survival methods employed by some of the commercial agents active today. It is the opinion of one of the survivors that dodging or circumventing the law was possible only for those already established, while newcomers found it extremely hard to break through and set up their own independent business because government control was after all relatively strong during the early 1960s.[23] Few agents started in business during this period. Those who did conducted their business from abroad and dealt with Egypt indirectly. Such businessmen represent professional men who were originally technocrats in the government sector or in the military and who were given the opportunity to travel and establish contacts abroad. Some had been engineers, while others had come from the armed forces.[24]

It must be remembered that the early 1960s were the formative years of the public sector and increased government control. As discussed in Chapter 3, the early formative years of the state sector had been characterized by a great dearth of socialist and ideologically committed managerial and technocratic staff. Hence a large segment of the managerial stratum and state technocrats had been recruited from the ranks of former businessmen, while some of those recruited from the army or civil service had managed to form alliances with private businessmen – usually internal wholesale merchants, contractors and commercial agents.

To understand the accounts of the surviving commercial agents one must place them within the context of the public sector's history, discussed briefly above, and in greater detail in Chapter 3.[25] The major infiltrations of this group into the public sector occurred during its formative months. As with other illicit activity, it was made possible by the public sector's incompetence, incompleteness and lack of a socialist ideology. The major differences between the two other forms of infiltration, internal trade and contracting, and commercial agency in foreign trade, is that while the first two were legally permitted in the private sector, the latter was prohibited by law and managed to survive through legal circumvention and through the structural deficiencies of the public sector – namely the manner in which it was founded and the recruitment of its personnel and managerial core. Meanwhile, despite Egypt's proclaimed socialist ideology and acute antagonism to the West, it continued to rely heavily on foreign products. Imports from the West continued. The public sector was still unable to cope with its new role; hence the private sector continued to be indirectly and illicitly involved in public tenders, i.e. the sale of imports to the government and state sector.

Legal circumvention was possible due to two sets of factors. First, there had been a continuity in Government civil servants responsible for the control, registration and legal sanction of commercial agency activity. The first law promulgated during the Egyptianization process, the second during the nationalization phase. A third set of laws and regulations which allowed and regulated commercial agency activity was issued during the 'open door' policy in recent years (1974); the same civil servants were employed by the Minister of Trade and were responsible for registrations till mid-1977. Secondly, the very nature of the activity performed by commercial trade agents did not lend itself to tight state control. (This is true particularly of those agents already established in the field.) The major assets of the business were contacts and a bank account abroad. The inner workings of the business will be elaborated in a subsequent chapter. Capital was never solidified for any length of time. Thus, as reflected in the various representatives' accounts, there was not much that state control could do to prevent their activity. Unlike the industrial bourgeoisie, internal commercial traders and contractors, whose property and capital were more conspicuous and could be nationalized or sequestrated, the commercial agent, save for a room or apartment in the centre of town used as an office, had nothing much to lose from nationalization or sequestration, nor did the state have much to gain in terms of capital.

In fact, in most cases a commercial agent did not even need to have a room in town, since this form of activity was perhaps the most accessible to members of the 'state bourgeoisie' occupying official government and managerial posts.

With the exception of some cases when former contractors became themselves state administrators or when they were engaged in the smuggling of goods,[26] the domain of exports and imports is where high government officials could 'directly' participate in illicit activity inconspicuously. In an attempt to describe this type of situation, J. Waterbury writes,

> With the great increase in state activities in import/export, a host of middlemen arose to help fulfil state needs, for fat commissions. The public sector not only tolerated such figures but fostered them so that public sector officials could also get a piece of the commissions. One former army officer, who worked during the 1960s for a state export company, later went private, acting as middleman between Egypt and the USSR in citrus exports and allegedly took a £E100,000 commission on a single deal. Variations on this theme are numberless, and symbiotic relations between public officials on fixed salaries and private entrepreneurs with no legal and profitable investment outlets had proliferated.[27]

However, although this activity was perhaps the hardest to control and attack, since there was hardly any material evidence to incriminate those involved, and although it was flourishing within the existing system, it could not expand to its maximum, given (a) the obvious constraints of state capitalism and (b) the heavy emphasis on bilateral relations with the Soviet Union and on barter trade agreements. Commercial agents needed a change in foreign policy which entailed free trade, especially with their patrons in the Western industrialized states. Moreover members of this group were originally surviving agents of the traditional bourgeoisie, who had been accustomed to operate in a free enterprise system, who knew how to deal with it, and who had different aspirations from those of the new corps of technocrats and military men in the state bourgeoisie. While the latter, out of lack of experience and proper foreign contacts, may have been satisfied with the available avenues of profit-making and enrichment, the traditional bourgeoisie, which had experience, contacts and higher aspirations, preferred to enter joint venture enterprises with foreign capital, purchase patents and licences from foreign manufacturers, or resume their once highly profitable industrial production of light consumer goods.

During the aftermath of the Sinai War, as previously mentioned, state control had greatly weakened and allowed for private business activity on the part of the state bourgeoisie and private sector profiteers. Travel abroad had become less restricted: a mass of skilled labourers, qualified technocrats and disenchanted businessmen chose to go to the oil-rich Arab countries where they could make money and do good business.

According to a number of commercial agents, the period following the 1967 war was a good time for business as well as for travel abroad. Some agents had begun their business immediately following the war. Some began their business from abroad while others were able to penetrate local business activity and begin from within. With regard to travel abroad, Kuwait had been a pole of attraction for Egyptian businessmen, ever since oil had first been discovered there, later to be followed by Saudi Arabia and Libya. One businessman worked in the military factories upon graduation as an engineer in 1968/69; his father, also an engineer, and previously a commercial agent, had travelled to Kuwait where he now resides and had set up his own business. Meanwhile the son had managed to cut his service short in the military factory after a year and begun his own business locally in partnership with the manager of his father's old company.[28]

Another temporary migrant to Kuwait during this period was an army officer who began his service at the time of the revolution, travelled to England where he obtained a degree in political science, and upon returning to Egypt in 1955 worked for the Ministry of Foreign Affairs. He resigned from his job, and from 1958 to 1968 he worked in the field of exports. In 1968, after the defeat, he had felt insecure and believed that prospects for business and investment looked rather bleak, so he travelled to Kuwait where he was able to make a great deal of money through export/import activity. Travel to Kuwait was very common among those who had not been absorbed into the public sector.[29]

A third temporary resident in Arab countries was a graduate from commerce, who upon graduation in the latter part of the 1960s travelled to join relatives in Abu Dhabi and Kuwait. In Kuwait he made a great deal of money through business activity, and in 1969, equipped with quite a lot of money, he returned to Egypt to work in the field of commercial representation. He registered as a consultant and worked through public sector firms. In his own words,

> beginning with the mid-sixties onwards was the best period to conduct business in Egypt . . . especially during the late sixties and early seventies. A lot of people made good money even though they limited their activity to avoid being conspicuous.

The agent believed that those who had not begun by then were not likely to succeed today.[30]

Another case of a temporary emigrant was that of a landowner's son who, having graduated in engineering, worked for the military factories till 1968. After resigning from his post the engineer became involved in his own private business, concentrating essentially on the field of contracting while also promoting the sale of international equipment. Shortly after establishing his business locally, the engineer had travelled to Saudi Arabia where he was able to make good money and obtain contracts with foreign firms, French in particular.[31]

Another example of this category of technocrats travelling abroad was an engineering graduate who travelled to Germany for the completion of his studies after which he began his career there. In the late 1960s, having started out in the Middle East as a salesman for the German company, he was able to set up his own private office in Tripoli, Libya, where he made enough money, according to the 41-year-old businessman, to keep him in luxury for the rest of his life. When liberalization got under way in Egypt in the early 1970s, he decided to return home and begin business there.[32]

With respect to the internal situation and chances of conducting business,

those who were able to begin business from within were either the sons of previously established businessmen or sons of contractors who had worked in co-ordination with the public sector. One such businessman, describing the state of business activity after the 1967 war, maintained that although government control had weakened and several businessmen were able to conclude deals, their activities were geared towards transient, unsystematic, short-term business transactions. This agent was the son of a manufacturer of chemicals and cosmetics, and an exporter/importer as well as a commercial agent for l'Oréal, whose business had been nationalized. In 1967, immediately after the war, he had decided to revive his father's business. He concentrated on the cosmetics department and re-established a relationship of commercial agency representation with l'Oréal. According to his own testimony, he made very good profits at the time.[33]

Another businessman, who had been an engineer working in the field of contracting as an employee in a foreign firm, began his own private business in 1968. The company he set up was initially engaged in assembling and running electrical and mechanical equipment in both the private and the public sector, civil works (waterworks, road building and maintenance, etc.), in addition to commercial agency for mechanical goods and equipment.[34]

A third businessman beginning his business enterprise in Egypt after the war is the son of a chair manufacturer. Having completed his degree in commerce, he set up his own company in 1969. At first the activity of the company centred mainly around internal trade and the distribution of local products. Gradually the company began to establish contacts abroad and became involved in foreign trade and commercial agency representation.[35]

A chemist, whose father was in the contracting business, set up his own independent office in 1968 after having worked with a foreign firm. The chemist began as the scientific consultant for Nestlé, and by the end of the Nasser period he had already begun to represent large American multinationals for chemicals, pharmaceuticals and equipment for pharmaceutical industries. By 1971 he had established a company for agency representation and imports.[36]

Throughout the Nasser period therefore, the activity of commercial agency representation had progressively proliferated both in times of political victory and of crisis. Although the Nasser regime had not been successful in creating an industrial bourgeoisie despite all the encouragements offered, it had certainly indirectly and unintentionally succeeded in creating a commercial bourgeoisie which had managed to survive even during the nationalization period. During the 1960s, although limitations existed, the business of commercial representation continued to be prosperous for some. It was prosperous both for those who had continued to function as agents privately, i.e. in the guise of consultants, and for those from within the state organs who were recipients of bribes and who purchased in the name of the government, either in collaboration with the private sector 'consultants' or separately. It is, however, only in the 1970s, with the Sadat regime and the liberalization of the economy, that the activity witnessed its second golden age, in private hands, with law no. 93 (1974).[37]

The boom of this activity during the late 1950s, its survival during the early 1960s and its proliferation during the latter part of that decade can be largely explained by the failure of the Nasser regime to either create an industrial bourgeoisie within a free enterprise system, or to accomplish a complete socialist transformation with a state or public sector representing the interests of the masses. The Nasser regime had instead unintentionally and indirectly succeeded in strengthening the commercial bourgeoisie which later became very significant within the political and economic transformations that occurred during the Sadat regime. The second boom of commercial agency representation during the 1970s cannot be totally explained through the development of the country's internal political economy and the inner contradictions of the previous regime, but needs to be understood within the broader context of global developments. Hence one must merge a political economy approach with a dependency perspective. The group of commercial agents studied greatly thrived under the 'open door' economic policy of *infitah*. The policy came about as a result of both external and internal pressures. Meanwhile commercial agents were at one and the same time cause and effect of recent economic and political developments. They contributed politically in bringing about the 'opening', while they greatly benefited from the outcome of the new policy.

Notes

1. Interview with former inspector-general for the application of the commercial law for agencies no. 107 (1961), on Wednesday January 25, 1972.
2. Interview with a commercial agency representative, 2 January 1978.
3. Berque, p. 564.
4. Robert Tignor, 'Nationalism, Economic Planning and Development Projects in Interwar Egypt', p. 201.
5. Berque, p. 625.
6. Law no. 24 (1957), *The Official Journal*, no. 154, July 11, 1961.
7. Hussein Khallaf, *Innovations in Egypt's Contemporary Economy*, p. 426 fn.
8. Interview with one of the largest and most prominent commercial agents on Monday January 23, 1978, and Friday April 14, 1972.
9. Interview with the Inspector-General for the Application of Commercial Agency Laws and also the director of the Commercial Registration Office for Agencies from 1957 to July 1977, on January 25, 1978.
10. Interview with owner and director of a commercial agency firm, 7 March 1978.
11. Interview with the owner and the director of a commercial agency firm, 20 February 1978.
12. Interview with the owner and the director of a commercial agency firm, 28 January 1978.
13. Interview with the owner of a commercial agency firm, February 24, 1978.

14. Interview with the general manager and director of the General Trading and Chemical Company on April 9, 1978 and the manager of the chemical department on April 4, 1978.

15. Law no. 107, for 1961, in *The Official Journal*, no. 154, February 11, 1961.

16. Mostafa Immam, 'The Consultancy Market and the Trap of Middle Men', p. 515.

17. Abdel Razek Hassan, 'The National Economic Map – Between the Public Sector and Private Sector', p. 73.

18. Interview with the former judicial inspector for the application of law no. 107 (1961) and presently the director of the Personnel Department in the Ministry of Trade. The information yielded by this key informant was confirmed by the facts discovered when interviewing the population under study. Furthermore the Ministry of Interior was approached in order to investigate the existence and size of the group registered individually as consultants in the early 1960s. Although only recent records were kept (i.e. within the last five years), through a talk with the head of the Statistical Department and surveys of the present classification categories employed, it appears that consultant and technical advisers were acceptable categories. Moreover the categories had been employed since 1958 when the law requiring all Egyptians working for foreign establishments to register with the Ministry of Interior was first issued. The actual function of the individuals registering under that category was, however, only revealed through interviews with those concerned.

19. Interview with a commercial agent (the daughter of a prominent industrialist and former minister during the post-war and Egyptianization periods), Sunday 5 February 1978.

20. Interview with a commercial agent on Tuesday 7 February 1978.

21. Interview with the general manager (director) of the General Trading and Chemical Company, on Sunday 9 April 1978.

22. Interview with a commercial agent, 27 July 1977.

23. Interview with a commercial agent, 9 January 1978.

24. Interview with four commercial agents, 1, 20, 25, and 27 February 1978.

25. See Chapter Three on the formation of the public sector.

26. Adel Ghoneim, 'Some Light on the Tendencies of Nationalist Capitalism', p. 104.

27. John Waterbury, 'Public Versus Private in the Egyptian Economy', p. 11.

28. Interview with a commercial agent on Monday 6 February 1978.

29. Interview with a commercial agent on Monday 26 February 1978. This agent returned to Egypt in the mid-1970s and established three companies, all of which are family partnerships. The agent is one of the most prominent on the market today, he had a monopoly over imports and sales of interior decoration and furnishing materials, and other household items.

30. Interview with a commercial agent on Wednesday 1 March 1978. The agent is one of the most prominent on the market today and is known as the king of cars. He owns four companies, two of which are in the field of tourism, one for the import of cars and another for the import of foodstuffs and consumer goods. The agent's office, which is luxuriously furnished, has some 50 employees. In addition he runs a luxurious showroom and owns a storehouse in Port Said.

31. Interview with a commercial agent on Thursday 19 January 1978.

32. Interview with a commercial agent on 27 October 1977. This agent, who actually began business in 1976/77 after a period of exploratory study of the situation, now owns two offices and represents eight German industrial corporations.

33. Interview with a commercial agent on Saturday 11 February 1978. It is worth mentioning that this agent is today one of the most prominent businessmen and the owner of four companies in the fields of cosmetics, international trading, investment and management, and imports and distributes medicine and pharmaceuticals.

34. Interview with a commercial agent on 24 December 1977. Today the agent has greatly expanded the section for commercial agency representation.

35. Interview with a commercial agent on Saturday 18 March 1978. This agent today represents some 47 companies in Egypt, dealing with an extremely wide variety of goods from hairpins to ships, cargoes and solar power equipment. The company employs 150 people, and runs a service department and four showrooms.

36. Interview with a commercial agent on Saturday 4 February 1978.

37. Law no. 93, for 1974, in *The Official Journal*, no. 30, 29 July 1974.

Part 2
The Contemporary Situation

5 Policy Changes

Under *infitah*[1] the new policy changes are gradually transforming the centralized State capitalist economy of the past into a liberalized one enhancing free enterprise. The position of the private sector generally is to be strengthened with special attention being given to foreign investors, joint ventures and commercial agents operating in a liberalized foreign trading system.

The changes in Egypt's socio-economic and political structure in recent times must be viewed as the outcome of both the country's internal historical development and its relation to global and regional developments. A full understanding of current legal policy changes will only be possible if one attempts to define Egypt's position within the international context, its relationship to the United States as the hegemonic power in present-day monopoly capital,[2] and the extent to which Egypt meets the requirements of capitalist expansion and penetration through both government and multinational activity.

First: Egypt within the international context

In the first part of this book we saw how Egypt went through a relatively radical experience of economic nationalism and state planning. The experience had at times shown promise of success, largely due to the strong position and autonomy of the state under Nasser during the latter part of the 1950s and first half of the 1960s, as well as the financial and moral support obtained from Soviet Russia. Russian support worked to Egypt's benefit at the height of the Cold War, but by the mid-1960s, under a situation of global détente, the United States had reluctantly begun to recognize Egypt as a Russian sphere of influence and Egypt soon became a Soviet stronghold.[3] This in no way meant that the United States had become totally uninterested in the prospects of a renewed 'friendship' with Egypt,[4] given its highly strategic geo-political position and control over important waterways; nor did it mean that despite the inner contradictions and weaknesses of the regime by the mid-1960s, it would be allowed to disrupt the carefully nurtured network of moderate regimes and guardians of American oil interests in the area.[5]

Although the long-term potential of 'Nasserism' as a radical movement, particularly in the much later stages of the regime, is questionable, one must admit the contribution Nasserism made as a precursor to the struggle against imperialism.[6] It is only after the defeat in 1967 that Nasser ceased to be the idol of the revolutionary masses, and that formerly anti-imperialist Arab governments shifted towards the right and 'moderation'.[7]

The United States, along with its allies, had been 'constrained', so to speak, to employ forceful intervention in the case of Egypt as a means of 'defending' its interests in the area.[8] The need to establish and consolidate a moderate regime as part of the overall US strategy was the chief motive behind the use of force, rather than the interests of multinationals searching for investment areas. A 'favourable climate' for investment was absent given both internal and external instability. Moreover the country hardly constituted 'a good market' for localized production given the low and stagnant per capita income of the vast majority of the population. During the Nasser period the average per capita income for the urban population was £E73.4 p.a. and for the rural population, which was in the majority, average annual per capita income was £E17.1.[9] In addition labour conditions were not particularly attractive or cheap since productivity per head was relatively low in addition to the absence of skilled and qualified labour.[10] Furthermore, as a reflection of the country's decadent economy, on the eve of the war, most of its services (ports, roads, communication) were already in deplorable condition. A multinational firm could at most hope for a liberalized foreign trade system allowing it to export its goods to Egypt.

From a US strategic viewpoint, however, the establishment and consolidation of a 'moderate' regime in Egypt had become a question of prime importance and could not be accomplished solely through forceful military intervention but required an integration of the country in the 'free world' camp by, first, the achievement of external stability through peace with Israel, and, second, securing internal political stability through heavy United States aid and other forms of international loans. This would 'remedy' the existing economic imbalances. Making investment safer and encouraging activity on the part of the multinational companies, first in their capacity as exporters and later as local producers.

With regard to the first requirement, America's eagerness to foster a peace treaty between Egypt and Israel does not require much in the way of evidence. The problem was not, however, to have a treaty signed, but to secure its continuity. The achievement of a sustained peace treaty and continued political moderation necessarily required internal political stability which could only be brought about through visible economic improvements. Thus the objectives of United States assistance to Egypt as presented in the introductory paragraphs of the Agency for International Development 'Middle East Peace and Security Supporting Assistance to Egypt' during the fiscal year 1976 were explained in the following manner (p. 13):

> Peace in the Middle East is a major United States foreign policy goal . . . . Egypt has demonstrated its desire and willingness to work toward a negotiated peace by playing a key role in the two interim settlements

already concluded . . . . in its leadership role in the Arab world the government of Egypt has taken both a courageous step and a calculated risk by proceeding with its recent second step agreement with Israel . . . . It is of paramount importance to the achievement of lasting peace in the area that implementation of this agreement succeed and that it lead to more comprehensive understanding and agreement in the future. . . . . The ability and willingness of Egyptian society to proceed with further steps toward peace will depend in large measure on the success achieved by the government in its efforts to direct the nation's energies toward economic development rather than confrontation as a way of achieving national goals.

An even more explicit paragraph regarding United States interests and goals is one describing Egypt today as

a force for moderation in the councils of the world community. Its decision to concentrate on developing its own country sets a positive example for future events in the Middle East. . . . Egypt suffers from a serious shortage of foreign exchange with which to sustain its economic recovery and undertake a development programme. . . . The new agreement between Egypt and Israel will, in itself improve Egypt's economic situation . . . Egypt's economic recovery (however) requires resources far beyond its own or any small donor's ability to provide.

Along with Arab assistance,

United States economic assistance also is needed urgently to bring Egypt through the crucial period of its post-war recovery and development.

The following paragraph sums up the US position after the signing of the peace treaty with Israel and in the congressional presentation of the AID for the fiscal year 1980,

the intense and continuing role of the United States in achieving a comprehensive peace settlement reflects the strategic importance of Egypt to United States foreign policy in the Middle East. Our high level of aid to Egypt demonstrates our political commitment. A growing economy increasingly able to meet the basic needs of the Egyptian people will enhance confidence in and support for President Sadat's peace efforts.[11]

Indeed the level of United States and consequently international aid to Egypt has never been as high as in recent years.[12]

The very large amounts of foreign loans do in themselves constitute a very real threat to economic independence and are a source of anxiety to dedicated Third World policy-makers and intellectuals who believe that according to previous experience, heavy loans have done a disservice to the receiving countries.[13]

There are numerous levels of analysis with regard to the whole issue of foreign loans, some of which are purely economic, such as the effect of loans upon a given nation's balance of payments, etc. I will be essentially concerned with the political aspect here, namely how loans can be a tool for political interference on the part of donor states. The greatest danger and the one with the longest-lasting effect is the power that donor nations enjoy in shaping the host country's socio-economic structure by partly causing and partly dictating policy changes.

The conditions often accompanying loans are a good indication of the extent of foreign influence exerted to shape local policy. Letters of intent on the part of recipient governments usually accompany applications for loans. On June 10 1978 Egypt presented its letter of intent to the IMF in order to obtain a loan of £E600 million over three years. The letter included Egypt's full acceptance of the IMF's long-suggested stabilization plan which among the many structural and fiscal changes included the following:

1. a more realistic pricing system, largely covering costs and profits;
2. encouraging agricultural development under private farming;
3. a decrease in government subsidy;
4. decentralization of employment policies.

Similarly, the conditions for obtaining loans from the 'consultative group', under the direct influence of the IMF, all pressed for the devaluation of the Egyptian pound, a liberalized foreign trade system, and the encouragement of both foreign and local private investment. Meanwhile an agreement between the United States and Egypt signed on September 28, 1978, whereby Egypt was to receive a loan of US$95 million for a cement project to be managed by the public sector Suez Cement Company, contained the following conditions among many others:

1. Not less than 20 per cent of the company shares must be sold to the private sector.

2. The price of local cement shall increase in order to compete with imported cement and Egypt shall periodically consult the IMF for further price changes.

3. US$4.6 million worth of the public sector company shares shall be sold to investors in order to fund the project.

4. The Egyptian cement sales department shall present AID with a yearly plan for the distribution of cement which the latter must accept.[14]

Donors of loans to Egypt are interested in creating the 'right climate' and 'sound' socio-economic preconditions for the delocalization of capital or foreign productive investment. Among many others, the preconditions I especially want to emphasize here as necessary ones in the preliminary stages of 'delocalized' production are:

1. Increasing the exports of multinationals as a first step in penetration until such time as they may begin to produce locally. (This primarily entails a liberalization of foreign trade.)

2. Supporting the dominant political élites who have opted for 'moderation' and creating the international managers who will administer the future 'modernized' sectors of the Egyptian economy.

The normal sequence of a firm establishing its subsidiary abroad is: (1) to export its products to the future host, (2) to set up its own commercial and marketing representations, and (3) to set up its productive units.[15] The multinationals' export phase is, when needed, accompanied by encouragements on the part of their governments. In Egypt, up to 1979, the largest AID programme has been the CIP (Commodity Import Program): US$250 million for 1977, and US$1,155 million for 1978.[16] In 1977 approximately 55 per cent of the total CIP was being utilized to finance consumables (industrial raw materials, foodstuffs, etc.) and 45 per cent for capital equipment (replacement machinery, trucks and tractors, etc.).[17] From 1975 to March 1979, the total sum of obligated money under CIP was US$1,205 million, US$686.9 million of which was expended.[18] The CIP for 1980 still promised to be the largest in comparison to all other programmes and amounted to US$200 million, subject to increase if required especially by the private sector.[19] Other donors facilitating Egypt's imports are: the IMF, providing approximately US$250 million per annum between 1978 and 1981; and Japan, West Germany and other European nations, providing US$75 million. The IBRD is also expected to contribute.[20]

Commodity loans are not only encouraging greater imports but are also encouraging the rather reluctant American multinationals to step into the Egyptian market. Money loaned under the AID CIP is certainly not 'condition free'. According to the rules and procedures applicable to commodity transactions, AID money will be employed to import goods exclusively from the US unless otherwise authorized by AID in special cases. Meanwhile the shipment and insurance of the commodities will be done by American private companies and from ports designated by AID and included in its geographic code of 'free world' areas. AID will provide various other delivery services such as inspection and auditing. Freight companies and aviation companies involved in transport of goods will also be American.[21] Peerless Pumps, a large American multinational specializing in pumping machines for petrol, was initially uninterested in the Egyptian market for a number of reasons; following the October war and *infitah*, the 'climate of investment' was still not favourable. However, with AID's increased loans to Egypt after 1974, Peerless Pumps as well as other American firms became positively interested in penetrating the local market. Their initial interest was to sell their products and compete for the available CIP money allotted to the Egyptian Government. By 1977 the company was greatly satisfied with its export activity.[22]

Judging from the geographical distribution of foreign trade, it is obvious that since 1974, the importance of US exports to Egypt is growing. In 1973 Egypt's total imports from the United States were worth US$109.1 million. In 1974 the amount more than doubled and became US$270.6 million and in 1975 reached US$301.7 million.[23] In 1976 US goods constituted 20.5 per cent of Egypt's imports and 20.6 per cent in 1977, which is very close to the percentage of European imports traditionally occupying the first position.[24]

The second precondition, namely the consolidation of the dominant political élite who had opted for 'moderation', has been the explicit aim, as mentioned earlier, of AID, as well as other forms of assistance. Undoubtedly military assistance is to play a very major role. However the details and exact figures of such assistance are not available. The daily papers have on a number of occasions reported the United States' great concern and interest to modernize and develop Egypt's armed forces and military industries.[25]

Meanwhile it must be remembered that the state political power which opted for 'moderation' and 'peace' had been largely controlled by the state bourgeoisie during and after the 1967 war, thus some very visible concessions had to be made to its various groups if their political power was to be consolidated economically. The group closely related to the state bourgeoisie that had pushed hardest for a *rapprochement* with the West and an internal free enterprise economy, and whose very existence and expansion depended heavily on a free trading system and the import of Western capital, had been the foreign trade commercial agents. There seems to have been a continuous relation between the commercial agent interest group and transformations in Egypt's socio-economic structure. The activities of commercial agents had facilitated a renewed entanglement with Western capitalism. Meanwhile as Western capitalism penetrated in greater depth, first in the forms of loans and commodities, this interest group was further consolidated and was to constitute one of the best choices for the future managers and administrators of the modernized sector.[26]

The 'delocalization of capital' requires international uniformity in the productivity process as well as a uniformity in the organization of productivity.[27] Both requirements are met through:

1. the transfer of technology to local industry;
2. the reorganization of the local productive sectors; and
3. the creation of the 'international managers' who will run the new modernized sectors of the economy in perfect uniformity and loyalty to the multinational company.

The creation of an 'international managerial' élite from local resources is both politically and economically profitable from a multinational viewpoint.[28] Meanwhile given the assumptions that (1) the very first stage of delocalization normally takes the form of creating local commercial firms,[29] and that (2) these firms have the closest contact with multinationals and their products, then owners and managers of local commercial representation firms constitute the very best choice for the potential international manager. In the specific case of Egypt, this line of business is not only one of the most prosperous in the private sector, but its members, as we shall see in a subsequent chapter, also have a certain amount of political power rendering an alliance with them, from a multinational viewpoint, highly profitable.

Second: legal and political changes under *infitah*

The green light for the implementation of the new 'open door' economic policy appeared in April 1974 with the *October Working Paper* presented by President Sadat. The document officially approved the new policy of openness to the entire world, especially the West. The 'paper' encouraged the revision of past ideological orientations and economic policies which appeared to have failed and were incompatible with the desired economic development. In the new economic development strategy there would be wider vistas for foreign investors and the private sector.[30]

The expressed hope for increased foreign investment in Egypt in the October Paper was not based on mere wishful thinking. A number of events were occurring at the time which were taken as encouraging signs: diplomatic relations with the United States were resumed; Japanese and West German trade delegations expressed their interest in the Egyptian market, as did Iranian and American businessmen. Immediately preceding the October Paper, David Rockefeller, Chairman of the Chase Manhattan Bank, in the course of a trip to various Arab countries, had made some favourable remarks publicly on prospects of foreign investment in Egypt.[31]

In the summer of 1974, in the course of President Nixon's visit to Egypt, a joint declaration had been made by the presidents of both countries, which outlined prospects of future economic cooperation. The US President declared that his country encouraged its entrepreneurs to invest in Egypt in the fields of petrochemicals, transport, food and agricultural machinery, tourism, banking, and a host of other economic sectors. Projects falling in the various fields of cooperation exceeded US$2 billion. Both presidents agreed that the idea behind mutual economic cooperation was to combine American technology and capital with Egypt's absorptive capacity, skilled manpower and productive investment opportunities, all of which would result in Egypt's economic development.[32]

The first major legislative step taken after the *October Working Paper* was the promulgation of a new investment law (no. 43), which was approved by the People's Assembly on June 9, 1974. The law offered even more attractive privileges for foreign investors than the 1971 version. Although the new law pointed out areas of priority where it hoped the foreign investors would participate, they were encouraged to invest in all fields of industry and metallurgy provided they obtained the approval of the investment authority. The law also made provisions for the establishment of free zones which would be regarded as extraterritorial land for investment projects. Firms operating therein were to be exempt from Egyptian taxes and customs duties. Meanwhile capital transfers abroad could be made with no restrictions. Free zone commodities would be sold at world prices to the Egyptian market.

Generally all projects falling under the new investment law, whether in the fields of banking, tourism, housing, construction or industry, enjoyed a number of privileges and guarantees:

1. Projects falling under the foreign investment law would enjoy complete immunity and protection from nationalization and sequestration.
2. Projects under the above-mentioned legislation would be deemed as private sector ones and would, therefore, not be subject to any of the public sector laws and regulations pertaining to internal organization, labour representation and the distribution of profit.

3. Joint ventures of foreign investment projects would be allowed to import necessary equipment directly and would also be allowed to open bank accounts in foreign currency, the use of which would not be restricted by permits or licences. Such accounts were to be used for the purposes of paying imports of commodities and capital goods, as well as foreign loans.

4. Foreign projects were to be exempted from the tax on commercial and industrial projects and the taxes appended thereto. Likewise the shares would be exempted from the proportional stamp duty and from the tax on the revenues from mobile capital as well as the taxes appended thereto. Such exemptions were to be for a period of five years from the first tax year following commencement of production. The period of exemption would be extended to eight years provided it was regarded as good for the public interest by the authority of investment.

5. The machinery, equipment and transportation equipment necessary for projects approved under the provisions of the law would be exempted from customs duties and any other taxes and dues.

6. Profits distributed by each project would be exempted from the general tax on income. This exemption applies only to profits up to a maximum of five per cent of the taxpayer's share in the invested capital.

7. Interest due on the foreign loans concluded by the project, even if in the form of a deposit, would be exempted from all taxes and dues.

8. Buildings utilized for administrative purposes, and above the average housing constructed under the provisions of this law, would not be subject to the rules limiting rents as stipulated in the laws governing rental of premises.

9. Foreign experts and employees brought from abroad to work in any of the projects enjoying the provisions of this law would be permitted to transfer from Egypt a portion of the wages, salaries and compensations which they received in the republic of Egypt provided it did not exceed 50 per cent of their gross earnings.

10. Foreign investors could export their capital abroad after the passage of five years from the beginning of the project. They could transfer their capital in five annual equal instalments in the same currency originally received.[33]

One month after the promulgation of the law on investment, a second major and crucial step was taken towards the liberalization of the economy, this time in the field of foreign trade. Law no. 63 for the year 1974 allowed both naturalized and native-born Egyptians to represent foreign companies in Egypt and thus abolished the old 1961 law no. 107 which had prohibited this activity.[34] This new law aimed at facilitating foreign trade by removing the task of commercial agency representation from the public sector and placing it in private hands. If the first law of foreign investment had concentrated essentially on an external opening to foreign capital, law no. 63 clearly marked the beginnings of the new emphasis the 'open door' policy was to make; namely internal liberalization which would allow the private sector to take on a vital role in the Egyptian economy.

A third step taken within the same year in the field of foreign trade, further decentralized and liberalized the activity. Law no. 137 (1974) allowed Egyptian individuals and private sector companies possessing foreign currency at parallel market rates to import all commodities that would promote the development of the country and provide the necessary material and equipment. Egyptians permanently residing abroad would also be allowed to import goods into the country against hard currency which would be employed towards touristic or personal expenditure, and/or the export of non-traditional goods.[35]

After the first three above-mentioned steps towards bolder external and internal liberalization, an extremely rapid flow of politico-legal measures was introduced. As the liberalization was being put into practice, new regulations were issued by the week in the fields of customs duties, as well as the imports allowed for the private sector. The latter appeared to be encroaching increasingly upon the goods that had been reserved for public sector companies.[36]

Despite the bold steps towards liberalization, the government had not totally endorsed the proposed IMF stabilization plan which essentially hoped to see the pound float, state subsidy shrink to a minimum, and the private sector rejuvenated, while the public sector was to be reorganized and geared towards the services. Meanwhile the country's deteriorating economic conditions manifested no improvement. Egypt continued to import huge amounts of foodstuffs to meet its very urgent needs, which the state resold at subsidized prices. With world prices greatly increasing,[37] along with the movement away from bilateral trade agreements,[38] and the introduction of a new foreign trade system which encouraged quite a lot of uncontrolled imports, mainly of consumer goods, Egypt's import bill increased tremendously. Once again the country was resorting to short-term commercial credits at a disadvantageous interest rate. Most of the loans had been obtained from the oil-rich Arab states following Kissinger's second attempt at enforcing a package deal on Egypt for disengagement, which the latter had refused.

By the end of 1975, following Egypt's change of position on the second disengagement plan, which it now accepted, it became quite clear that the country could no longer count on long-term loans from neighbouring Arab countries. Both internal and external pressures were becoming too heavy for Egypt to endorse a full stabilization plan and rely heavily on US aid. Meanwhile several IMF missions had come to Cairo to study the situation. Finally by the end of 1975 a major concession was made towards a relaxation of price controls and government subsidy when the price of petrol was increased.[39] At that stage Egypt's receipt of bilateral credits had totalled US$4.4 billion.[40]

On the internal political scene a few ministerial changes indicated the new orientation of the 'open door' policy. In April 1975 Prime Minister Higazi was replaced by Mamdouh Salem the former Minister of Interior. Higazi, one of the originators of the 'open door' policy, had concentrated on external opening while greatly defending the public sector before Parliament and emphasizing its leading role in the Egyptian economy during the difficult years from 1967 to 1973. Higazi had been relieved from his post on the allegation that the policy had been moving too slowly.[41] Abou Wafiya, a leading Member of Parliament, had at the time emphasized that external opening must be preceded by an internal opening.[42] The director of the Planning Institute, Ismail Sabri Abdallah, a prominent economist, who had formerly been a Communist Party member and leader, was replaced by an American-educated Egyptian economist.[43]

Another interesting ministerial change was the appointment of Dr Ahmad Abou Ismail, as Minister of Finance. The new minister, as a member of the Assembly Plan Committee, had previously advocated the sale of public sector enterprises to private persons. The following suggestions were subsequently made by the Right in the People's Assembly:

1. complete floating of the pound;
2. opening foreign trade to the private sector and allowing private entrepreneurs to deal with foreign suppliers and markets;
3. restricting the Egyptian stock and commodity exchange;
4. raising the ceiling on land ownership;
5. raising the ceiling on personal incomes by rescheduling tax rates;
6. raising business and corporate profits tax;
7. allowing foreign banks to open branches in Egypt in both local and foreign currencies;
8. allowing the private sector to enter as local partners in joint ventures;
9. allowing foreign investment in any sector of the Egyptian economy, as long as the project was not incompatible with planning goals; and
10. allowing foreign firms or joint venture enterprises to lease or own Egyptian agricultural land for commercial purposes.[44]

Immediately following the ministerial reshuffle, law no. 262 of 1975 was promulgated. The law encouraged the public sector to expand its capital by offering new stock issues to private individuals.[45] In September of 1975, law no. 111 was promulgated abolishing the general organizations which had been in charge of planning, coordinating and supervising the public sector. This law represented yet another step towards liberalization and decentralization, thus serving to reorganize the public sector.

Despite the various steps in the way of economic reform, Egypt continued to confront very serious difficulties, and *The Financial Times* reported that the country was once again late in meeting payments and in servicing its £E700 million revolving credit. By January 1976 the Prime Minister, Mamdouh Salem, reported to Parliament that some of the IMF proposals had been accepted.[46] During that month of January a cut-down on subsidized goods was attempted, only to be immediately repealed. Although a complete devaluation of the Egyptian pound and massive reductions in government subsidies for basic goods were rejected by the government, the Minister of Economy Dr Shafei is reported to have said 'we have a full understanding with the IMF and IBRD. An IBRD team had participated in the elaboration of our five-year plan.' The minister indicated that the government would be working towards a policy of price stabilization through increased production.[47]

The cornerstone of the new plan for stabilization was to further liberalize fiscal policies, i.e. float the pound, as well as further liberalize foreign trade. With regard to the convertibility of the pound, a partial float was accepted. In May 1976 the commercial market was to replace and include the parallel market. Within this market the value of the pound would be determined on a daily basis.[48] The accompanying measures proposed by the government for the implementation of the stabilization plan included: (1) limiting government expenditure; (2) moving away from price controls; and (3) increasing interest rates on bank savings. Up until the beginning of 1977 the above proposals were still being debated and had not been endorsed by the government.[49] In 1978, the Deputy Minister of Planning and Deputy Prime Minister declared that the government had decided to cut down on a number of subsidized goods and to adopt a more realistic price policy based on sound economic thought. He also declared the government's intention to increase its savings through (1) an increase of interest rates on bank deposits; (2) increasing the productivity of the public sector; (3) encouraging the private sector to participate and in fact take over or complete some of the projects begun by the public sector; and (4) gearing the available local and foreign investments towards projects yielding rapid returns.[50]

A year before the declaration, in 1977, the foreign investment law no. 43 (1974) was amended by law no. 32 (1977). According to the new amendment, projects in the sphere of modern development in need of foreign expertise such as industrialization, mining, energy, tourism, transportation, land reclamation, housing and urban development, investment companies, banks, construction, contracting, technical consultancy, with entirely Egyptian capital and owned by Egyptian nationals would enjoy the privileges and exemptions of foreign investors.[51] However, the industrial private sector proper not investing in the above areas remained subject to law no. 21 (1958)[52] which was issued during the beginnings of state planning and control under Nasser. The law is in many ways restrictive.

With regard to agriculture, which had traditionally been the stronghold of the private sector, several new legal measures were introduced to further strengthen the position of the private sector, to minimize government participation and control, and to enhance the position of the 'progressive' farmer, agri-businessman, as well as small and medium farmers. The following are some of the structural changes occurring during the *infitah* period in the areas of land distribution, loans and the banking system, tenancy laws, taxes, marketing facilities and prices.

With regard to land distribution a major step was taken in 1974 when the government decided to abolish land sequestration and to return land held by the government to its original owners.[53] Meanwhile the distribution of reclaimed land to university graduates, a trend which began before the official proclamation of the new policy,[54] increased greatly after 1974. By the end of 1974 a total of 248,858 feddans had been distributed to settlers in the newly reclaimed land and by 1979 total estimated land to be distributed to small holders was 160,000 feddans.[55] The most recent census on land distribution indicates that the group which increased was that falling within the 5–10 feddans bracket.[56] Landowners generally have been favoured within the new policy. A law passed on June 23, 1975 allowed landowners the possibility of increasing their holdings to 200 feddans of reclaimed or new lands.[57]

In terms of loans to farmers, in 1976 the rural bank was established to replace the cooperative in its function as a direct supplier to farmers. In the past, credit had first been delivered to the cooperatives who then decided upon the various loans. Since 1976 farmers were allowed to treat directly with the banks.[58] Small and medium farmers (5–10 feddans) were the happiest with the new arrangement as the old cooperatives had not serviced them satisfactorily.[59]

With regard to tenancy, in 1975 a law was passed in favour of landowners, who now had greater freedom to evict tenants from the land. The law indirectly encouraged owners to raise land rent.[60]

Finally in the area of rural cooperatives, the private sector has been increasingly encouraged to step into the domain of marketing facilities whether as exporters, importers or internal wholesale intermediaries. This is especially true of the crops which were not originally part of the cooperative system, such as fruits and vegetables. There are, however, indications that even with regard to crops that are regulated by the cooperatives, such as cotton, there appears to be far less centralization than during the 1960s. In 1973 certain decisions were made regarding the cooperative marketing of cotton, whereby individuals or companies were allowed to purchase cotton directly from the cultivators. The new policies favour both large cotton plantations as well as those operating as intermediaries.[61] Within the last few years both international organizations and the Egyptian Government have called for decentralization and have also pointed out the various defects of the cooperative system for marketing which appeared to disfavour small and medium farmers. The latter sold their exportable or marketable crops at inferior prices to those obtained by the cooperative when selling to the international or local markets.[62]

Already by 1979 there were signs of the decreasing importance given to agricultural cooperatives. In 1979 several decrees were issued from the Ministry of Trade to liquidate a number of cooperatives, including the company for agricultural markets and services. By March/April 1979, five cooperatives had been dissolved or were on their way to being dissolved.[63] The fiscal and economic policy of 1980 invited and greatly encouraged the private sector to participate actively in the agricultural sector generally, but more specifically in the area of trade and marketing as well as land reclamation and the necessary transfer of technology.[64] According to the new fiscal policy, the government decided to reserve £E75 million for loans to individuals, university graduates and cooperatives at a minimal interest rate of 3.5 per cent. Meanwhile in order to encourage the transfer of technology all imported tractors, agricultural machines, irrigation machines as well as other necessary equipment and commodities for land reclamation and/or cultivation, were to be exempted from taxes.[65]

Previously, land reclamation had been a task totally undertaken by the government. Along with land redistribution the government had planned a scheme for the horizontal expansion of agricultural land, i.e. expanding the agricultural area around the Nile Valley in addition to the employment of modern technology to turn some of the desert land into agricultural land. During the period from 1953 to 1959 some 79,000 feddans were reclaimed at an annual rate of 13,000 feddans of new land. Under the first five-year plan (1960/1 to 1964/5), 536,000 feddans were reclaimed at an accelerated pace of 107,000 feddans per annum.[66]

In the area of foreign trade, which was to undergo important ramifications, the private sector was also greatly enhanced. The new foreign trade policy was clearly moving away from centralized planning. Different modes of payment, methods and channels of import were open to both the private and public sectors. According to the various laws promulgated during the late 1970s, the structure of foreign trade in the public and private sectors respectively was as follows.

The public sector
Imports for the public sector generally enter through two channels: (1) public sector commercial firms, which are presently nine in number, and (2) public sector productive companies involved in the various investment projects. In the latter case, such firms import directly or through a system of public tendering. The firms import through a dual regulatory system: one requires permits and licences which are issued from two sources, while the other requires no permits. With regard to the first system of imports, purchasing committees are one of the sources in charge of issuing import licences. These committees are assumed to be responsible for the selection of the best offers. Payments for such imports must be at official rates. No imports under this system may be made without the intermediary of a commercial agent save for the following cases:

1. commodities imported for defence and military production, which must be determined by the Ministry of War;[67]
2. unmanufactured raw tobacco;
3. commodities produced under licence or patents whereby the importing public sector firm must obtain its raw material and equipment from the parent company;
4. commodities imported under the surplus agricultural products law.

Commercial agency representation in public tenders must be reserved for the public firms for the import of the following commodities: all commodities imported under the trade agreements and protocols – wheat, wheatflour, unpacked tea, cooking oil, animal fat, chemical fertilizers, agricultural pesticides, potatoes, fertilizers, tobacco, military and defence commodities.

The second source of permits and licences for public sector (and private sector) imports is the import licensing committee attached to the Ministry of Trade. Payments for imports under such licences must be from the company's own resources and exchange rates can vary.

The public sector (as well as the private sector) is allowed to import certain goods without an import licence provided payment for such goods is made through foreign exchange at parallel market rates and purchased from commercial banks directly. Commodities purchased under the no-licence system must have a local registered commercial agent.

The private sector

Imports by the private sector are also subject to a dual system of regulations with regard to licensing and rate of foreign exchange payments. Imports by private sector industrialists, artisans, and those working in the field of tourism can be paid at semi-official rates (parallel market rates) provided they obtain a licence or permit from the commercial agency purchasing committee in the public sector Misr for Imports and Exports Company.

Private sector importers may purchase foreign goods for the purpose of internal trade provided the payment of such imports are drawn from the importers' own reserves of foreign exchange. Law no. 417 (1977) allowed the private sector to import a list of specified goods directly.[68] Imports effected under that law did not require a permit and the importer could purchase the required foreign exchange at parallel market rates directly from the banks. Commodities imported under this law would be represented locally by a commercial agent for the foreign firm.[69]

Another system of imports allows the private sector to import directly certain goods without obtaining licences and permits or foreign exchange from the banks. Imports under this system are not included in the Ministry of Trade statistics. Commodities imported under this system theoretically include purchases made for personal use and not for commercial purposes.[70]

The system of exports on the other hand, although clearly encouraging the private sector to participate, a situation existing even prior to *infitah*, is relatively more restricted and regulated. Exporters have to produce contracts with foreign importing firms before any permits can be issued from the Ministry of Trade. In addition a list of 35 commodities ranging from raw materials, certain foodstuffs and manufactured goods are excluded from exports while another 44 commodities are subject to a three-month permit to be re-evaluated yearly. Another 13 articles, which include art objects, foodstuffs and publications, all require special permits. Another 32 articles, including spare parts, manufactured and semi-manufactured goods, all require special permits from the Central Authority for General Mobilization which specifies the quota and any special restrictions. The remaining export goods not included in the above-mentioned lists and falling under the category of agricultural and animal products are subject to strict control.[71]

Infitah, which was more than the culmination of Egypt's past political economy or a mere reflection of the new regime's political orientation, aimed at an overture to foreign investment and a rejuvenated private sector within a liberalized economy. Major legal internal innovations appear to promote and consolidate the following strata:

1. Foreign investors and their local partners.
2. Egyptian commercial agents and importers.

3. Egyptian entrepreneurs investing in the 'modern' sector requiring foreign technical expertise; included within this category are those investing in contracting activity, agribusiness, mining, transport and tourism, banking and finance, manufacture under patents or licence, energy, and technical consultation.

Moreover in addition to the internal ideological level as reflected by the legal innovations, Egyptian commercial agents and businessmen have been greatly advantaged by structural international developments. The 'delocalization' of capital very obviously required local representatives of multinational interests as a starting point in the integrative procedure.

The schemes for peace and development in the Middle East promoted by the West, and America in particular, very clearly concentrated upon the integration of Egypt in the 'free world' camp. All means were employed to create a group of commercial agents. American aid was pumped into the economy, especially in the area of trade, which not only enhanced the import of American goods but also helped create the much needed group of loyal businessmen to help with the expansion of capitalism, promote American and European goods and secure the Arab world against Communist expansion.

Notes

1. The Arabic word for the open door economic policy.
2. See Nicos Poulantzas, *Classes in Contemporary Capitalism*, pp. 42–69.
3. See M. Hussein, pp. 202–16 and 224–7 and for Russian dominant presence in Egypt also see Oliver Carrée, 'Pouvoir et Idéologie', pp. 254–8.
4. See M. Hussein, pp. 226, 227.
5. Fred Halliday, *Arabia without Sultans*, p. 21.
6. Ibid., p. 21.
7. Ibid., pp. 22, 28.
8. For an interpretation of American involvement in the Six Day War see V. Ernst, *Impérialisme au Moyen-Orient*, and M. Hussein.
9. Hassan Riad, *L'Egypte Nassérienne*, p. 41.
10. Robert Mabro and Samir Radwan, *The Industrialization of Egypt*, pp. 145, 147, 149–150.
11. AID, 'Congressional Presentation, FY 1980: Egypt' (unpublished), p. 10.
12. AID, Ibid., p. 12.
13. Ramzi Zaki, *The Crises of Foreign Loans: A View from the Third World*, pp. 375–86, and 360–98.
14. Goudah Abdel Khaliq, 'Development, Self-Reliance and Social Justice' (unpublished), pp. 10–22, 24, 25.
15. Charles Albert Michalet, *Le Capitalisme mondial*, p. 131.
16. AID, 'Security Supporting Assistance Loan Activity Data, FY 1977' (unpublished), p. 40 and CIP, *Monthly Summary, 4/30/78* (unpublished).
17. CIP, 'Report on Type of Commodities to be Imported as of December 31, 1977' (unpublished).

18. AID/Controller, 'Summary of Economic Assistance to Egypt FY 1975 to 3/31/79' (unpublished).

19. Ministry of Finance circular no. 8, 1978, 'United States Commodity Loan Funds Allocated to the Private Sector' (unpublished).

20. AID, 'Congressional Presentation by FY 1980, Commodity Import Program' (unpublished), p. 16.

21. AID, Regulation 1, *Rules and Procedures applicable to Commodity Transactions*, part 201, Sub-part B, conditions governing the eligibility of procurement transactions for AID financement.

22. Interview with the regional sales manager for the Middle East and Africa of Peerless Pumps, on October 24, 1977 in the Cairo office of the company's commercial agents.

23. The Central Bank of Egypt, *Annual Report 1975*, table 6 in the statistical section.

24. The Central Bank of Egypt, *Annual Report 1977*, table 22 in the statistical section.

25. See *Al Akhbar* no. 1814, August 11, 1979, p. 1, where it was reported that the United States was exporting a very large arms deal to Egypt as part of a joint agreement on cooperation between the Egyptian and American defence and armed forces to modernize and develop Egypt's manufacture of weapons. The American delegation was headed by Minister of Defense McGovern. Also in the same issue another report was written to the effect that Egypt was presently receiving one-third of American loans and aid to the entire world. Also see *Al Akhbar*, no. 8475, August 13, 1979, pp. 1, 11, where an official from the Egyptian Ministry of Defence reported that the American delegation was extremely keen to meet Egypt's demands for modern weapons. The country had of course already received the outcome of a number of military assistance deals in the last few years.

26. Other resources for the creation of the 'international managers' may be found in the 'reorganized' public sector management as it enters into joint ventures with foreign capital. In the case of Brazil, for example, the public sector management proved very successful in meeting multinational require-ments for successful joint venturing business. The managerial élite of state corporations such as Petrobras very quickly learnt to adapt to international managerial ideology. See P. Evans, 'Multinationals, State-Owned Corporations, and the Transformation of Imperialism: A Brazilian Case Study', pp. 55–9.

27. Michalet, pp. 175–8.

28. Ibid.

29. Ibid., p. 131.

30. Ministry of Information – State Information Service, *The October Working Paper Presented by President Mohamed Anouar Al Sadat*, pp. 53–63.

31. Waterbury, 'The Opening: Part I: Egypt's New Look', pp. 6, 7.

32. Ibid.

33. The General Authority for Investment and Free Zones, *Law no. 43 of 1974*.

34. *The Official Journal*, vol. 30 (Bis) A, July 29, 1974.

35. The Ministry of Trade and Anis Mishriqi, *The Customs Guide*, p. 120.

36. Up to 1976 according to the decree 1072, the following commodities could not be imported by the private sector and were the exclusive responsibility of the public sector: wheat, flour, maize, beans, sesame,

unpacked tea, sugar, oil, animal and edible fat, tobacco, cotton, spun cotton, manufactured jute, coal, petrol and its by-products, chemical fertilizers, insecticide, imports for defence and the military, armaments. In 1978, according to the ministerial decree no. 1036, the quantity of goods reserved for the public sector had decreased and no longer included maize, beans, sesame, sugar, non-agricultural insecticides, spun cotton and manufactured jute. Furthermore the decree allowed the private sector to import some of the prohibited goods if allowed by the deputy minister in charge. Decree No. 1036 for 1978, article four in *Al Ahram al Iqtissadi Supplement*, September 15, 1978.

37. Waterbury, 'Egypt's New Look', p. 5.
38. Ali El Gritly, *Twenty-Five Years*, pp. 148, 149.
39. Waterbury, 'Egypt's New Look', p. 6.
40. Waterbury, 'Luring Foreign Capital', p. 13.
41. Waterbury, 'Egypt's New Look', p. 11.
42. Fouad Morsi, *This Economic Opening*, p. 156.
43. Judith Tucker, 'Economic Decay, Political Ferment in Egypt', p. 4.
44. Waterbury, 'Egypt's New Look', p. 9.
45. Waterbury, 'Public versus Private in the Egyptian Economy', p. 24.
46. Waterbury, 'Public versus Private', p. 7.
47. Ibid., p. 8.
48. Ibid., pp. 8, 9.
49. El Gritly, pp. 264, 265.
50. The plan and fiscal policy in *Al Ahram al Iqtissadi* supplement, 1 January, 1978.
51. See *Law no. 43 (1974) concerning the investment of Arab and foreign funds and the free zones as amended by law no. 32 of 1977*, article 3,6 (the General Authority for Investment and Free Zones).
52. See the Egyptian Federation of Industries and Chambers, *The Industrial Directory* (1974), pp. 46–66. And interview with the director of the federation, February 2 and 4, 1980.
53. Morsi, p. 278.
54. Ibid.
55. World Bank Report no. 931b, *Egyptian Agricultural Development Problems: Constraints and Alternatives*, table 18 in statistical appendices. In recent years (1979–81) *Al Ahram* daily paper has on very many occasions reported the distribution of reclaimed land, see for example *Al Ahram*, February 6, 1980, p. 1, where it was reported that 175,000 reclaimed feddans were distributed to university graduates and landless farmers.
56. A. Hassan Ibrahim, 'Agricultural Capital Project Analysis Course', p. 9, table 1.
57. M. C. Aulas, 'Egypt Confronts Peace', p. 4.
58. A. Hassan Ibrahim, 'The Impact of Certain Agricultural Policies on Income Distribution in the Rural Areas' (unpublished, to appear soon in published form), see tables 10–13, in the manuscript.
59. Interview with Dr A. Hassan Ibrahim (agricultural expert in the Institute of National Planning) January 5 and 8, 1980.
60. Morsi, p. 279. According to Dr Ibrahim's recent field observations, a new trend is now emerging whereby owners lease their land for a single crop at very elevated prices. For example one crop yield of wheat would cost the tenant £E150 per feddan.

61. Morsi, p. 278.

62. Raymond Baker, *Egypt's Uncertain Revolution under Nasser and Sadat*, pp. 214–17. Also see World Bank report no. 1815, *Egypt, Arab Republic of Egypt: Economic Management in a Period of Transition* (6 vols.) vol. 1, November 1977, pp. 60–1.

63. Legal publications, *Legislations for 1979, Including Laws Ministerial and Presidential Decrees*, pp. 84–8.

64. See *Al Ahram al Iqtissadi* supplement, January 1, 1980, 'The Fiscal and Economic Policy of 1980'.

65. See *Al Ahram*, Saturday November 24, 1979, 'Fiscal and Social Policies for the New Government Budget', p. 1.

66. Mahmoud Abdelfadil, *Development, Income Distribution and Social Change in Rural Egypt (1952–1970)*, pp. 126, 127.

67. Under the amended decree for imports in 1978, the private sector was being increasingly allowed to participate in the import of such strategic commodities.

68. The following is the list of specified goods: leather manufacturing requirements, furniture manufacturing requirements, car and transport spare parts, medical equipment, hospital equipment, and production requirements (a miscellaneous category including cocoa and photographic apparatus).

69. According to a discussion with the director of the Foreign Trade and Affairs Department of the Central Bank, the law was issued upon the advice of the International Monetary Fund in order to facilitate and encourage imports by the private sector. Interview conducted on May 6, 1978.

70. For the structure of imports within the new foreign trade system see Anis Mishriqi, *The Customs Guide*, the Ahram distribution department, 1977. The guide includes all the recent export/import and customs regulations. Also see the unified decree for imports and exports in *Al Ahram al Iqtissadi* supplement of September 15, 1978.

71. 'The unified decree', pp. 29–44, and appendices 8–10.

6 The Avenues of Investment for Businessmen and Opportunity for Commercial Agency Activity in the New Economy

The 'open door' policy very clearly expressed a desire to see a strong private sector emerge in the new economy. A sectoral survey will shed some light on the performance of the private sector generally, and commercial agency activity specifically. Thus the aim of the present chapter is twofold: firstly to evaluate the performance of the various sectors in the economy and the position of the private sector therein, and secondly to point out new avenues for commercial agency activity as well as areas of control.

Industry, agriculture, petrol, services and foreign trade; joint venture ownership

Despite facilities, privileges and encouragement given to foreign investors, the influx of foreign capital has not been over-abundant and has tended to focus on specific areas of the economy, the most important of which have been tourism, the tertiary sector and services (training in particular), banking, and more recently a few industrial projects such as textiles and chemicals. Egyptian capital under law no. 43 projects constituted 52 per cent of total investment excluding banks. Arab capital constituted 17 per cent, while foreign capital constituted 31 per cent.[1]

Projects under the joint venture law no. 43 are very profitable areas of investment, given the privileges and facilities offered. This explains both the interest of Egyptian private capital in the area, as well as the migration of human expertise from national public enterprises to joint venture ones, creating a 'new class of businessmen'.[2] In addition, 25 per cent of public sector industrial companies are presently negotiating with foreign investors for the establishment of joint ventures and a third of engineering enterprises have finalized agreements. In most cases the foreign partner will insist on ownership as well as administrative and executive predominance, especially in the case of large projects.[3]

Generally most joint venture projects that have begun production are clustered around services (banks), chemical industries (plastics in particular), metal industries (aluminium products) and textile industries (ready-made clothes). Meanwhile projects in banking, the contracting sector and chemical industries have already invested the majority of the estimated capital upon approval.[4]

Banking has not only attracted foreign capital, but has also been the subject of controversy both in public debates and the press. Foreign and joint venture banks steadily increased from nine banks in 1975 to nineteen in 1976/77,[5] and finally to 35 banks by the middle of 1978.[6]

Foreign investment banks' financing of projects has been extremely limited. Most of their loans have been short-term ones for the finance of foreign trade, imports in particular, as well as some limited export activity.[7] Meanwhile they have duplicated the functions of national banks, servicing the same clients – namely, businessmen in foreign trade. The foreign banks have not only drained the national banks of their best personnel but are also draining the country of potential investment capital drawn from Egyptian clients and transferred abroad.[8] The above findings were corroborated by the Central Bank's study submitted to the Ministry of Economy, wherein it proposed a joint supervision and limitation of their activity.[9]

The major clients of the banks, both depositors and borrowers, are private sector Egyptian commercial agents. The banks' participation in public sector investment is reduced to short-term loans made to the Central Bank or other local banks to help them meet import requirements in foreign currency. With regard to the private sector, the majority of financing has gone to the trading sector in short-term loans.[10]

Under the joint venture and foreign investment projects foreign banks are not the only factor enhancing the position of private sector businessmen in trade. The customs policies adopted are another added factor. According to law no. 43, all investment commodities imported for projects under its regulation are to be exempt from customs duties, while in the area of tourism all commodities, including consumer goods, are exempted.[11]

Industry, agriculture, petrol, services and foreign trade under national ownership, both private and public

Industry

One of the striking changes in industrial development during the operation of the *infitah* policy has been the relative decrease of industry's contribution to domestic income in comparison to other sectors of production. The contribution to GDP of the other primary productive sectors, namely agriculture, oil, trade and finance, have increased markedly.[12]

Industrial rates of growth at constant 1959/60 and 1970 prices have declined from 8.5 per cent in 1960–65 to 4.3 per cent in 1970–75, while the rate of growth for trade and finance increased from 11.1 per cent to 13.3 per cent.[13]

Recent developments in industry and investment policies in various sectors have been interpreted as both cause and effect of increased dependence on the world capitalist system. Liberalization of trade has led to competition with local industry and hence the latter's decline. Meanwhile investments were being rerouted from industry to trade.[14]

Industrial policy has generally changed from an import substitution policy, to an export-oriented one which is largely controlled by and dependent upon the international capitalist market. This kind of policy has historically been linked to the development of multinationals. Moreover the ownership of the industrial enterprise is also gradually shifting from a previously state-owned one to a private one. However the public sector still continues to be the single largest industrial investor in the Egyptian economy.[15]

All the above changes have had a number of detrimental effects upon the working class. The decrease of industrial activity has in a sense halted the development of the working class. Moreover the various anti-public-sector measures and various liberalizing commercial policies have also withdrawn a number of benefits previously enjoyed by the state-sector workers. The inequalities of income between the traditional state sector and the new modern sectors have been a source of great discouragement to the state workers, who are not only not participating in the ownership of the enterprises but are in addition underpaid in comparison to the 'modern sectors' and unable to claim their rights through strikes or union activity at least by law.[16] Moreover signs of unemployment have appeared,[17] a phenomenon which had rarely existed under the Nasser regime, and discrepancies in income disparities continue to grow larger.[18]

Meanwhile the industrial and productive sectors manifesting the largest growth rates are those partly financed and run by foreign capital, examples of which are petrol, the extractive industries, engineering and chemical industries.[19] Thus the private sector composed of joint Egyptian and foreign capital under law no. 43, although still small at present, is gaining in significance in the overall economy.[20]

With regard to the private industrial sector proper, i.e. the existing small-scale purely Egyptian industry which was not subject to the new investment laws, it is the World Bank's opinion that progress made in that domain is fairly slow. This portion of the industrial sector, called 'residual'[21] by some and small-scale nationalist by others,[22] concentrates on fairly small establishments manufacturing leather, furniture, wood, clothes, food processing, printing, some metallic products, textiles and chemicals.[23] With the exception of the chemical industries,[24] this sector has faced the harshest competition within the internal market due to import liberalization of finished goods. The number of private sector enterprises in Egypt declined after 1974, but picked up again during 1975–76. It is the World Bank's opinion that this sector has been largely neglected under the new policy, both with regard to procedures required to facilitate the setting up of an establishment, and in terms of statistical surveys and studies.[25]

Moreover it appears that those industries within this sector which have any sense of survival will have entered into joint venture enterprises with foreigners.[26] This area of investment is not only slow in growth but is in addition deemed to be of limited profitability.[27] This sector's share of total industrial investment is extremely small, averaging about four per cent per annum. The 1976–80 draft plan envisages an investment of £E300 million by the private sector, with the share of joint ventures estimated at £E860 million out of a total planned industrial investment of £E2,865 million.[28] Workers in this sector are, however, quite privileged and enjoy relatively high salaries, and are able to negotiate and protest.

Agriculture

Despite the fact that in recent years Egypt's agriculture has been a slow-growing sector with average rates of 3.5 per cent in the 1950s and 2.5–3.7 per cent in the 1960s and the first half of the 1970s,[29] and despite the government's recognition of the numerous problems confronting the expansion of this very vital sector in its initial stages, the new open door policy has given very little attention to agricultural development policies.[30] The agricultural sector has been a latecomer in government official planning (namely 1976–77). In addition, agriculture has traditionally been the stronghold of the private sector, a trend encouraged even more in recent years. Government investment in agriculture, irrigation and drainage, compared to total investments, has fallen from 25 per cent in the mid-1960s to 12 per cent in 1971/72 and was projected at 8.6 per cent for the period of the 1978–82 plan. Major government expenditure on agriculture since the mid-1960s has concentrated largely on land reclamation projects (50–60 per cent of total public investment).[31] However, the government is seeking to increase the productivity of established farmlands. Major choices for agricultural expansion and development are contained within the so-called 'Green revolution' and 'food security' policy guidelines, both of which aim at increasing the supply of local market requirements of agricultural products, increasing the surplus for export, ameliorating existing industries, providing work opportunities as well as reducing constraints confronting the sector.

Recent trends in land exploitation, farm mechanization, the interlinkages between local industry and agriculture, and the agricultural balance of trade, all point towards:

1. The increase of areas cultivated with non-traditional crops and the decrease of cotton cultivation. This has led to a decrease in government marketing and distributive activity as well as increased private sector capitalist farming and trade activity.[32]

2. Increases in farm mechanization and technological innovation,[33] a major portion of which is being met by imports.

3. Large increases in agricultural imports – leading to the appearance of a trade deficit for the first time in 1974.

The available statistics vary with regard to the exact figure of the trade deficit. However, all agree that it first appeared in 1974 and was caused by the vast increases in agricultural imports, particularly of consumer goods.

The various trends in agricultural development have created greater opportunities for the import of agricultural commodities as well as the import of foreign technology, all of which constitute new avenues for commercial representative and mercantile activity. In addition, foreign capital has also been attracted to the agricultural sector. Some of the major governmental projects, both in horizontal and vertical expansion, are being jointly funded by the World Bank and the United States AID, as well as Western multinationals. Foreign investment is mainly active in land reclamation and agribusiness projects concentrating on the cultivation and processing of fruit and vegetables as well as fish-farming and animal production.[34] It has been reported that multinational firms such as Coca-Cola, FMC, Massey Ferguson, as well as other European firms, are involved in independent projects for the production and processing of citrus fruit and vegetables for export.[35] In addition to participation in the major government projects, the US AID is also involved in 62 research projects with the Ministry of Agriculture. The projects are financed and supervised by the American Food for Security Programme under PL480.[36] Meanwhile American and Egyptian cooperation in agricultural development was crowned with the creation of a joint council for agribusiness staffed by Egyptian and American businessmen.[37]

The Egyptian private sector as mentioned earlier has always dominated the agricultural sector. In recent years, however, this sector has in addition witnessed the emergence of 'gentlemen farmers'.[38] Locally two names appear as the most prominent in the area of agribusiness, namely Othman Ahmad Othman (former Minister of Housing, Honorary President of the Arab Contractors Public Sector Company, and eventually First Deputy Prime Minister for Food Security Projects and President of the Engineers' Syndicate) and Al Tounsi.[39] Both are city-dwellers.

The phenomenon of the 'gentleman' farmer – city-dwellers and businessmen involved in farming and agro-industry – is gaining weight. The avenues open to importers of agricultural technology and equipment are also very promising. A number of contemporary Egyptian commercial agents are already cooperating with and selling the products of internationally well-known firms in the field of agriculture, such as Massey Ferguson and FMC. A large number are involved in the import of agricultural consumer goods, machinery, equipment, fertilizers, and pesticides. A much smaller proportion are involved in the export of agricultural products such as perfume and ornamental flowers, rice, peanuts, seeds, coconut oil and honey. Meanwhile the commercial representative of Massey Ferguson has initiated[40] a joint venture project for the local assembly of tractors between Massey Ferguson and the public sector El Nasr Automotive company.

The position of the agricultural workers continues to be quite distressing. Although some improvements were made in the mid-1960s, during the following decade this class became once again underprivileged, disorganized and unable to benefit from previously state dominated privileges. Seasonal labourers, of course, suffered most, and will continue to do so, so long as:

1. Consumerism continues to pervade the economy both urban and rural, which also means a decline in productivity, less labour opportunities and increased trade deficits.

2. Low levels of relative income continue to be the general rule.

3. There is a decline in the role of agricultural cooperatives and cooperative farming, which might have allowed for better farming conditions for small farmers at the very least, while workers might have also benefited in indirect ways since cooperatives had become effective means of indirectly taxing agriculture. They allowed cash crops to be purchased at tax-element-inclusive prices. One may speculate that there might have been sufficient state revenue under the right ideological environment to ameliorate the conditions of agricultural labourers. It is agreed that in the period 1965–70, transfers of income from agriculture to the state treasury were of the order of £E330 million.[41]

4. There does not exist the kind of democratic environment that might allow seasonal and other agricultural workers the right of political expression.[42]

Some individual solutions are found in the mass exodus of agricultural labourers to oil-producing countries. However, this is not a radical or collective solution, since it merely leads to more consumption by some, while political collective action continues to be absent.

As the position of small farmers and agricultural labourers is on the decline in the agricultural scene, middle-sized farmers and landowners, as well as gentlemen farmers and agricultural importers/exporters, are gaining power.

Oil

Petroleum has grown rapidly since 1979 and has come to dominate the Egyptian economy in terms of financial importance. The contribution of this sector to government revenue increased from ten per cent in 1975 to 27 per cent in 1978 and reached 49 per cent in 1979.[43]

The petroleum sector has attracted considerable amounts of foreign investment, particularly in 1979 when foreign oil companies invested £E371 million. From 1977 to 1979, foreign investment constituted four-fifths of total investment in oil and monopolized the areas of research and exploration, while investment in refining and distribution was reserved for the Egyptian public sector.[44] Almost all the Egyptian investment in such companies comes from the government and only a small proportion from the public sector EGPC.[45]

The Egyptian private sector proper does not invest in the productive oil sector as such. In recent years, however, it has been involved in ancillary activities, in the area of services such as inspection, rental of machinery and equipment, transport, and catering for the oil companies stationed in the desert.[46] According to some commercial agents involved in the above services, the activity is highly profitable. Thus with regard to catering it is possible to provide a US$12 meal for oil company personnel in the Western desert against a price of US$25.[47] Similarly, rental of machinery to foreign oil companies during the exploration period and the provision of local servicemen (engineers for equipment inspection) is also highly profitable.[48]

According to the investment and free zones statistics, by 1979 43 projects in the field of mining and petroleum had obtained approval with a total capital of

£E57.8 million, constituting 2.3 per cent of total investments.[49]

Moreover the petroleum sector has also opened new avenues for imports and commercial representation activity. Large numbers of commercial agents were involved in the import of machinery and equipment related to the sector.

Services

Housing and construction

The housing sector has been rather stagnant, and for the past two decades supply lagged far behind both need and demand.[50] However what has been recently called the 'housing problem or crisis' did not manifest itself as acutely as in the early 1970s.[51] In 1976 the urban housing shortage was estimated to be one million units, notwithstanding some 3,000 existing units which were in deplorable condition and subject to decay. The housing problem has been especially acute with regard to the lower income groups.[52]

Despite the fact that national investments in housing and construction industries progressively increased from 1973 onwards, with the exception of 1976,[53] the percentage of such investments in total national investment has declined over the last three decades.[54] The public sector has been dominant in construction industries such as cement, porcelain, metal, steel pipes and glass.[55] With regard to construction, since the early 1970s the government has essentially aimed at encouraging the private sector.[56] This trend is even more pronounced in the housing five-year plan (1980–84) where the private sector is expected to construct 90 per cent of total required housing units.[57] Meanwhile the projected percentage of low-income housing is only 55 per cent of total production. The remainder is aimed at middle and high income housing.[58]

In addition to the encouragement of the local private sector, the new housing policies have also aimed at importing foreign technology in the area of construction both through the import of advanced machinery and equipment and the setting up of eleven prefabrication factories.[59] Meanwhile the World Bank is financing a number of housing projects to be carried out by the Ministry of Housing, namely in the construction of new cities.[60]

Since 1974 a certain fraction of businessmen in the housing sector have found new avenues of investment, as well as sources of rapid enrichment. The open door policy has not only encouraged foreign investors but also a large inflow of tourists, notably from Arab countries. Thus the phenomenon of furnished flats at exorbitant rents emerged, some reaching thousands of pounds per month when rented on a daily basis. An interesting trend has been the construction of luxury apartment houses for sale, again constituting a very handsome profit for investors since normally such flats will be sold at about £E100,000 in affluent residential areas, while land and construction costs will not be more than £E10,000 per flat. Land speculation is another very lucrative area of investment.[61] The construction of luxury apartment houses and administrative complexes for rent is also an extremely profitable area which has attracted not only local private sector investors but also foreign investors.[62] Rents for such apartments in Cairo have been estimated at £E1,500 per month in 1977, which is the equivalent of New York rents.[63] The housing shortage has created another source of revenue for a number of private sector speculators in the form of downpayment or 'key money', which is a sum paid over and above the rent to the owner of the house and often to a former tenant when vacating the apartment. The abovementioned sums have soared in recent years. Contracting is another area of substantial profit-making, particularly for those enterprises which are equipped with modern machinery. In addition quite a large number of private sector contractors are involved in subcontracting, i.e. taking over some public sector operations or simply mediating between customers and the public sector against exorbitant fees.[64] The latter type of activity accounts for about £E50 million of private sector productive capacity.[65]

Finally the whole area of foreign trade in the housing sector, where the private sector has been most active, is an added avenue of investment and enrichment. In recent years the private sector has saturated the market with certain specific commodities such as sanitary equipment and tiles to the extent of threatening local industries, while with regard to certain other commodities it has created artificial shortages. A black market for cement has recently appeared, leading to spectacular increases in the price of cement, from £E6 per ton of Egyptian cement in 1974 to US$54 per ton of imported cement through the commercial companies in Port Said in 1977.[66] A large number of agents are involved in the importing of machinery, equipment and raw material necessary for housing and construction, a smaller number are involved in contracting activity.

Tourism
The tourist sector has since 1975 attracted increased government planning and attention. This sector has been regarded by many government officials as a vital sector in the Egyptian economy and an important source of foreign currency.[67]

Statistics on tourism are unfortunately highly hypothetical. However, it may be safely maintained that the tourist sector has become a significant component of gross domestic product.

Table 6.1 compares various gross domestic product figures in a number of economic sectors from 1974 to 1980/81.

A large proportion of projected and planned investments in the tourist sector were to be obtained through foreign loans. Foreign loans in that sector appeared for the first time in 1975. In 1978 foreign capital was to constitute 46.4 per cent of total investment.[69]

Net revenues from tourism have increased (from £E109.4 million in 1975 to £E229.2 million in 1978).[70] However, the real contribution of tourist receipts is difficult to assess because of the substantial outflows of tourist receipts in the form of associated imports. In 1974, despite large increases in tourist receipts, income generated from this sector only constituted 1.9 per cent of gross national product.[71] It might be mentioned here that a comprehensive assessment of the economic and social returns of tourism in Egypt is limited by the lack of statistics.[72] This is possibly a rare calculation.

Table 6.1
Comparison of Gross Domestic Product Figures

Commodity Sectors	2332	2828	3359	4089	4869	6867	9594
Agriculture	1280	1468	1744	2038	2286	2530	2427
Industry and Mining	746	880	993	1120	1319	1650	2144
Petroleum	112	149	247	468	626	1908	3105
Electricity and Public Utilities	65	88	96	106	121	132	157
Construction	129	243	279	357	517	647	761
Distribution Sectors	807	1032	1355	1679	2233	3059	3809
Cans, Comm. and Storage	180	220	260	322	395	586	768
Suez Canal	3	40	141	169	294	406	543
Trade, Finance and Insurance	630	772	954	1188	1544	2067	2498
Service Sectors	1058	1196	1451	1766	1919	2175	2775
Housing	203	209	222	244	262	287	321
Other Services	855	987	1229	1522	1657	1888	2454
GDP at Factor Cost	4197	5056	6165	7534	9021	12101	16178
Net Indirect Taxes	142	162	562	810	774	604	768
GDP at Market Prices	4339	5218	6727	8344	9795	12705	16946

Source: Ministry of Planning and IBRD estimates.

The 1980/81 figure was derived by assuming the same growth rate as for other services.[68]

Major outflows of tourist revenue may be grouped under four headings:

1. commodities (namely food and beverages);
2. import of services (hotel administration, outflows of profits to some of the hotel shareholders);
3. other expenditure (advertising abroad, foreign tourist bureaux abroad); and
4. local consumption of imported goods, particularly by those most closely involved and employed by the tourist sector.[73]

Direct commodity imports and other capital outflows for hotels (food, beverages, spare parts, office equipment, fuel and oil, advertising, services and wages have been estimated at £E7.81 million in 1975, while indirect imports (imported components of local industries which service tourism) were estimated at another £E1.58 million in 1975. Thus total direct and indirect imports for hotels in the tourist sector was of the order of £E9.39 million, constituting 7.8 per cent of total touristic expenditure.[74] Hotels are of course not the sole area of investment in tourism. Other areas are restaurants, transport, communications, night clubs, casinos, shops, etc.). From 1976 to 1980 foreign imports, whether in the form of capital, equipment, machinery, transport or commodities, constituted 30 per cent of total tourist investments.[75] In 1977 alone foreign currency at official rates allocated to the public tourist sector for imports was £E4 million.[76]

Tourism has offered the private sector new avenues of enrichment in recent years. This is especially true of the whole area of imports whereby, according to a law promulgated in 1973, commodities imported for the tourist sector (including building materials and all other necessary furnishing, equipment, household and kitchen ware, etc.) are to be exempt from customs. This has encouraged a number of importers to circumvent regulations and smuggle in large amounts of commodities under the heading of tourism.[77] As mentioned earlier, another area of profit-making and investment has been renting furnished flats at exorbitant prices, to Arab tourists in particular.

Consultancy
An area where the private sector has become active is the whole area of technical, legal, administrative and economic consultancy. The activity, although existing in the past, was rejuvenated with the 'open door' policy and the invitation to foreign investment. The major task of consultancy is primarily to guide prospective foreign investors and their local partners as well as local investors. Moreover, although according to a number of observers, the numbers of consultants are fairly large and increasing, the activity is, however, still not regulated and thus knowledge of exact numbers involved not possible. Individuals involved in consultancy are not necessarily professionals or specialists. A significant number of those in business are simply speculators who do not prepare studies or offer consultation, but mediate between prospective foreign investors and the investment authority for the securing of

approvals against very high fees. Such individuals do not normally have permanent bureaux, nor are they registered. Thus they do not pay taxes. Recently some of the professional syndicates (engineering, legal and trade) have attempted to promulgate laws to regulate consultancy. However, such efforts have been uncoordinated and therefore difficult to implement properly, given the absence of a professional syndicate union.[78]

Foreign trade

The area of foreign trade is an especially crucial sector in national development and one which has a very direct impact on the balance of payments and rates of national investment. This is especially true in the case of Egypt, where economic production is specialized and therefore highly dependent on foreign trade as a promoter of development and growth.[79] In recent years this sector has manifested substantial qualitative and quantitative changes.

Imports

An analysis of the patterns of imports within the years 1974–77 reveals a steady increase in the annual rate of payments for imported goods. During the years immediately preceding the 'open door' policy (1970–72) annual rates of payments for imports were of the order of £E377.6 million. Under *infitah* annual rates of payments greatly increased.[80] Thus total payments for imports increased from £E622.3 million in 1973 to £E1,252.8 million in 1974 and £E1,691.1 million in 1975. In 1976 payments decreased slightly to £E1,642.2 million only to increase again in 1977, reaching £E1,899.8 million.[81] The largest payments for imports were made for foodstuffs, including wheat and grain, closely followed by machinery.[82]

The large increases in payments have been attributed to several factors, among which have been the great international price increases from 1974 onwards, particularly with regard to machinery, capital goods, and manufactured goods generally.[83] Meanwhile absolute quantities of commodities imported have not only increased, but with liberalization of foreign trade there were qualitative changes with regard to commodities imported. Since 1974 there has been a steady increase in the import of consumer goods as well as luxury goods.[84] This is largely attributable to the new liberalized trading system which allowed private individuals to import goods directly without official foreign exchanges or government control. The percentage of imports made under this new system increased from three per cent in 1975 to 25 per cent of total imports in 1978. About 55 per cent of the commodities imported under that system were essentially luxury goods and other consumer goods. Payments for such commodities under the direct liberalized system increased from £E65 million in 1977 to £E150 million in 1978.[85]

Apart from increases in world prices, increased amounts of commodities imported, and increases in both consumer and luxury imports, another extremely important factor contributing to the large increases in import payments has been the manner in which imports are conducted or the institutions are involved in the import process, and their effects upon price increases, regardless of whether the imports are made to the account of the public or private sector. Hence my concern here is not only with the type of commodities the private sector imports in a liberalized foreign trade system, but the extent of private sector participation in foreign trade. In other words the question I address myself to here, and which is in fact related to the major concern of this present section, is the extent of the control and participation of private sector commercial agents in foreign trade, imports in particular. In the following section based on the available statistics, along with interviews conducted with officials directly involved in the control and registration of imports, I will reconstruct the degree to which imports are effected through the mediation of private sector commercial agents.[86]

National statistics on the participation of each sector in imports do not exist, hence a numerical estimate is not possible. It is, however, possible to obtain indications by inference, i.e. through

1. a study of the statistics issued from the various licence committees;
2. statistics from the public sector commercial companies;
3. data obtained from the Central Bank and Ministry of Trade;
4. interviews with chairmen of the public sector firms, licence committees registration staff, and the Central Bank Director of the Foreign Relations Department.

The statistics and data obtained are for the years 1976/77.

Of imports purchased by the public sector, those for small manufacturers and artisans amounted to £E12.3 million at parallel market rates for 1977.[87] Although according to trade regulations such imports should be made through the mediation of the public sector Misr trading company, it appears that this is not actually the case. According to informed sources, during the *infitah* period the overall annual turnover of the company declined from £E6 million to $E3.5 million. This was largely due to the fact that the private sector was now very active in their field. The Misr Company for Import and Export is essentially specialized in foodstuffs, which is the only domain that has remained active. According to our informant the company formally has 1,004 agency contracts with foreign suppliers. Most of their commercial activities, however, are carried out by the private sector through illicit subcontracting. This arrangement suits both the private and public sector for the following reasons:

1. The number of contracts formally registered as theirs is far too great for them to follow up or service adequately.
2. Quite a large number of the foreign suppliers require exclusivity in their representation which the public sector cannot provide if it has to meet the salary requirements of its employees.
3. The public sector personnel are not as flexible, mobile and experienced as the private sector, and thus are not effective in market surveys, salesmanship and follow-up activity.
4. Furthermore the public sector, unlike the private sector, cannot accept payments for imported goods in local currency since they already suffer from

foreign exchange shortages. Many local clients will prefer to deal with private sector agents who can accept payments in local currency.

5. The private sector is quite happy to operate through subcontracting which saves it the trouble of bureaucracy and formal registration, as well as enabling it to avoid taxes.

6. Normally the public sector gets a share of the commissions obtained through subcontracting. The private sector is satisfied, for it still manages to gain its commission tax free, and the commission paid to the public sector will normally be about one per cent – not a real burden if we take into consideration that commissions received by the private sector will normally range between five per cent and 30 per cent, occasionally even reaching 50 per cent. The public sector is also quite happy with the arrangement, for instead of losing their agencies totally, they can at least earn a one per cent commission, which managers can proudly add to their annual turnover.[88]

Another category of imports is composed of those effected directly through the commercial banks, according to the ministerial decree 417. Although the decree meant to allow this form of imports for both the private and public sectors, according to the Director of the Foreign Affairs and Trade Department in the Central Bank, who in accordance with regulations is kept informed by all the commercial banks on the letters of credit issued and the names of the applicants, 99 per cent of the imports are carried out through the private sector. The director explained that the decree was supposed to encourage public sector companies to import directly without having to go through the commercial firms. However, this did not happen, since when they did attempt to contact foreign suppliers directly, the latter referred them to their local private sector agents.[89] The total amount of payments for imports under this system was £E7.5 million in 1977 at parallel market rates.[90]

A further category of imports comprises those effected through the licence committee. These imports were ones falling under the ministerial decree 227 for 1976, allowing the private sector to import without currency transfers from banks. Total payments for such imports in 1976 were £E163 million, and in 1977 increased to £E265 million. In 1977 payments for spare parts and transport equipment (22 per cent), engineering equipment (19 per cent), and foodstuffs (12 per cent), were the largest in order of importance.[91] Although this system of imports was essentially designed for both the private and public sector commercial companies wishing to import in order to trade internally, no public sector commercial company had, up until 1977, availed itself of this facility.[92] Furthermore, private sector applicants for licences were both importers involved in internal commerce and commercial agents who frequently imported for the public or private sectors when the latter were short of foreign exchange.[93]

A significant proportion of imports are effected by the public sector through its commercial agencies. The only commodities that are allegedly being imported by public sector commercial firms are certain strategic commodities and subsidized foodstuffs imported at official rates. Such imports are subject to licensing from the public sector purchasing committees. Total amount of payments for supply commodities (tea, flour and wheat) and agricultural goods at official rates in 1977 was £E135.7 million, plus £E46.8 million for the requirements of the armed forces. Thus the total amount of the above imports at official rates was of the order of £E182.5 million for 1977.[94]

A final category which we shall look at is that of imports effected by virtue of licences obtained from the purchasing committee of public sector companies. Payments for such commodities are made at the parallel market (semi-official) rate. The total payments of such imports are extremely difficult to determine since there is bound to be duplication in the above-mentioned sources of statistics if we are to take into consideration the fact that private sector agents may import to their account and then proceed to deliver the goods to the public sector against local payments. However, in an approximate sense one may consider the total payments for imports through the purchasing committee, which may be through the private or public sector, to be the remaining amount of total import payments for 1977; £E1,899.8 million, 1977 total, minus £E467.3 million, sum of all the above import payments, equals £E1,432.5 million.

It is difficult to determine how much of this total represents imports through the mediation of the private sector. Only two sources can be utilized as indicators: first, statistics of the various public sector commercial companies; and second, the Central Bank. Both sources yielded contradictory data. According to the public sector companies' statistics, the nine importing companies were involved in the import of £E890.9 million worth of commodities in 1977,[95] thus leaving the private sector with £E541.1 million only. According to the Director of the Foreign Affairs and Trade Department in the Central Bank, approximately 90 per cent of the application forms submitted to the bank from the purchasing committees of the public sector companies were accompanied by the names of private sector agents.[96]

Although the first source appears as official statistics, this researcher is inclined to question its validity based on the interviews conducted with public sector managers and directors which seemed to point at the unreliability of the statistical figures, the encroachment of the private sector through sub-contracting, and the fact that the companies were not yet willing or prepared to act as pure commercial enterprises, i.e. import and market the goods internally, since they did not have the means or experience.[97] Furthermore the total value of £E890.9 million presumably not only includes imports for the purchasing committees, but also imports to the account of public sector commercial firms and for the private sector, the latter being only nominally under their control.

Although nothing absolutely definitive and translatable in accurate figures can be said about the hegemony of private sector commercial agents over imports, one can certainly conclude from the available information that they control or are involved in the vast majority of the country's import transactions. It may also be worth mentioning here that commercial agency representation has absorbed the vast majority of private sector joint stock company activity. By the end of 1977 the total number of private sector productive companies registered with the Ministry of Trade was 336. Those companies were involved in such activities as trade, industry, agriculture, contracting, pharmaceuticals and services. Out of the total of 336, 87 private sector companies were established under law no. 43 of 1974 regulating joint ventures and foreign investment.[98] Commercial representative agencies were registered in a separate department of the Ministry of Trade, and by the end of 1977 the total number of companies registered was 766.[99]

The number of registered agents has greatly proliferated since the presidential decree no. 1906 for 1974, which was amended by the decree no. 14 for 1976. The decree set up a special registration office for the agencies and stipulated the manner in which agents were to be registered, the preconditions for registration and the necessary fees to be paid. By the end of 1976, 244 commercial representative companies had registered their names at the Ministry of Trade. By the end of the following year the number had increased to 766, and by 1978/79 the number of commercial agencies was in the order of 1,170.[100] This of course does not include the number of agents who were not registered.[101]

Exports
The increase in payments for imports was not met by a similar or sufficient increase in export proceeds, which inevitably continued to burden the balance of trade. In 1974 revenues from exports totalled £E653.9 million against a total of import payments of £E1,252.8 million, thus giving rise to a deficit of £E598.9 million. In 1975 while payments for imports continued to increase, reaching the amount of £E1,691.1 million, proceeds from exports declined to £E612.8 million due to a crop failure in agricultural produce, increased internal consumption and a fall in agricultural prices. The deficit consequently rose to £E1,078.3 million.[102] In the following year there was a slight increase in export proceeds, reaching £E629.7 million, accompanied by a slight decrease in import payments to £E1,646.2 million, resulting in a slight improvement in the deficit, which, however, still remained at the alarming figure of £E1,016.5 million. In 1977 the deficit once again increased to £E1,123.6 million despite an increase in export proceeds totalling £E776.2 million. Payments for imports had once again increased to £E1,899.8 million.[103]

Exports and the private sector
Innovative policies and facilities offered the exporting sector have not been as great as the import sector within the overall foreign trade area. Thus, according to a World Bank report, the actual developments in the external sector serve to underline the fact that the authorities have had no coherent overall strategy for encouraging exports. Some *ad hoc* measures have indeed been taken which have assisted the development of certain types of export commodities, but their cumulative impact has not been very significant. The most important measures were the creation of the parallel market in September 1973, in which exporters of specified commodities were given a premium of 50 per cent over the official exchange rate, which produced an effective exchange rate of £E0.58 per dollar

(compared with £E0.39 per dollar for the official rate) and subsequent changes in the parallel market rate and coverage for exports. Thus, in 1976, the parallel rate was altered in successive steps to £E0.70 per dollar, while in the budget for 1977 the scope of the market was widened to cover all export commodities, except raw cotton and petroleum.[104] However, the report goes on to point out that 'changes in the effective exchange rate do not in themselves constitute a comprehensive export promotion policy. Egypt's export effort remains subject to serious handicaps.'[105]

In 1977 private sector exports of industrial commodities constituted only ten per cent of total national industrial exports.[106] Meanwhile there are no statistics available on the percentage of private sector exports in agriculture. However, one may safely assume that, although increasing in recent years, it is still fairly small since cotton continues to be the major export, constituting 64 per cent of total agricultural exports in 1977. Cotton is marketed by the public sector. Private sector exports mainly consist of fruits, vegetables, ornamental flowers and medicinal plants whose percentages have been increasing.[107]

Although the number of exporters registered by the Ministry of Foreign Trade and Economy is fairly large – 9,675 exporters since the early 1960s to December 1979 – only 200–300 of those have actually been operating recently and are fairly successful.[108] According to a key informant in the Ministry of Trade, the cumulative registry does not keep a very accurate or rigorous count of the names that were dropped out of the registry due to death or failure on the market, or change in profession.

The new political economy of Egypt under *infitah* has very clearly strengthened the position of the private sector. Meanwhile from the sectoral survey of the economy it becomes clear that the country has become increasingly dependent on foreign capital in the form of imports of commodities and technology, as well as loans and investment.

Moreover, under *infitah*, a new ascendant bourgeoisie is emerging whose various strata are linked to the so-called 'modern' sector of the economy, i.e. those sectors mostly dependent on the external market and foreign capital in its various forms. The activities of the new bourgeoisie are mainly centred around:

1. import trade and commercial representation;
2. joint venture projects, especially in housing, agriculture, food, construction, the pharmaceutical industries, and wood manufacturing;
3. capitalist farming and agribusiness;
4. servicing in the oil sector;
5. real estate speculation;
6. contracting;
7. consultancy.[109]

The new bourgeoisie, linked to foreign capital, emerged as the natural offshoot and extension of certain fractions of the state bourgeoisie and their 'protégés', who dominated the mid- to late Nasser period. The new bourgeoisie appears to have merged with fractions of the state bourgeoisie. Note the new trend of public sector managers entering in joint ventures with foreign capital, in addition to mutual cooperation in the areas of contracting as mentioned earlier in the chapter, as well as in foreign import trade, through subcontracting.[110] The major conflict within the bourgeoisie lies between certain fractions of the new bourgeoisie and national industrial capital.

The most significant fraction of the new emerging bourgeoisie, and one which will be singled out in the remaining chapters of this work, is that composed of commercial agents and importers. This fraction is of particular importance for three reasons:

1. They feature as the initial 'liaison group' between foreign capital and the Egyptian economy. They are the link between multinationals in metropolitan societies and the Egyptian market, and have been greatly enhanced and privileged as the economy extended and developed its exterior linkages. Note that both foreign government and private loans from local foreign banks have greatly favoured commercial transactions.

2. They control the key sector in the present economy, namely foreign trade imports. As was pointed out in each of the sectors surveyed, the import of commodities and technology feature as the present bases for further development. Moreover foreign trade constitutes about 26 per cent of national economic activity, which shows this sector's crucial position in the Egyptian economy.[111]

3. Unlike all other fractions of the new bourgeoisie, commercial agents are legally privileged and protected by the present state inasmuch as the activity has been exclusively reserved for Egyptians. Thus while all other fractions and economic groups in the new class share their activities with foreign entrepreneurs, local commercial agents have a monopoly over their activity. Moreover state protection of the activity in no way implies state control or regulation, given the new liberalized foreign trade system and regulations.

Notes

1.   The Ministry of Economy, Foreign Trade, and Economic Cooperation, Economic Studies Unit, *A Study on Law 43 Investment Policies*, p. 21 and table 5 in the statistical appendix. (The study will be referred to under the names of the advising committee: Dr El Emary, Dr El Gritly and Dr Handoussa.)

2.   Ibid., pp. 16, 39.

3.   Ibid., p. 40.

4.   Ibid., p. 12.

5.   *Al Ahram*, Wednesday 13 July 1977, p. 11, in the supplement on banks.

6.   Abdel Moneim Othman, 'From the Statistics of the Central Bank: the Real Picture of the New Banks in Egypt', p. 14.

7.   See El Emary, El Gritly and Handoussa, pp. 59–63. Although the report depicts the failings of the bank, it is nevertheless impartial inasmuch as it justifies and explains the causes for the various shortcomings, a number of which are, according to the report, due to internal conditions in Egypt.

8.   Fatma Annan, 'The Egyptian Banks are in Difficulty', pp. 10–13.

9.   Othman, p. 4.

10.   Interviews with managers of the American Express (Monday March 20, 1978, the Chase National Bank (Tuesday March 28 1978), Citibank (Monday April 3, 1978), and Bank of Commerce and Credit International (BCCI) (Tuesday April 13, 1978).

11.   El Emary, El Gritly and Handoussa, p. 31.

12.   The Egyptian Central Bank, *Annual Report 1976*, table 5 in statistical section.

13.   Galal Amin, 'The Economic Opening in Egypt' (unpublished), p. 7.

14.   Ibid., p. 8.

15.   Saad Hafez, 'The Reflection of the Ruling Class upon the Structure and Direction of Industry in Egypt', pp. 64–85.

16.   Ismail Sabri Abdallah, 'Some Socio-economic Changes appearing upon the Egyptian Economy (1974–84)' (unpublished).

17.   Ibrahim El Issawy, *Egypt's Future*, pp. 63–72.

18.   Abdel Khaliq, 'The Most Significant Indices of Structural Transformations in the Egyptian Economy with the Open Door Economic Policy: 1971–77', pp. 35, 36, 37.

19.   Note that engineering and chemical industries are not only the ones manifesting the highest levels of production (see p. 3), but are also the areas where foreign and joint venture capital have been most concentrated.

20.   El Emary, El Gritly and Handoussa, p. 26.

21.   See World Bank report no. 1818 Egypt–Arab Republic of Egypt, *A Survey of a Small-Scale Industry* (December 2, 1977, document of the World Bank), pp. 1–41.

22.   See Fouad Morsi, *This Economic Opening*, pp. 129–51.

23.   Ibid., p. 4.

24.   The engineering and chemical industries, which comprise some 1,000 public and private sector establishments, appear to have had a better position than many other industries with regard to foreign competition. Through the Federation of Egyptian Industries, the above-mentioned industries were able to pressurize for the restriction of a number of imports falling in their domain of production. In 1978 law no. 321 was passed prohibiting the import of some 81 commodities in the fields of metals and engineering products, chemicals, textile products and relevant or necessary equipment, as well as four miscellaneous products. See ministerial decree no. 321 for 1978– The Ministry of Trade (unpublished handout); also see *Al Ahram al Iqtissadi* supplement, September 15 1978, 'The Unified Decree for Import and Export', pp. 52–7; and *Al Ahram*, Friday March 22 1978, p. 1, wherein the chamber of chemical industries expresses its gratitude to the government for having passed the protective ministerial decree no. 321.

25.   World Bank report no. 1818, p. 3.

26.   The World Bank report does not give any figures on the degree of migration from this sector to the joint venturing sector. However, based on this researcher's own observations and an interview with the Director of the Research and Statistical Department of the Federation of Industries, this appears to be a prevalent trend.

27.   El Emary, El Gritly and Handoussa, p. 16.

28.   World Bank report no. 1818, p. 24.

29.   World Bank report no. 1815 *Egypt, Arab Republic of Egypt: Economic*

Management in a Period of Transition (six vols.), vol. 1, November 1977, pp. 22–3.

30. World Bank report no. 931b EGT, *Egyptian Agricultural Development, Problems, Constraints and Alternatives*, p. 4.

31. World Bank report 1815, p. 62.

32. Non-traditional crops such as fruit, vegetables, medicinal plants, perfume and ornamental flowers are not subject to government cooperative marketing. Unlike cotton and various other traditional crops, non-traditional crops are supplied on a free unrestricted market, i.e. the government does not set purchasing prices for the cultivators. Meanwhile landowners cultivating such crops may evict tenants from the land.

33. Evidence for the increases in general farm mechanization and technological innovations and the Egyptian Government's general encouragement may be found in an AID project report which updates the latest governmental official figures on mechanization through its own team research in 1978. See AID project paper, *Egypt Agricultural Mechanisation Project* 263–003 (unpublished material obtained from the Ministry of Agriculture). Also see A. H. Ibrahim, 'Agricultural Capital Project Analysis Course'.

34. For a listing of government projects in horizontal and vertical expansion, some of which include foreign funding, see World Bank Report no. 931b, pp. 47–56, and the Ministry of Agriculture – the Agency of Aquaculture, 'A report presented to the minister on the achievements made with regard to fish farming till August 1979' (unpublished), and interview with Mr Arif Zulfiqar (World Bank representative in the Ministry of Agriculture) Cairo, December 27, 1979, and The Ministry of Agriculture, 'The joint projects between the Egyptian Ministry of Agriculture and the United States Agency for International Development' (unpublished).

35. Interview with Dr Al Kholly (Professor of Agricultural Economics and Chairman of the Department in Shebeen El Kom University who has offered consultation to the Ministry of Agriculture) on November 17, 1979 in the Ministry of Aquaculture.

36. The Ministry of Agriculture, the Department of Agricultural Foreign Relations – The American branch. 'A listing of the research projects under the US Aid PL480' (unpublished).

37. *Al Ahram al Iqtissadi*, no. 572, June 15, 1979, p. 17.

38. This concept is borrowed from Ashok Rudra, 'In Search of the Capitalist Farmer'. The concept is used to designate professionals, businessmen, retired bureaucrats engaged in any of the various agricultural activities.

39. Interview with Dr Al Kholy, November 17, 1979. This is not an exhaustive listing and essentially singles out Othman A. Othman. Knowledge on the various fields of activity was picked up from the media as well as through chats with knowledgeable businessmen. A more rigorous account of other areas of business activities would require an examination of all companies and businesses registered within the last few years. Such information may be found in *Al Waqi'e Al Massriya*, which publishes periodically basic information on newly established companies. However, the scope of the present work does not require such extensive research.

40. By 'initiated', I mean here that the commercial agent in question mediated, established the initial relation between the two contracting parties and obtained the approval of the foreign investment authority against a

commission. (Interview with a businessman also involved in that area of activity, on Saturday February 7, 1981.) According to my informant the project has been running at a loss. Recently, in *Al Ahram al Iqtissadi*, no. 632, February 23, 1981, p. 8, it was reported that the Investment Authority and Ministry of Industry decided to annul the project and contract four years after its initial approval.

41.   Mahmoud Abdel Fadil, *Development, Income Distribution and Social Change*, pp. 106–107 and Atteya El Sirfy, *Seasonal Workers*, pp. 143–4.

42.   Sirfy pp. 143–44.

43.   World Bank report no. 3123 EGT, Arab Republic of Egypt – *Domestic Resource Mobilisation and Growth Prospects for the 1980s* (November 3, 1980), pp. 28, 33.

44.   Ibid., p. 31.

45.   Ibid.

46.   Accurate statistical estimates of the number of Egyptian entrepreneurs or the amount of capital involved in this area are not available. Meanwhile although the trend is relatively new (since 1979), it is, according to a key informant involved in the activity, quite significant and promising, judging from the competition met on the market. Moreover, also according to this key informant, most competitors offering engineering, inspection and rental services were commercial agents of foreign companies specializing in petroleum. Interview with a commercial agent (a key informant also involved in that area of activity) on Saturday February 14, 1981.

47.   Discussion with a commercial agent who was not part of the initial population under study, on January 20, 1981.

48.   Interview, on March 10, 1981, with a commercial agent who was part of the original sample and who, in 1979, established a new company in partnership with a foreign investor for the rental of cranes and the provision of inspection and engineering services in the area of petrol. The commercial agent in question also hopes to enter the area of transport as an auxiliary service to the petrol sector. The interviewee is the commercial agent of a foreign multinational oil company and has in past years supplied the oil sector with machinery and equipment.

49.   Computed from El Emary, El Gritly and Handoussa, table 1 in the statistical appendix, and the Investment and Free Zones Authority, *Facts and Figures V* (July 1979). It must be pointed out that the various servicing activities related to petroleum do not all have to be registered under the law no. 43 projects. Meanwhile in the statistics of the Investment Authority, mining and petroleum are not distinguished nor is the nature of the companies clearly defined.

50.   Essam Montasser, 'The Housing Sector as a Component in Egypt's Development Planning', p. 44.

51.   Mohaya Zaytoun, 'The Housing Problem in Egypt and Trends for its Further Development', p. 37.

52.   Milad Hanna, *I Want a House Problem which has a Solution*, pp. 33, 40. Estimates for the exact shortages have varied. However, all sources will agree that demand far exceeds supply.

53.   The Egyptian National Bank, *The Economic Bulletin*, vol. 33, no. 1, 1980, table 1/6 G in the statistical appendix.

54.   Zaytoun, p. 9.

55. Hanna, pp. 83, 84.
56. Hossam Issa, *Capitalisme et sociétés anonymes en Egypte*, p. 119.
57. Fatma El Sheikh, *Housing in Egypt: some Economic and Technical Aspects*, p. 15.
58. Issa, p. 98.
59. Hanna, pp. 155, 156, and Montasser, p. 53. All prefabrication factories were purchased by the Ministry of Housing. Units produced are extremely costly.
60. Issa, p. 113.
61. Hanna, p. 151.
62. Zaytoun, p. 42, and Essam Rifaat, 'The Mafia in the Real Estate Market', in *Al Ahram al Iqtissadi*, no. 584, December 15, 1979, pp. 4–6.
63. Loutfy Abd El Azim, 'The Real Face of Tourism', p. 5.
64. Hanna, p. 90.
65. Issa, p. 66.
66. Hanna, p. 85.
67. Dr Mohaya Zaytoun, 'Towards an Objective Basis for the Determination of the Role of Tourism in the Development of the Egyptian Economy'.
68. World Bank report no. 4136–EGT, *Arab Republic of Egypt Issues of Trade Strategy and Investment Planning*, p. 408.
69. Ibid., pp. 57–8.
70. The Egyptian National Bank, *The Economic Bulletin*, vol. 33, no. 1, 1980. Table 3/4 in the statistical appendix.
71. Zaytoun, 'Towards an Objective Basis for the Determination of the Role of Tourism', pp. 333, 334.
72. Khalid Ikram *Egypt: Economic Management in a Period of Transition*, p. 309.
73. Zaytoun, pp. 337–9.
74. Ibid., pp. 340–5.
75. Ibid., p. 349.
76. The Ministry of Economy and Economic Cooperation – the general administration for the financial budget, 'Financial instalments for the import of intermediate, investment and consumer commodities according to the 1977 budget and agreements of the purchasing committees issued from 1/1/77 to purchasing committees issued from 1/1/77 to 31/12/1977' (unpublished).
77. *Al Ahram al Iqtissadi*, no. 533, November 1 1977, p. 13. It is rather difficult to determine the percentage of commercial representatives involved in the import of touristic commodities since no clear distinction can be made between such goods and more general items.
78. Mostafa Immam, 'The Consultancy Market and the Trap of Middle Men', pp. 16–20.
79. Abdel Khaliq, 'The Most Significant Indices of Structural Transformations in the Egyptian Economy', pp. 13, 14.
80. Ibid., p. 23.
81. Central Bank of Egypt, *Annual Report 1976*, p. 26, and *Annual Report 1977*, p. 14.
82. Central Bank of Egypt, *Annual Report 1976*, p. 26, and *Annual Report 1977*, p. 15.
83. El Gritly, pp. 238, 239.
84. Abdel Khaliq, pp. 24–30.

85.   Ibid., pp. 78, 79.

86.   In this section I merely want to establish the degree of control enjoyed by the private sector and its participation in foreign imports. The question of how its control constitutes yet another source for the increase in import payments will be dealt with in passing and discussed again in a subsequent chapter describing and analysing in detail the activities of the commercial agents.

87.   The Ministry of Economy and Economic Cooperation; the general department for finance, 'Total transfers and letters of credit through banks for the payment of commodity imports 1977' (unpublished report obtained from the Central Bank of Egypt.)

88.   The information concerning the encroachment of the private sector on public sector agencies and the reason for it was obtained through an interview with a senior official of the commercial agency for the import of private sector commodities, on Wednesday April 12, 1978. (The official, commenting on the manner in which statistical data were constructed in each of the various departments, was highly critical of their validity and ascertained that managers normally liked to exaggerate their yearly activity and turnover by registering the number of transactions more than once.)

89.   Interview with the Director of the Foreign Affairs and Trade Department of the Central Bank of Egypt, Thursday May 4, 1978.

90.   An account of the value of total letters of credit issued by the commercial banks in accordance with the ministerial decree 417 (unpublished documents obtained from the Central Bank of Egypt).

91.   The Licensing Committee, *Statistics of the Total Value of Imports without Currency Transfers during 1976 and 1977.*

92.   Interviews with four employees in the Department of Licence Registration, in the Licensing Committee, on Sunday April 16, 1978.

93.   Interview with the Director of the Foreign Affairs and Trade Department in the Central Bank of Egypt, May 6, 1978. (The information obtained from this interview on the topic was also corroborated by the interviews with commercial agents.)

94.   The Ministry of Economy and Economic Cooperation, 'Statistics of import permits for 1977 out of the 1978 budget in free currencies at official rates and a report of the allotted parcels of foreign currency transfers to meet the payment of consumer, investment and intermediate imported commodities for 1977' (unpublished material obtained from the Central Bank of Egypt files).

95.   The Ministry of Trade, the Supreme Council for Foreign Trade, *A Report on the Activities of Foreign Trade Companies in the Field of Imports during 1977 Compared with 1976.* This figure presumably includes imports for public sector productive companies, the private sector manufacturers and imports for internal trade.

96.   The Director of the Foreign Trade Department, who is in charge of approving all the application forms for the opening of letters of credit for the Public Sector Purchasing Committees' payments of imports. In the absence of statistics classified under public or private sector, this director appears to be the best authority on the matter.

97.   Interview with public sector managers and directors of commercial agency companies on Sunday April 9, 1978, Tuesday April 4, 1978 and Wednesday April 12, 1978.

98. The Ministry of Trade, Department of Companies Registration and Statistical Inspection.

99. The Ministry of Trade, Department of Commercial Representation.

100. The listing of names and the total numbers registered were obtained from the Ministry of Trade and Supply. The Department of Commercial Representation.

101. The existence of non-registered agents in operation was discovered through interviews conducted with some of these agents.

102. Central Bank of Egypt, *Annual Report 1975*, pp. 14–18.

103. Central Bank of Egypt, *Annual Report 1977, statistical section*, table 18, balance of payments estimates, general summary.

104. World Bank Report no. 1815, Egypt–Arab Republic of Egypt, *Economic Management in a Period of Transition* (6 vols.) vol. 1, November 1977, p. 43, para. 4.29.

105. Ibid., p. 43, para. 4.30.

106. Computed from the Central Bank of Egypt, Annual Report 1977, table 20 in appendix, and the Ministry of Industry and Mineral Resources, *Total Private Sector Exports from 1/1/1977 to 31/12/1978* (printed statistical handout obtained from the Federation of Egyptian Industries).

107. See section on agriculture, pp. 5–6.

108. Information obtained from the Ministry of Supply and Foreign Trade, the Legal Department and the Department of Statistics, in February 1980.

109. There are other new activities emerging such as banking but on a very limited scale. There are about three private sector local banks.

110. A deeper insight into the type of merger existing between the state bourgeoisie and the new modernizing bourgeoisie would require the setting up of a social matrix depicting kinship ties between agents of the two classes. There are presently some indications of this broad trend. An attempt to develop such a matrix will be made with regard to commercial representatives in a subsequent chapter.

111. Mohamed Doweidar, *The Egyptian Economy between Underdevelopment and Development*, pp. 619, 620.

7 Commercial Agents within the New Socio-economic Structure

A rigorous, comprehensive and accurate analysis of the contemporary Egyptian social formation in its entirety is beyond the scope of the present work. However, an analytical starting point lies in the realization that such a formation may not be understood by itself but must be placed within a world system. In the preceding two chapters it was pointed out that the contemporary economy was becoming increasingly dependent on Western capital in all its various forms. Given this very crucial relationship to the Western advanced economies, Egypt's economic system cannot be examined autonomously. Similarly, and as a consequence, its social structure may not be analysed separately or apart from a world system. This is not to say that the Egyptian social formation and its internal socio-economic structures are a mere extension of Western metropolitan societies or that they are exogenously created.

Egypt as a peripheral economy

Third World social formations such as Egypt's having symbiotic relations with the advanced Western capitalist countries have been conceptualized as peripheral or dependent formations within which peripheral capitalism features as the dominant mode of production. According to Amin, major characteristics of peripheral economies are that, by virtue of their involvement in the world capitalist system, they become disarticulated, extroverted and astructural. Moreover Amin explains the significance of disarticulation, extroversion and astructuration in the periphery in contradistinction to the structures in the centre. Hence he maintains that

> the disarticulation or astructuration of the underdeveloped economies has become one of the common places of current writing. . . . Interindustrial tables of the underdeveloped countries are 'empty' or the 'technical coefficients' are negligible.[1]

This is on the level of forward and backward linkages in the industries of the underdeveloped countries as opposed to the developed ones. On the broader level of the economy at large Amin views the developed economy as an integrated whole, a feature of which is a very dense flow of internal exchanges, the flow of external exchanges of the atoms that make up this entity being on the whole marginal as compared with that of internal exchanges. In contrast to this, the underdeveloped economy is made up of atoms which are relatively juxtaposed and not integrated, the density of the flow of external exchanges of these atoms being relatively greater and that of the flow of internal exchanges very much less. It is said that this economy is 'autocentric', whereas that of the underdeveloped countries is 'extroverted'.[2]

Amin in addition points out that just as the economies of the underdeveloped societies are disarticulated, so also their social structures are 'mutilated', the important element of which is the absence of a strong national bourgeoisie and the dominance of the metropolitan bourgeoisie.

Finally, taking into account historical variations, all peripheral social formations share the following features:

1. the predominance of agrarian and commercial capitalism in the national sector of the economy;
2. the creation of a local bourgeoisie in the wake of dominant foreign capital, which becomes integrated into a foreign system of production far more advanced than the remainder of the local economy, thus perpetuating the existing unequal distribution of wealth locally and internationally;
3. the tendency to a peculiar bureaucratic form of development.[3]

Although the concept has its problems and has been criticized for being loose, theoretically unsophisticated, and not sufficiently developed and refined to explain all aspects of Third World societies, it is, however, a very useful framework and approach for comprehending and analysing the internal class structures, particularly the bourgeoisies, of such societies. A more refined centre/periphery approach specifically concerned with class analysis posits that class structures in both metropolitan and peripheral societies cut across each other and are interlocked. A fundamental feature of peripheral societies is the existence of 'liaison groups' which link the class structures of their own societies to that of metropolitan societies. Through interlocking class structures the free flow of capital and goods from the metropole to the periphery is greatly facilitated. Thus as Petras puts it, 'the peripheral nation contains classes of double nationality: state rule is shared with economic subjects possessing external political allegiances, i.e. the multinational corporations.'[4]

Commercial agents are a very good example of a liaison group. They are strongly linked to the external capitalist system and also have their own internal cohesion.

A model of commercial agency activity

The agency contract and formal registration
According to the decree of the Ministry of Commerce no. 247 for 1976 (item II),

it is forbidden for the purchasing committees of the public sector to accept an offer from a foreigner, or foreign company, unless it is presented through an Egyptian commercial agent (*Wakil*) from the private or public sector who must be registered in the registry of the commercial agents.[5]

The very first stage in the sequence of procedures required for formal registrations and the practice of commercial agency activity is the effectuation of an agency contract with the foreign suppliers. The contract stipulates the responsibilities and obligations of both parties. The Egyptian partner is responsible for the local promotion, sales and representation of the foreign firm in various public tenders, as well as other business transactions involving import. He must, in addition, observe the interests of the company he represents. Hence, over and above his sales and promotion services, and the establishment of contracts with the relevant local authorities, he must according to the agreement also provide his 'principals' with all the necessary required and relevant information on development in the Egyptian economy, the political structure and market surveys. The local agent must also keep his 'principals' informed of all the recent legal developments and clarify the laws when required to.[6]

Normally 'contracts' will be made for the duration of one year, subject to renewal if both parties are satisfied and so desire. The agency agreement or contract will specify the goods which the local agent will be responsible for promoting, representing and selling. While supplying firms demand exclusivity, i.e. the local agent may not represent another firm manufacturing similar products, the 'principals' may on the other hand have many more than one agent and are not accountable under Egyptian law for any breach of contract or harm they may inflict upon their agents.

The agency contract includes a clause on the commission due to the local agent for each of the commodity and project items sold.[7] However, the formal contract is not the only document regulating the relationship between the two parties and is usually worded to meet the requirements of registration, local authorities issuing public tenders and government tax collectors. Meanwhile the actual commission received by agents is decided upon through mutual 'gentleman's agreements' and informal contracts between the two parties involved. The obvious purpose and function of this dual contract system is tax evasion on the part of local commercial agents,[8] something which is extremely common among such businessmen. In one case where it was possible to obtain evidence, the commission actually received was twenty times that declared.[9]

The commission as a form of payment

In exchange for the various services provided by the Egyptian agent, he receives his remuneration in the form of commissions on the various commodities sold rather than a fixed salary. The commission will vary according to the nature of each product sold. Products having a high turnover rate such as foodstuffs, fertilizers and consumer goods generally, will have a lower commission attached to them, normally 1–2 per cent of the total price. When the products sold are very expensive and have a low turnover rate, such as highly sophisticated machinery, scientific and medical equipment, or whole industrial plants, the commission will normally be 5–20 per cent of the total price according to formal contracts.[10] The real situation, as revealed by interviews, showed that such commissions for sophisticated equipment and machinery range between 40 and 50 per cent of the total price, even more in exceptional cases.

It is important to note that the commission is not extracted from the manufacturing firm's price or profit, but is obtained by the agent through the sale of the imported product to the local client over and above the manufacturer's delivery price. Thus when the agent presents a given offer to local purchasers the price will include the commission informally agreed upon with the supplying firm. The total price of the goods sold locally is received by the producer or supplier, who then subtracts the agreed commission due to the agent and places it in the latter's bank account abroad. Only the amount declared in the formal contract is subjected to the Egyptian authorities' control; i.e. the representative must keep the office of registration informed of commissions received and the banks where they are deposited. The foreign banks in question must be accepted by the Central Bank and either have local branches in Egypt or transfer arrangements with the existing Egyptian banks. Commissions received will be brought into the country in their original currency form, and after having paid the required income tax, commercial agents may unrestrictedly employ the foreign currency for further purchases of goods, various forms of investment, savings and private consumption.

On very rare occasions, some commercial agents will offer their services against a regular salary. This occurs when dealing with American firms exporting goods against AID money, loaned to the Egyptian government under the CIP programme which places certain restrictions and regulations on its sales transactions, among which is the prohibition of the commission as a method of payment.[11]

Formal registration and the nature of the business establishment

Once all the necessary legal conditions are met, commercial agents will register their establishments at the Ministry of Trade against a fee of £E390.80. Many, however, are not registered.[12]

The registered establishments may be partnerships or singly owned ones. Partnerships are the most prevalent model. Partnerships take on various legal forms, the most common of which is that of the simple commandite partnership. Such partnerships are characterized by their highly personalized nature. Partners personally select each other, while the consideration of persons is primordial, i.e. the company is automatically dissolved with the death or incapacitation of any of its members. In commandite partnerships certain members are more active and legally responsible than others.[13] Numbers of partners range from two to fifteen with an average of six members per company.

The most significant aspect of the types of partnerships existing is that they are essentially family affairs.[14] The normal trend is to register one's immediate family, i.e. wife and children, the latter often being non-active partners. The purpose of establishing such family partnerships is to make a formal distribution of profits among their members, thus minimizing taxes.

The registered capital of the majority of agents[15] ranged from £E1,000 to £E30,000, with an average of £E11,352 per establishment, which is extremely small, in absolute terms as well as relatively, if we consider the kind of profits members of this group make. Suffice it here to mention the example of one such commercial firm[16] whereby the single owner obtained an adjudication (among several others) from the railway authority worth £E20 million in a single year, wherein his *formal* commission was two per cent. Another firm had managed to obtain a tender for the Alexandria Port Authority for the sale of cranes worth $8 million and obtained a service fee worth ten per cent of the total.[17]

Commercial agents' major local customer

Nearly all commercial agents essentially sell their goods to the public sector whether productive companies (including military factories) or ministries. Despite the bureaucratic complications involved, commercial agents in fact prefer to deal with the public sector since it is still the country's largest importer and purchaser of foreign commodities, and since payments are secured, even if slow. Most of the offers and sales to the public sector purchasing committees and ministries are theoretically, and according to import regulations, done through public tendering.

The tendering system (public commercial adjudications)

According to import regulations, public sector purchasing committees must publicly advertise the commodities they wish to purchase and inform the various public sector commercial firms of the date of public adjudication. Usually advertisements for public tenders will be found in the daily papers accompanied by the exact date and place. Once the tender has been published, commercial agents are invited to purchase the tendering book which contains all the necessary specifications (technical descriptions, delivery due dates, conditions of delivery, i.e. CIF, FOB, or C & F, method of transport and the price range). The average price of such books is £E20–50.

When the agent has purchased the book, he contacts the appropriate productive firm, sends the specifications and waits until his 'principals' study them and prepare a quotation or offer within the time limit specified. Before the offer is submitted in its final form, it will be revised by the local agent, who may have some useful suggestions to make regarding its format, price and information that is preferably deleted. Finally the offer is placed in a sealed envelope and submitted by the local agent to the public sector or ministerial purchasing committee which must under no circumstances open the envelopes before the public session, when all the competitive offers have been submitted by agents who may attend the session or send an office salesman to support the offer verbally. If the agent is formally registered and eligible for the representation of commodities required, he will enter the adjudication under his or the firm's name. If for some reason, however, he has failed to register some of his agency contracts, he may still attempt to participate illegally in the adjudication through subcontracting and the mediation of public sector commercial firms. One such businessman operated in this manner for a whole year through two public sector commercial firms with whom the commission was shared. Two other agents interviewed declared that although they were formally registered they had not registered all the branches of specialization and preferred to subcontract some of their informal agency agreements to the public sector thus avoiding the tendering process and all the paperwork involved, as well as evading taxes.[18]

Upon delivery of the offer, each tenderer must submit a letter of guarantee worth two per cent of the total value of the price as a bid bond valid for a period of one month over the validity period of the offer. The guarantee money paid is a proof of the supplier's seriousness in meeting the requirements of the purchaser.

Once the purchasing committee has the complete set of offers on the date specified, based on the salesman's arguments and the terms of the quotation, it makes a choice of the best offer either on the spot or at a subsequent date after having studied the offers more carefully. If the competition between a number of select suppliers is very intense from the point of view of price, specifications and quality, the committee may call for a 'negotiation' session wherein suppliers through their commercial representatives are invited to compete in the reduction of their prices and advancement of delivery dates. Once the choice has been made it must in the final analysis be approved by the relevant ministry or government authority. That is the theory. In practice the procedures are often very different due to the existence of a great deal of corruption, unfair competition and the monopoly of certain commercial agents over specific imports or purchasing committees. The field situation was replete with such examples, a number of which were mentioned by members of the business group themselves who either accepted it or on very rare occasions sought to render regulations more watertight and less permeable through the mediation of the Chamber of Commerce. Meanwhile a number of scandals and cases of corruption were reported in the press, the most notorious being the Boeing and Westinghouse scandals in which a number of public figures were accused of excessive extortions on the prices of goods unjustifiably sold to the public sector. The transactions had allegedly caused great harm to the national economy and those involved in the scandals were placed on trial.[19]

Types of commodities commercial agents promote, import and sell
According to the formal registry in the Ministry of Trade for the years 1976 and 1977, which not only included the names of commercial agents, but also the commodities they represent, most commercial agents were involved in the promotion and import of machinery and transport equipment. In 1976 items in this category represented 48.62 per cent of the total number of items mentioned in the registry list. The next most important item was chemical products (including detergents, paints, food flavouring, cosmetics and pharmaceuticals,

which constituted the largest item within the broader classification of chemicals).[20]

For the year 1977 the same trend appeared with a total increase in the commodity items registered. This was due to the increase in the actual number of agents registered, as well as their feeling of greater security in registering the commodities represented.[21]

Commodities promoted and imported through local agents were also classified according to their end use. The broad classificatory categories were the following: light, heavy, miscellaneous industry, services (transport, health, communication), agriculture (tractors, fertilizers, pesticides), tourism (hotel equipment, touristic aircraft, buses), consumer and luxury goods.

For the year 1976, most commodities represented by local agents were in the field of services (42.44 per cent of the total items formally listed) with a special emphasis on transport equipment. The same trend continued for 1977 (38.42 per cent of the total items formally listed) while items falling under industrial commodities now occupied the first position (39.52 per cent).

The above trends of representation are of course directly related to areas of local demand. Both the areas of industry and transport had received large amounts of loans for the import of commodities. To mention only American AID inflows, the largest recipients of loans from 1975 to 1979 under the CIP programme were the Ministry of Supply ($430.9 million), the Ministry of Industry ($321.2 million), and the Ministry of Transport ($128 million).[22] The trends of commodity representation are also shaped by profit. This is especially true of pharmaceuticals whose turnover is extremely high when dealing with such over-the-counter drugs as cold remedies, vitamins, aspirins, etc., as well as other prescription drugs geared towards Egypt's most prevalent diseases such as bilharzia, diabetes, anaemia, and heart and intestinal problems.[23] Machinery and spare parts are also very profitable areas of representation.

Items falling under consumer and luxury goods in 1976 constituted 19.52 per cent and 6.74 per cent respectively, of the total items of commodities listed, and 8.42 per cent and 10.70 per cent in 1977. Statistics for these categories are, however, not very accurate since imported or represented luxury and/or consumer goods are often not mentioned in the formal list. The following items discovered through field research are examples of luxury commodities which were not mentioned in the formal listing and whose exact proportion could not be discovered: chocolates, Christmas cards, parrots, decorative fish, cosmetics, canned food, perfume, food flavouring, sauces, instant coffee, tea, processed cheese, butter, electronic musical equipment, cars, office equipment, gardening tools, cigarettes, cigars, colour television, baby food, clothes, watches, ultra-modern and sophisticated medical equipment such as electronic dentistry chairs, toilet soap, toys, sportswear and equipment, interior decoration and furniture, household appliances and houseware (sweepers, electronic appliances), and housecare products (furniture polish, floor detergent and carpet shampoo).[24] Although the pound value of luxury and consumer items imported through commercial agents could not be discovered from the field research, it is quite significant that 88 per cent of the respondents interviewed dealt with some of the abovementioned items. Regardless of the major areas of specialization for commodity representation, about 70 per cent had a department for foodstuffs. Meanwhile the majority of offices visited, 60 per cent, manifested a remarkable lack of specialization in goods represented. One such firm representing a Korean business group, as well as various European firms, promoted, represented and imported the following items: aircrafts, ships, tankers, hairpins, clothes and foodstuffs. According to the list of goods formally registered under the various commercial agency firms in 1976, 38.26 per cent specialized in a specific field of import, i.e. dealt with one or several inter-related commodities, 61.74 per cent did not specialize. In 1977 specialized agents accounted for 39.81 per cent, non-specialized for 60.19 per cent. This non-specialized multi-departmental organization is very much a function of the companies which local commercial agents represent, the majority of which are multinationals manufacturing a very wide variety of products. Moreover the lack of specialization poses serious questions as to the efficiency of such firms in sales promotion and servicing the goods sold. According to the regional manager in the Middle East and Africa for 'Peerless Pumps', an American firm specializing in oil, most representative local firms are extremely inefficient, requiring a great deal of supervision and assistance in sales promotion from the parent company, as well as technical and service personnel. However, local agents were indispensable and very useful for the establishment of contacts with the local ministries and authorities.[25] The field situation revealed that a great deal of such firms do in fact have foreign technicians and sales managers permanently attached. It therefore appears that the real function of agents is to establish the link or contact between foreign multinationals and the responsible local authorities in order to facilitate the flow of goods.

Although local commercial agents extract their profits from the national economy, namely the public sector, their primary customer, they are none the less extremely dependent upon and subservient to their multinational principals. On one level they are dependent upon them for paying and transferring the undeclared part of the commission abroad and for obtaining a formal agency contract in order to fulfil registration requirements. On a broader level they are dependent upon foreign capital loans and the foreign productive market exporting its goods to the local market. It might be argued that multinationals are in turn dependent upon their local agents for the sale of goods. This is not totally incorrect, but one must ask who is dominant in this interdependent relationship. Local commercial agents, who desperately compete for agency contracts among themselves, are not protected by law for any breach of the contract; they do not hold a very secure position since contracts are made on a yearly basis; and they are restricted by the exclusivity clause in the contract, while foreign firms may have more than one representative for a single commodity, thus giving them a privileged position.

From this account of the activity of commercial agents it becomes clear that, as a business group, they perfectly fulfil the function of a 'liaison group' who interlock the class structures of their own Egyptian society to that of metropolitan society. In addition they enhance the free flow of capital and goods from the advanced capitalist societies to the periphery. Their role in encouraging consumerism is only too obvious.

They are strongly linked to and dependent upon the external capitalist system by virtue of informal 'gentlemen's agreements' and parallel contract systems. Multinationals in fact enhance their illicit high profit-making and allow them not only to evade taxes but also to make headway in the Western capitalist system by placing their money in foreign banks. Meanwhile this group of businessmen is also well established internally. Through corruption they are able to build links and networks of contacts. Economically they constitute a power block. The state is not able to control their income, although they are making extremely high profits, basically from sales to the public sector. Not only do they evade taxes by all possible means, the capital invested in their business is fairly low, and the effort minimal. The kinds of goods they deal with are those whose sale is being encouraged by the huge amounts of conditional foreign loans pumped into the economy, which virtually force the Egyptian government to purchase specific goods.

Notes

1.   Samir Amin, *Accumulation on a World Scale: A Critique of Underdevelopment*, vol. 1, p. 262.

2.   Ibid., p. 288.

3.   Ibid., pp. 378–9.

4.   James Petras, 'Class and Politics in the Periphery and the Transition to Socialism', p. 25.

5.   Ministerial decree no. 247 for 1976, published in *Al Jarida al Rasmiya*, no. 275, December 5, 1976.

6.   On extra-contractual informal bases, commercial agents will also be responsible for making hotel reservations and provide transport for visiting foreign representatives.

7.   The form, structure and content of the contracts were discovered from looking at a number of such contracts in the Ministry of Trade Office of Commercial Representative Registration. Meanwhile copies of agency contracts were obtained from the commercial agency firm upon which an in-depth case study was conducted through participant observation and interviews.

8.   This information was surprisingly enough obtained from a number of commercial agents interviewed and appears to be normal practice.

9.   The evidence was obtained through an in-depth case study.

10.   Interview with a young salesman engineer in a commercial agency firm on January 9, 1978. He claimed that in the firm in which he was employed specializing in agricultural equipment and pesticides, there were cases where the commission had reached 80 per cent.

11.   See CIP regulations cited previously. Normally this regulation is ignored.

12. The names of some of the agents studied were not in the formal listing of the 766 names at the registry by the end of 1977.

13. Discovered through a survey of files of registered members in the Registration Office, Ministry of Trade, and interviews with commercial agents. Family connections were discovered either through the similarity of name or address, i.e. if the wife carrying a different name was listed, her address would be the same as that of her partner and children.

14. See Dr Kamel Amin Malash, *The Encyclopaedia of Companies*, pp. 130–2 and 147.

15. Point made by a key informant who is the only outsider in a family business.

16. The data on capital were obtained from the Registry Office of the Ministry of Trade as it was difficult to obtain the information through interviews in many of the cases.

17. Interview with an engineer employed in the commercial agency firm in question, on Saturday February 14, 1981.

18. Interviews with two commercial agents on March 1, 1978 and February 25, 1978.

19. For the Boeing case see: Assem Hanafi, 'The Legal Immunity of Ministers and the Accusations of the General Prosecutor', pp. 30–2; Essam Hanafi, 'The Boeing File', pp. 10–13; the *Guardian*, Friday November 24 1978, p. 6; and Ibrahim Amr, 'At Last the Boeing Case before Criminal Court', pp. 20–1. For the Westinghouse case, see the *Guardian*, 24 November 1978, p. 6, and *Al Ahram*, 1 May 1979, p. 1.

20. The classificatory system employed for the statistics on the goods represented by the commercial agents was borrowed from the *United Nations Commodity Indexes for the Standard International Trade Classification in its Revised Form* (ISIC-U.N., New York, 1963). A system of classification was necessary since the commodity items in the formal registry are listed in very great detail and not placed under broad categories. The UN index places each commodity trade item under broader categories such as machinery and transport, manufactured goods, chemicals, etc. Within each of the broad classifications the detailed trade items included are described.

21. This explanation was provided by the officials responsible for formal registration, who also added that the list of commodity items declared was, even in 1977, not exhaustive. Some agents preferred not to mention all the goods they represented in order to minimize the appearance of their business deals for purposes of tax evasion and also in order to give the impression of participating essentially in the economy's productivity and not simply encouraging increased consumption. Some agents will omit certain luxury and consumer goods from the list for which formal registration is not necessary, since these goods are normally not imported through public tendering. Examples of such luxury and consumer goods were discovered from the field situation. Meanwhile those commercial agents interviewed who in fact dealt heavily in luxury and consumer goods, and whose names were found in the formal registry, had in many cases not mentioned such items, but only those relevant to investment and production.

22. AID, *CIP Information Sheet*, June 30, 1979 (with summary of programme since inception), unpublished material obtained from the American Embassy in Cairo.

23.   Interviews with two commercial agents specializing in pharmaceuticals and hospital equipment on Saturday March 11, 1978.

24.   Most such goods are imported by the public sector. However, a number of government stores are also importing such luxury goods.

25.   Interview with regional sales manager of Peerless Pumps in the Middle East and Africa on October 24, 1977, in the Cairo Office of one of their representative agents.

8 The Commercial Agents' Socio-economic Characteristics and Internal Class Position

Although the group under study is legally, politically and economically privileged as a whole, it does within this context have an internal hierarchy.[1]

The social hierarchy within the commercial agent business group

The élites within the group under study were distinguished according to two groups of criteria:

1. the degree of political power, contact and influence they enjoyed, access to the state apparatus through kinship, friendship or colleagueship relations, and the scope of their economic activity, i.e. how successful they were on the market;
2. seniority in the business, superiority of experience, culture and family background.

The last criterion is a more or less subjective one and employed as a basis for an élite within an élite.

The first distinction of an élite and the categorization of commercial agents into a 'core membership group' and a 'marginal or peripheral group' is based on the construction of an ideal type which emerged out of the numerous discussions with members of the business circle. The 'core group' essentially refers to the larger entrepreneurs, the most successful and those enjoying a situation of monopoly over various areas of import. The most successful were determined according to annual turnover, which, based on discussions with two key informants, was in the order of above £E10 million per annum. This group is not only economically prosperous, but is, in addition, politically well-connected through kinship and other shared interests.[2] The following are some of the crucial examples of kinship ties existing between members of the group under study and high-ranking political figures. The precise relationship will be demonstrated with the help of kinship diagrams. Names have been omitted (Fig. 1):

(1)

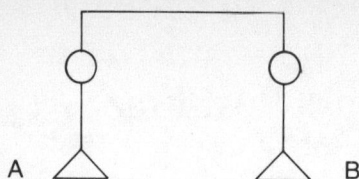

Businessman A, a prominent commercial agent specializing in agricultural machinery and products in addition to other areas of business activity, is the maternal cousin of B, Egypt's Prime Minister from 1978 to 1980 (Fig. 2).

(2)

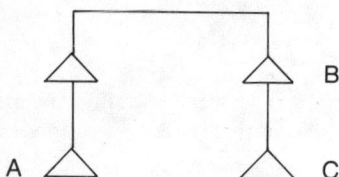

Both A and C, who are extremely prominent businessmen in agency representation and in other areas of business, are very closely related to B, former President of the People's Assembly, ex-Minister of Agriculture, and now Chairman of the Presidential Advisory Council (Fig. 3).

(3)

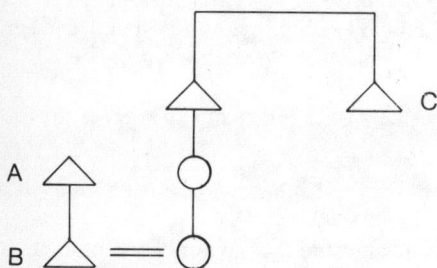

A, a commercial agent who had been involved in industry prior to the 1952 revolution is the father of B, the Minister of State and Culture (1979–), who is in turn related, through his wife, to C, ex-Minister of Agriculture, former President of the People's Assembly and present President of the Presidential Advisory Committee (Fig. 4).

(4)

A, a prominent commercial agent specializing in car spare parts, is related to B, former Minister of Economy and Deputy Prime Minister during the early 1970s (Fig. 5).

(5)

A   B

A, one of Egypt's youngest and wealthiest commercial agents working, among other business activities, in the oil sector, and who employs some 150 people, is related to B, a member of the revolutionary council and a Free Officer, who has maintained his prestige from those days. A is, in addition, involved in business with the former secretary of the late President Nasser.[3]

The marginal group is on the other hand composed of small beginners, not so much with regard to their age or date of commencement, but with regard to their anonymity on the local market and the absence of crucial political contacts. The marginal beginners, not needing to possess much capital and being attracted to commercial agency activity with the hope of accumulating wealth rapidly, are not always successful. This subgroup is characterized by a great deal of mobility. Hence, while the life expectancy of each individual firm is short, as they are phased out of the market in the face of the existing competition or are satisfied with a 'single hit and run' major deal, the marginal beginners are as a sub-group more numerous than the core group. As some firms drop out of the registry within months, others are quickly added and so maintain the numerical majority.[4]

The second distinction of an élite within the group under study was based on an 'empirical type', i.e. on the manner in which a certain portion of the core group (50 per cent) of the respondents studied distinguished themselves as against others. This élite within an élite referred to themselves as the 'insiders' to the business as opposed to the 'outsiders' and intruders. The 'insiders' was a category used to designate the old guard and their offspring, i.e. those who had begun their business activity prior to the revolution or with the Egyptianization movement of the late 1950s and survived throughout the Nasser era. The 'outsiders' were perhaps as successful economically, even though they began at a much later stage, namely in the mid-1960s or after the 1967 war. According to the self-selected élitist group, 'outsiders' lacked ethics, finesse and business experience. Their source of success lay in the political influence they enjoyed. Some were ministers or their offspring, state technocrats, high-ranking army officers, and their offspring, while a third category and the most despised of all were sons of wholesale merchants, black marketeers and contractors who had accumulated excessive wealth during the late Nasser period. Hence, within the core élitist subgroup, a distinction appeared, largely based on social origins, between the old clique from traditional bourgeois origins and the 'nouveaux riches' born with the state bourgeoisie.

The social origins of the commercial agent business group

In the light of the sample of commercial agents studied, the following were their social origins. Members of the various categories will, in some cases, belong to the first generation, i.e. they themselves will have been involved in commercial representation, industrial activity, or state sector management in the past. In other cases members of the categories will belong to the second generation, i.e. they will come from such families as large landowners,[5] or will be the sons of state technocrats, or the traditional industrial and trading entrepreneurs; in most of these latter cases they will have begun their business during the late Nasser era or *infitah* period. Some will have inherited their family business. Table 9.1 summarizes the percentages of different socio-economic categories.

Table 9.1
The Social Origins of Commercial Agents

	Categories	%
1.	Military officers	6%[a]
2.	Large land-owning families[5]	2%[a]
3.	Traditional trading and industrial bourgeois families[6]	50%[b]*
4.	State sector technocrats, managers and senior civil servants	30%[c]
5.	Liberal professions (accountants, lawyers, doctors, teachers and engineers many of whom had begun their careers abroad)	10%[b]
6.	Small-scale merchants and domestic wholesale traders	2%[a]

a. Namely belonging to the second generation.
b. Mostly belonging to the first generation with only 4 per cent belonging to the second generation and who will have begun work in their parents' enterprises.
  * Originally such agents were involved in business prior to the 1952 revolution or begun during the 1957 Egyptianization movement (20 per cent were of Levantine origin and 8 per cent of Greek origin); only 20 per cent had been originally in industry while the remaining 80 per cent were in trade.
c. 84.6 per cent belonging to the first generation (61.5 per cent of whom were engineers and scientists), and 15.4 per cent belonging to the second generation.

The clustering of most of the respondents' backgrounds under the traditional trading and industrial bourgeoisie and state sector technocrats, managers and civil servants is very indicative of the group's class background and the country's political economy in the recent past. The group under study, as pointed out in the earlier background chapters, truly began their activity and prospered during the Egyptianization movement following the Suez crisis. At this stage the traditional Egyptian bourgeoisie, which had developed in the interwar period, still existed as a class, and although it had been weakened it continued to enjoy economic power and a certain degree of political power.[6] The commercial business group involved in representation and trade became the most prosperous fraction of the traditional Egyptian bourgeoisie. While the political and economic power of the landowning fraction had been severely checked, and that of the industrialists placed under closer state control, new markets and business firms were being offered the commercial and trading fraction of the bourgeoisie. With the nationalization laws and the development of state capitalism, the traditional bourgeoisie had been dismantled as a class. Both its economic and political power were appropriated by the state and public sector, which very soon became the stronghold of a new class – namely the state bourgeoisie. The business and trading fractions of the traditional bourgeoisie, as well as other agents from the industrial fraction had survived the blow directed against the class as a whole and were in fact instrumental in the emergence of the state bourgeoisie as they taught the new bureaucrats and administrators the art of enterprising activity. The group under study had therefore manifested itself within two class formations, one existing during the liberal free enterprise economic system emerging within the 'post-colonial' mode of production, and the other existing during the centralized planned economic system emerging within nationalist state capitalism, i.e. the state bourgeoisie.

Meanwhile both members of the traditional trading bourgeoisie and state technocrats, managers and civil servants had had opportunities to establish their contacts abroad at an early stage, which therefore gave them an advantage over others. Moreover the fairly large percentage within the sample of first generation state technocrats, managers and civil servants is indicative of the migration of agents of the state bourgeoisie to join the new ascending bourgeoisie and of the potential internal connections such agents will still maintain with former friends and colleagues or clients of the state sector, thus greatly facilitating business transactions as well as cementing links between the new bourgeoisie and the state bourgeoisie.

The high percentage of both the traditional bourgeoisie and state technocrats in the listing of social background is also indicative of the anatomy of the new ruling class. The new ruling class of today is a merger between fractions of the old traditional bourgeoisie, who were restricted under Nasser and once again revived with the 'open door' economic policy, fractions of the bureaucratic bourgeoisie born with the state sector under Nasser and finally businessmen performing new activities and stepping into areas of investment with the least risk and highest profits, namely commercial agents. It is interesting to note, however, that the military as a social force in the ruling class is losing ground. This is not only true of economically powerful groups such as commercial agents, but also of purely political and high executive positions where the military institution had also been losing ground under *infitah*. Thus political recruitment to high-ranking positions changed markedly from Nasser to Sadat. The Free Officers were no longer a privileged group. It was the age of civilians. Academia and the bureaucracy became the dominant channels of recruitment. Sadat in addition recruited members of the business and free professions. Meanwhile, as there were fewer military men as ministers under Sadat, technocrats increased, mainly engineers and agronomists. There was also an increase in businessmen and economists.[7]

Moreover, it should be pointed out that the diversity in social origins, manifested by commercial agents, and the subjective élitist distinction within the 'core group' are not objectively important in terms of the group's cohesion. The gap between 'insiders' and 'outsiders' is largely bridged by the most universal and effective adhesive for binding groups together – namely, kinship and intermarriage.

Kinship and marriage within the group

The following kinship diagrams will be used as devices to present a few examples of the patterns of intermarriages within the group. Names have been omitted (Fig. 1):

(1)

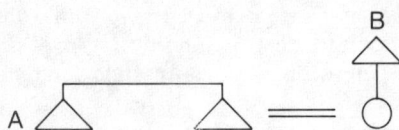

A, previously the chairman of the public sector Al Wadi (in the mid-1960s), is related to B, whose family had long been involved in trade and, prior to the 1952 revolution, owned large tanneries in Alexandria which were nationalized in the early 1960s. B and his brother subsequently worked for the public sector as appointed managers, only to resign after a year and begin activity in the area of trade and commercial agency representation once again (Fig. 2).

(2)

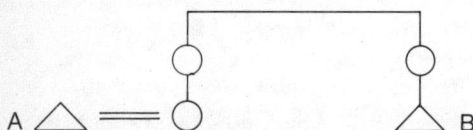

A, a prominent commercial agent also involved in contracting activity and who had previously been a state technocrat – a mechanical engineer appointed after graduation in the early 1960s in Aswan, is related to B, a commercial agent who had worked in the foreign service during the late 1960s and whose father had been Minister of Finance during the Nasser regime and an ambassador to the UN (Fig. 3).

(3)

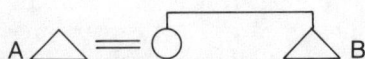

A, a prominent commercial agent who had begun business in car spare parts in the late 1940s and whose family had long been established in the business since the thirties, is related to B, former Minister of Economy and ex-Under-Secretary of State during the early 1970s and now a commercial agent. Meanwhile A and B's brother have set up a company together for the representation of British Leyland (Fig. 4).

(4)

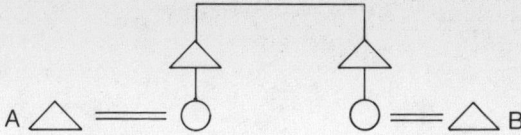

A, an engineer who had been working for the public sector General Transport Corporation from 1965 to 1971, and is now a prominent commercial agent, is related to B, a former computer engineer who is presently one of the top commercial agents, began his career with IBM and started his business abroad (England) in connection with an Egyptian millionaire (Fig. 5).

(5)

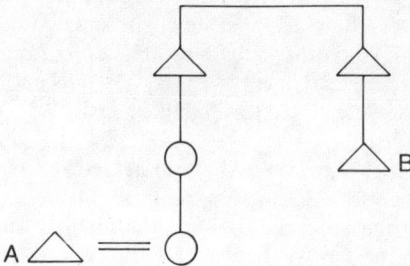

A, whose family had been involved in the manufacture of pharmaceuticals and cosmetics as well as trade prior to the revolution, and who after being nationalized was nevertheless able to be involved in commercial representation in the late 1960s, and is presently a minister, is related to B, a young commercial agent who is the nephew of a former President of the People's Assembly and ex-Minister of Agriculture.

Other members of the group under study are linked together by descent rather than intermarriage, examples of which are (Fig. 6):

(6)

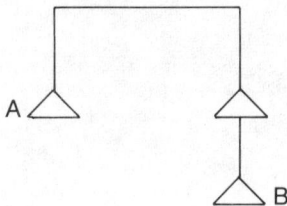

A, a very prominent commercial agent essentially for agricultural products and machinery, and who began business during the 1940s, is related to B who had previously been employed in one of the public sector export/import trade companies in the late 1960s and was subsequently employed by A till the mid-1970s, after which he began his own private business (Fig. 7).

(7)

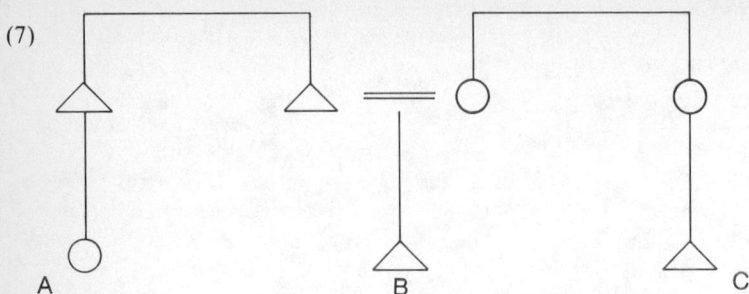

A, a commercial agent whose originally foreign husband had been in trade since the late 1940s is related to B, who is also her business partner. B, who had begun his business career in Arab oil-producing countries is also related to C, an extremely prominent commercial agent in the area of cars and involved in other areas of business activity, who had through the help of B begun business in Arab countries.

Meanwhile the family names of twelve of the commercial agents studied had been picked out on one or more occasions in the formal listing of registered agents. On four occasions the repetition of the family name was a definite indication of kinship given the similarity of the middle name. Moreover such family names as Othman, Higazi, Mahmoud were repeated three times each. Members of the afore-mentioned families are very prominent in several areas of business activity and are in addition politically prominent, i.e. the Higazi and Othman families include former ministers, whilst the Mahmoud family is through marriage related to former Foreign Minister Ismail Fahmy.

The group's broader class membership

The extent of multi-sector activity, participation and economic integrational activity within a group suggests the existence of a 'class' perspective, consciousness and membership broader than the single group. Given the various overlapping group memberships, the given group's narrow interest is expanded to include that of the class at large.[8]

The group of commercial agents under study not only control and mediate the vast majority of the country's foreign trade import transactions, but in addition are involved in various other business activities in the new 'modernized' sectors of the economy. The group of commercial agents studied may be adequately divided into two:

1. Single sector participants, i.e. those specializing uniquely in commercial representation activity.
2. Bi-sectoral participants, which refers to commercial agents who are also involved in internal marketing activity, i.e. they do not just import goods upon

order for prospective clients but import goods to their own account for the purpose of domestic trade. Such agents will have storage facilities, showrooms and their own retail shops to promote the sales of goods imported from the companies they represent and in some cases from other companies.

The majority of the businessmen in the group are multi-sector participants. The following areas were ones mentioned by the commercial agents as additional areas of economic activity in order of importance (note that a single respondent may be participating in one or more of the various sectors):

1. Export trade.
2. Import trade.
3. Joint venture enterprises (essentially assembling and packing industries).
4. Manufacture under licence (essentially foodstuffs such as Dolce ice cream, cosmetics such as L'Oréal, and pharmaceuticals such as Aspro).
5. Contracting.
6. Service and repair workshops.
7. Technical consultancy.
8. Small-scale manufacture. (These included paints, chemicals, leather and the manufacture of tools and car spare parts. Two of the respondents working in the domain of paints and chemicals claimed that they were presently concentrating on their commercial companies and were seriously contemplating ceasing their manufacturing activity, since it proved most unprofitable in view of the increasing competition of imported goods as well as other complications related to management, labour and taxes. One of them hoped to enter in partnership with foreign investors. The foreign partner would provide technical know-how and a small portion of the capital in the form of equipment, whilst the respondent would provide the greater part of capital and the existing collateral. The project's aim would be to modernize productive techniques and expand the output of the firm.)
9. Setting up turn-key projects. (The commercial agents would not only supply material and equipment to the local clients but would also be responsible for the study and erection of whole projects from A–Z. The agents would mostly import foreign experts and technology. The former, along with local experts and engineers, would prepare the feasibility study for the project, work out the cost, plan and perform the erection of the necessary buildings and equipment. The job largely resembles that of contractors.)
10. Agriculture (essentially involved in growing perfume flowers and vegetables for export, as well as a poultry project).
11. Tourism (essentially the ownership of tourist companies and management of hotels).

Only a few of the respondents interviewed were uni-sector participants, i.e. specializing in commercial agency representation to foreign firms on a contractual and commission basis, while a small number of agents were bi-sector participants, i.e. acting as both commercial representatives and importers for internal trade. Out of the respondents classified as either uni-sectoral or bi-sectoral participants, a large proportion had no plans for business expansion save for the increase in the volume of trade. Only a few of the businessmen studied had plans for future expansion and preferred areas of investment, i.e. had made concrete plans for future investment. Some, in fact, only required the permits from the local authorities. The following is a listing of the projects in order of importance:

1.   Joint venture enterprises (for car assembly, electronic equipment, tourism, chemicals, foodstuffs, plastics, the engineering industry – namely machine tools, agribusiness – namely poultry and slaughter-houses, and the oil industry).
2.   Manufacture under licence and the purchase of patents (for foodstuffs, electronic appliances and chemicals).
3.   The purchase of storage space in the free zone area.
4.   Internal trade and marketing activity.
5.   The setting up of packing industries in the field of chemical products and foodstuffs.
6.   Export trade.
7.   Setting up service and repair workshops.
8.   Tourism (hotel construction).
9.   Housing (the construction of modern apartment houses through modern techniques).
10. Banking.
11. Technical consultancy and assistance (including the import of advanced Western technology).
12. Private transport.
13. Setting up turn-key projects.

The phenomenon of multi-sectoral participation and investment within the group under study and the specific preference for areas directly linked to foreign capital and formally defined as the 'modern sectors' of the economy according to law no. 43, indicates that commercial agents do not simply constitute a business or economic group; they are members of the new ascending bourgeoisie consolidating its position with the *infitah* policy, the invitation of foreign policy and externally induced modernization.[9] Meanwhile members of the core group under study have not only fractionalized their capital into various other areas of investment, but are in addition interlinked with other businessmen, notably in joint venturing activity, through kinship ties, thus furthering their broader class consciousness and shared interests. From a survey of *Al Waqie Al Massriya* 1978 (WM) and other issues from different years wherein the establishment of new companies through ministerial decrees are registered, a number of family names were picked out as founders and administrators of companies which were the same as some of the commercial agents listed in the formal registry. The following are a few examples:

Names of founders[a] and managers[b] of joint venture companies	Corresponding names of commercial representatives in the registry
1. Mohamad Mahmoud Diab[a] (Dina-Vision Co. for the diffusion of select domicile TV, service-Decree No. 9 1978 in WM no. 22, 25/1/1978)	1. Diab Co. and partners (Reg no. 366, 21/3/1977)
2. Hashem Mostapha al Qollaly[b] (Nile Bank-Decree no. 12, 1978, in WM no. 23, 26/1/1978	2. Hashem Mostapha Al Qollali (Reg. no. 253, 10/1/1977)
3. Ashraf Hassan Allouba[a] (The Middle East consulting group Co.-Decree no. 57, 1978 in WM no. 94 22/4/1978).	3. Naela Hassan Allouba. (Reg. no. 221, 9/12/1976)
4. Anwar Zaki Wissa[a] (Orman Co. for land testing & chemicals - Decree no. 83 1978, in WM no. 99, 27/4/1978)	4. Adel Wissa and partners (Reg. no. 40, 2/6/1976)
5. Halim Said Bibawi[a] (Orlicon Misr Co. for smelting and shaping rods - Decree no. 121, 1978 in WM no. 111, 11/5/1978.	5. Tawfiq Bibawi and partners (Reg. no. 100, 2/8/1976)
6. Mohamad Abdallah Marziban[a] (Colgate Palmolive Misr Co. for the manufacture of soap - Decree no. 146, 1978 in WM no. 114, 16/5/1978) and Ahmad Mohamad Hamouda[a] (The Egyptian Andrews Brown Co. (Breek) for electrical erections - Decree no. 291, 1978 in WM no. 238 17/10/78)	6. Fouad Hamouda and Hussein Marziban and partners. (Reg. no. 422, 18/4/1977) and Mohamad Abdallah Marziban (Reg. no. 28, 15/5/1976)
7. Hassan Allam[a] (Allan/Garvis for general contracting - Decree no. 160, in WM no. 134, 8/6/1978)	7. Hassan Mohamad Allam & Sons Co. (Reg. no. 531, 20/6/1977) and Youssef Allam (Reg. no. 325, 9/3/1977)
8. Niazi Ibrahim Mostapha[a] (The Nile Co. for hotels and tourism - Decree no. 354, 1978 in WM no. 278, 10/12/1978)	8. Niazi Ibrahim Mostapha (Reg. no. 325, 9/3/1977) (continued)

Names of founders[a] and managers[b] of joint venture companies	Corresponding names of commercial representatives in the registry
9. Sherif Alexan[a] (The Nile Co. for hotels and tourism - Decree no. 354, 1978, in WM no. 278, 10/12/1978) and Said Sherif Alexan	9. Sherif Emile Alexan (Reg. no. 125, 6/9/1976)
10. Madiha Farid Shoukry[a] (Dong San Co. for construction and engineering - Decree no. 343, 1978, no. 288, 31/12/1978)	10. Mostapha Shoukry and partners (Reg. no. 232, 22/2/1977)
11. Maha Fathi Al Badrawi[a] (The Arab Co. for prefabricated houses - Decree no. 292, 1978 in WM no. 224, 30/9/1978)	11. Mohamad Talaat Al Badrawi (Reg. no. 220, 8/12/1976)

A number of other names were picked out which corresponded with non-registered commercial agents who were none the less part of the sample studied, or whose firms had been advertised in the downtown area such as Abd Al Aziz Higazi.

The group under study as earlier pointed out constitutes a stratum of the new ascending bourgeoisie with which it is tightly knit through shared interests and kinship ties. Both as an economic business group (i.e. involved in commercial representation and imports) and as a stratum of a broader class partly owning and controlling the modern sector of the economy, it is very strongly and organically linked to the bourgeoisies of Western capitalism. The group's potential assimilation within the bourgeoisies of advanced Western capitalist systems is a result of many levels of interrelatedness, among which are the economic (the contractual and business relation), the social (including contact with Western culture, interpersonal relations, and lifestyles and consumption patterns), and finally the ideological level (dealing with the question of identities and consciousness).[10]

The business group's relationship to the representatives of the dominant classes in Western capitalism and their culture

The economic level
The contractual and work relationship existing between the group under study and the firms they represent was discussed in Chapter 8.[11] The agency contract agreement is, of course, the obvious and fundamental economic link and the basis for mutual and shared interests.

Most of the commercial agents studied had signed contracts with large manufacturing multinational corporations. Examples of some of the more internationally renowned are: Thyssen (GMBH), Henkel International, FMC, Vetco, Johnson, Peerless Pumps, Perkins Elmar, British Electrics, Diesal, Phillips, National, Remington, Massey Ferguson, Suchard, Chicco, British Leyland, ITT, Beck Aircraft, Goodyear, General Motors, Westinghouse, Dreyfus, Trodax, Adidas, Unilever, SKF, Klokner, Seimans, BICC, Olivetti, Fiat, Allis Chalmer, Wallace and Turner, Volkswagen, Bosch, Aspro, Gillette and Nestlé.

Not only does the formal contract and commission bind agents and foreign companies together, but in addition foreign companies are instrumental in facilitating various financial transactions for commercial agents in foreign banks, serving as references for loans and transferring the undeclared portions of the commissions to foreign bank accounts. Most of the respondents studied declared that they had no need for banking facilities, since their 'principals' or supplying firms served as banks, i.e. provided both loans and exchange services. A few of the respondents dealt only with foreign banks both abroad and locally, while some dealt with foreign banks essentially, but also had local currency accounts in national banks; only a very small number dealt exclusively with local banks. Furthermore, a number of commercial agents had trading and commercial firms abroad.

Although commercial agents and foreign firms have shared interests, it must be pointed out that the relationship is asymmetrical. Local representatives often have very little initiative in their own agency activity and work very closely with the parent firm. Almost all commercial agency offices are equipped with a telex operator or share one with a nearby colleague. The volume of the daily inflow and outflow of telexes is indicative of the closeness with which both local and foreign managers work. However, as was revealed from reading the daily correspondence of one such firm for about six consecutive months, foreign multinational managerial departments acted as 'superintendents' guiding the local firm. In fact two of the foreign firms had sent their sales managers to the local firm in question for two years, in order to advise on market techniques, and to revise the office's filing system and administration.

The social level
Contact with Western culture and education
Most of the respondents interviewed had travelled, studied or trained in Western European countries or with foreign firms operating in other Third World countries prior to the nationalization movement.

With regard to study abroad and lengthy training courses a number of the agents had obtained Ph.Ds, M.Scs. or diplomas from the following Western countries in order of importance: Britain, the United States, West Germany and France. Some had been on medical training courses in African hospitals administered by British nationals.

Some of the agents had followed intensive professional/administrative courses in Switzerland, the United States and Germany.

Some had had training experiences with foreign firms operating in Egypt and academic degrees from foreign educational institutions such as the American University in Cairo, while others were sent to schools and universities abroad.

It is perhaps interesting to point out that most of the interviews conducted with the respondents were in English, which appeared to be the main language employed in the offices.

Local engineers and salesmen employed in the various local commercial firms are frequently invited to attend training sessions offered by their principals or other related technical and educational institutions. The cost of training is usually shared by both foreign multinationals and the local firms. Secretaries employed in the firms are usually foreign-educated, with a mastery of several languages. In a few cases, foreign secretaries were employed.

Lifestyles and consumption patterns of commercial agents

All the commercial agents interviewed lived in relatively elegant residential areas such as Zamalek, Maadi, Heliopolis, Garden City and Guizah. Quite a large number owned their own villas, while others lived in luxurious apartments consisting of more than a single flat. One of the businessmen owned a palatial mansion in the pyramids area. Quite a number of the agents do not just own houses in Cairo but also abroad and in some of Egypt's summer resorts such as Agami and Alexandria. A number of the businessmen owned houses in Europe. One of the agents, who spent only three months a year in Egypt, owned four houses in a number of European countries, where he resided for the rest of the year. Swimming pools and patios are found in some of the more luxurious houses. One agent, whose annual income was £E½ million,[12] owned two villas with swimming pools. In addition he owned three cars, one of which was equipped with a telephone, not a unique case in present-day Cairo. Most agents own more than a single car and often of the latest models. Since parking and traffic are problematic, quite a few preferred to hire chauffeurs. One of the respondents who owned three cars had a chauffeur for every one of them. This is of course over and above the very large numbers of house servants.

Holidays are also taken by members of this business group, either locally or abroad. Holidays and cruises on private boats are often used to conclude business deals. One of the businessmen owned a yacht on which he annually invited business friends to join him on pleasure cruises abroad. Yet another, it was discovered, also owned a boat, but in addition he owned a luxurious caravan which he employed for internal as well as external trips. Almost all the agents spent a good deal of time abroad, whether on business or pleasure trips.

Almost all the offices visited were luxuriously furnished, had all kinds of modern equipment and automatic gadgets, expensive stationery, and high salaried Western-style secretaries.

All this must of course be contrasted with the kind of income earned by the vast majority of the Egyptian people. The income of agricultural labourers, who constitute the majority of the employed poor, is £E140 per annum according to the 1976 census,[13] while average per capita income in 1975 was £E128.35.[14] 1,547,000 rural families and 2,442,000 urban families were living beneath the poverty line, i.e. earning £E270 and less per annum in 1974/5.[15] The most recent census of income distribution conducted by the World Bank stated that for 1982, per capita income was US$690.[16]

Personal relationship with foreign managers
Several of the businessmen interviewed maintained that they had established close relations of friendship with foreign managers. Such friendships involved the exchange of favours, the mutual interchange of gifts, and shared social lives and activities. The exchange of favours involved facilitating the travel of the representative's friends and relatives abroad, whether on purely pleasure trips or training sessions, in addition to mailing services (delivering parcels and letters abroad). On the Egyptian side commercial agents facilitated accommodation (at times receiving such friends in their homes), as well as general circulation and shopping.

Social entertainment is also shared both on the company and personal levels. In a purely Western-style fashion, visiting 'friends' and foreign business managers are often entertained through 'cocktail' parties and dinners in first-class hotels, night clubs and restaurants. One of the agents interviewed, whose firm was studied in greater depth, manifested all the above patterns of friendship relations and had in addition met his German wife during such business parties abroad. Marriage to foreigners is not a rare phenomenon.

The ideological level
All the above levels of interrelatedness become dramatically reflected in members of the group's ideology, consciousness and attitudes. Most of the businessmen maintained that there were no major professional problems with their principal supplying firms. A few explained that no real problems or conflicts could exist between them since they shared common interests. One commercial agent, whose firm was studied in greater depth and who also owned a sister firm in West Germany, explained the role or job of commercial representation as follows:

> The real function of commercial agents is to act as feelers for the foreign company as to the economic and political situation in Egypt. We are in a sense ambassadors for the parent firms and will help them decide whether or not Egypt is a profitable market.[17]

This kind of statement is indicative of the interviewees' primary allegiance and how his own self-identity is defined.

The question of identity and class-consciousness is an important aspect of the process of 'delocalizing' capital and the creation of international managers. Through propaganda, training sessions, education abroad, and sharing the aspirations of foreign managers, problems of national differences are resolved and a loyalty to the corporation or business group is created. Hence the children of such managers may reach the stage of being identified as the children of 'Coca-cola' or 'Ford', rather than belonging to a given nation state. While local managers do not rank highest on the decision-making and power hierarchy of the firm, efforts are constantly made to assimilate them and keep tight contact and communications with them. Firms organize periodic cocktail parties, trips, annual seminars and travel abroad for them, giving them a taste of Western-style life and the chance to mix with Western associates. In this way the Egyptian manager acquires their manner of operation, value system and lifestyle. This sense of belonging is further nurtured by inviting the wives and families of the various managers to participate in all the social activities organized by the firm.[18] It is no wonder that multinationals and/or related technical institutions are willing to spend so much on training courses and scholarships for overseas participants. The administrator of the AID participant training programme is reported to have said 'We get more for our training dollar than we do for a dollar invested in a truck.'[19]

Although on a global level the group does not own the means of production it does fulfil the 'function' of global capital through its activity, and is simply placed on the lower echelons of the global bourgeois hierarchy. Locally the group very definitely partly owns and controls the means of production, both through its membership in the ascendant new bourgeoisie as well as its connections with the state bourgeoisie still controlling state property.

The group's class position is therefore quite complex and constitutes a good example of what Petras calls 'liaison groups', linking class structures of both peripheral and metropolitan societies. These groups, according to him, provide the 'access' points for foreign economic entry and political influence.[20]

Commercial agents and political power under *infitah*

The extent of political influence and access to political decision-making enjoyed by the group under study is, for obvious reasons, not amenable to accurate quantitative measurement.[21] It is, however, possible to give some very significant indications of the power they enjoy, as well as the influence they exert upon national decision-making. Through fieldwork and articles in the press it was discovered that some members of this group, although numerically small, were currently or had in the recent past engaged in 'overt' political activity or were close relatives of such people. By 'overt' political activity I mean the holding of ministerial, undersecretarial, and/or high-ranking government administrative and military positions. Meanwhile a larger number of the group, although not themselves in overt political positions, are extremely well-connected through family, friendship, business and mutual interest networks. The group also enjoys the ability to exert political influence through its participation, collectively and individually, in a number of official legislative, executive, planning and advisory organs.

A survey of the official listing of commercial agents revealed twelve names which this researcher could identify with some degree of certainty as having held ministerial and high-ranking government positions in the very recent past (i.e. last five years) as well as several first degree relatives of present holders of political power.[22] Meanwhile another two such offices, which were not registered in the formal listing, and which were owned by an ex-minister, former governor of one of the Delta provinces, Waguih Abaza, and former Prime Minister Higazi, who ended his services in the Cabinet in 1975, were discovered through advertisements in the downtown area and Abassia.

Meanwhile during interviews and discussions with the officials in charge of the formal registration of commercial agency firms under the auspices of the Ministry of Trade, who had both personal contacts and firsthand knowledge of the owners of registered firms, this researcher was informed that for the most part, those involved in the business were retired high-ranking officers in the army, while others had held ministerial posts in the recent past, such as former Prime Minister Higazi, former Minister of Education, former Minister of Higher Education, former Deputy Prime Minister and Minister of Economy Marziban, and former Governor of Al Sharkiya province Waguih Abaza.[23] Other names were added by a young commercial agent, when he was asked to describe the nature of competition on the market and some of the firms that appeared to be successfully competing, i.e. acquiring a great number of the deals and dominating various fields of commodity imports. Hassan Ibrahim, former member of the Revolutionary Council and Director of the Economic Organization following the Egyptianization movement as well as Vice-President of the republic in the 1950s, now has a commercial firm in the Garden City area, and specializes in cement. The business had begun long before the *infitah*. Another prominent name mentioned was that of Egypt's most successful contractor, Othman Ahmad Othman, who had been the Minister of Housing immediately after the 1973 October war. Engineer Othman, who is Honorary President of the public sector Arab contractors, also owns and manages a number of private sector companies, one of which specializes in commercial representation in the field of earth-moving equipment, cranes and construction machines.[24]

The former President of the Egyptian Chamber of Commerce (a semi-official government organization), who is himself involved in the commercial representation of foreign cigarettes, recommended two commercial agents for interviews, since they were both very successful and, according to him, highly respectable. They were Al Shadly, former Minister of Supply, and Ahmad Effat, former Minister of Maritime Transport.[25]

An interview with another commercial agent – one of the oldest and most prominent – revealed that he was the President of the American Egyptian Business Council, and was a very close friend of Dr Qaissouny, the recent Minister of Economy and Finance. According to this respondent, his advice was often sought for legal innovations and for the shaping of current business and economic policies such as customs duties and regulations. The manager of the firm also testified to the close connection between the respondent and Dr Qaissouny. The former had in fact been summoned by the latter to write a report in article form on the present tendering system and manners in which relevant regulations could be improved. A copy of the article was given to this researcher. The four-page article was essentially a critique of current tendering systems' responsibility for existing inefficiency, slow and corrupt decision-making, and proposed reforms.[26] Some of the reforms, it must be said, were, according to interviews with other commercial agents, already being practised by a number of the public sector purchasing committees.

Another commercial agent from the sample studied was, in addition to his business activity, the Special Assistant to the Governor of Guizah for investment projects. Guizah received large investment funds from the Industrial Bank, a subsidiary of the World Bank, for the implementation of new projects.

Interviews with two key informants on the business revealed that kinship ties were not the only form of relationship and association commercial agents had with political figures. Other forms of ties existed, such as mutual and common business interests between officials and commercial representatives, as well as political and occupational colleagueship.

The following is an example of how personal and political contacts may be employed to exercise political influence, i.e. to shape specific allocations of state resources in order to improve one's relative position. The example is used here, not so much to stress political contacts as a sole source of power, more to point out how they are in fact used – i.e. the direction of the flow of influence and the significance of personal and political contacts within the Egyptian context.[27] There are endless examples recounted by the businessmen themselves. However, the example cited below is an interesting one in as much as (a) it involved more than obtaining an order for the import of goods, and (b) it was based on the actual testimony of the person involved in the exertion of political influence.

The respondent's firm is part of a broad business group owned by a Lebanese who operates in the whole of the Middle East with a headquarters in Athens. Being a foreigner, the Lebanese businessman operates in the Egyptian market through his subsidiary firms, one of which is managed and partly owned by the present respondent.

The respondent, who is the son of a former minister, is involved in the commercial representation of some 50 foreign firms from Europe and the United States as well as setting up 'turn-key jobs', i.e. he is not only responsible for the supply of material and equipment to local clients, but also supplies studies and plans for whole projects and erects plants, supervising the initial phases of operation. An American firm had offered its technological and 'know-how' services for a joint venture project which involved a local public sector firm. The project, which had been initiated by local planning and according to the public sector firm's demand, was to use sugar cane waste for the production of paper, which Egypt is importing in increasing amounts. This respondent had initially been cooperating with the American firm which provided its services against AID money loaned to the Egyptian authorities. The American feasibility study and plan had been accepted and gained the approval of the Egyptian investment authority and the firm was preparing to enter the public tender for the supply of equipment. Meanwhile the respondent interviewed, who claimed to have provided a number of services to the American firm, was extremely disappointed with the salary they proposed to pay. The firm had refused to cooperate with the respondent on a 'commission' basis since AID regulations precluded it, which, according to the respondent, did not appear to be the real cause since they could have had a gentleman's agreement with him as normally occurred with other firms. The respondent became determined to thwart the project and compete through another of the supplying firms he represented, this time French. Following some contact, meetings and travel, the respondent was able to obtain another 'feasibility' study from the French company, which claimed that it could convert sugar cane waste into animal fodder, a project which had not been originally planned for by the public sector company in question, the investment authority, or the industrial planning organization. However, this respondent was able to contact a number of his father's friends and old colleagues, as well as the president of the investment authority, and thus obtained the preliminary approval for the animal fodder project and annulled the previous project.[28]

'Covert' political participation of commercial agents as an indication of power

Members of the business group under study also enjoy the potential and actual power to exert political influence through their group or individual membership in various private, public and semi-public advisory, legislative and executive organizations, examples of which are: the Egyptian Chambers of Commerce and the Union of Commercial Chambers; the Association for Egyptian Businessmen; the Merchants' Syndicate; the Union of Importers; the Egyptian–American Business Council; the Chamber of Engineering Industries; the Committee for Pharmaceutical Imports; the Economic Committee in the People's Assembly. These are dealt with in turn below.

The Egyptian Chambers of Commerce and the Union of Commercial Chambers
The Egyptian Chambers of Commerce were established in 1951 as official and public foundations. Their purpose was to secure, organize and supervise commercial and industrial activity in Egypt. The chambers exist in all the provinces. Half their members were appointed by the Minister of Economy, while the remaining half were elected through secret ballots. All merchants had the right of membership.

The chambers were essentially responsible for the collection of data and statistics on commercial and industrial activity which they presented to the government. The government was obliged to take the chambers' opinions into account when deciding to alter or establish organs directly related to trading or industrial activity. Meanwhile the chambers could make suggestions to the government with regard to commercial and industrial legislative policies generally, as well as tax regulations and custom duties. They could also make suggestions to the government on more general issues related to the promotion of trade and industry, such as road maintenance and construction. The chambers were also responsible for the regulation of members' activities and their adherence to general state regulations and ethical practices, in addition to the protection of their rights when necessary. The chambers could establish branch organizations under their supervision for those members specializing in a particular form of trading or industrial activity. These splinter groups or branch associations were to look after the interests of these particular members.[29]

In March of 1955, the General Union for the Egyptian Chambers of Commerce was established through a ministerial decree. The Union was established to coordinate the various interests of the individual chambers, and to formally represent each of the chambers before the local authorities, as well as foreign states and their respective chambers. The Union could also function as an arbitrator when requested by contending chambers or individual merchants. The Union was composed of the presidents of the various chambers, except for those of Alexandria and Cairo, which would be represented by the President of the Union and the Secretary-General. An additional six members of the Union were appointed by the Minister of Industry and the Minister of Trade, while both ministries appointed at least one representative in order to supervise the activities of the Union.[30] Thus the Union appeared to be under tighter government control. Whilst the various individual chambers express the interests and views of their members, i.e. merchants and industrialists, the Union essentially represents official government policy.[31]

Suggestions made by the various chambers of commerce to the government with regard to desired policy changes and legal innovations are not binding. However, according to the former President of the Cairo Chamber (up to February 1978) the chambers are represented in the People's Assembly economic and legislative committee and are also in direct contact with the Ministry of Trade. Also according to this former president, since the beginning of the *infitah* policy, the chambers have acquired a very influential position; they played a very important role in the shaping of Egypt's recent tax and customs laws, in addition to other regulations concerning imports. One of these regulations requires special attention, for it was the subject of great public debate, and the ultimate outcome of the law is indicative of the power enjoyed by importers. The regulation in question was the result of ministerial decree no. 119 signed in 1977 by the Minister of Trade, Dr Zakariya Tawfiq Abd Al Fatah and the Deputy Minister, El Sayid Al Masri. The decree was promulgated with the aim of restricting imports, particularly luxury goods, by setting a maximum of 30 per cent for the profits earned by importers on any imported commodity. The contravention of the decree would be penalized by imprisonment and a fine. In addition the Deputy Minister had himself supervised the implementation of the law by conducting a number of field inspections. The decree had been met by a great deal of opposition from importers supported by the chamber of commerce where a number of meetings were held to condemn the new decree. Merchants and importers complained that the restriction was not realistic, insulting to their integrity and respectability and contrary to the spirit of *infitah* which they claimed was 'freedom'. Meanwhile, Mostafa Murad, who was then the President of the Chamber as well as the head of the opposition party in the Assembly, was also able to bring sufficient pressure to bear on the Ministry of Trade for him to allow a public hearing with importers in the General Assembly in order to discuss the law and its application. After raging debates and discussions in the Assembly, the decree was passed, but made practically ineffective.[32] Its executive, Sayid Al Masri, was transferred to the Ministry of Supply,[33] and in recent ministerial changes, the Ministry of Trade was subsumed under Commerce and Supply.[34]

Moreover the Chamber had, of course, been invited to formulate the 1974 law no. 63 which allowed commercial activity. More recently, according to its former President Mr Ezzat Ghaydan, the Chamber has been successful in influencing the Minister of Trade to amend the initial regulatory decree no. 1906 by decree no. 14 in 1976 which abolished the obligation on retired political public officials to let two years pass before they become involved in agency representation; they can now become involved in commercial representation immediately after retirement.[35] The Chamber has also pressed the ministry to abolish the two-year condition altogether, allowing all political and public officials to become commercial representatives upon ending their government services, whether through resignation or retirement. The amendment is still under study.[36]

With regard to the status of the President of both the Chamber of Commerce and the Union for Egyptian Chambers of Commerce, the former President of the Cairo Chamber who is now President of the Union is himself involved in the commercial representation of foreign cigarettes, while the newly elected president of the Cairo Chamber is involved in the manufacture and export of cosmetics[37] and his son is the representative of Marlboro cigarettes and the partner of the Union's president.[38]

The Association for Egyptian Businessmen
The Association was informally created late in 1977 and formally established early in 1978 under the auspices and supervision of the Union of Chambers. The Association is essentially composed of commercial agents and appears to act as a pressure group within the Union, lobbying for the specific interests of its members. It wishes to acquire an independent status as legal counsellor to the Economic Committee in the government association, and calls for more liberalized policy changes than even the chambers of commerce would approve. The Association is presided by former Minister of Supply Al Shadly[39] and seconded by one of the prominent car spare parts commercial agents who is also a partner to the brother of the former Minister of Economy. According to the latter respondent interviewed, the function of the association was to advise the government on various legislative measures pertaining to business and trade. It was the respondent's belief that the association would very soon acquire a very influential position in Egypt's economy. Indeed there were already signs of its growing political influence. In the course of a visit and interview with a commercial agent who was also a member of the above-mentioned Association, this researcher was able to obtain a report

prepared by the respondent and signed by others, which was discussed during the Association's meeting in October and passed on to the Minister of Trade and the General Assembly. The study essentially called for the predominance of the private sector in all foreign trade representation activities without any form of discrimination; i.e. commercial agents should be able to supply military and strategic goods which were according to law preserved to the public sector firms. Moreover the report argued that since supply was generally short and the public sector firms inefficient, their various purchasing committees should not be given the right of agency representation, but that the domain should be left to the private sector while purchasing regulations should be made more flexible and liberal.[40] It is interesting, and probably not coincidental, that following an amendment of import regulations at the time (ministerial decree no. 1036 for 1978), private sector commercial agents were allowed to import a greater number of goods formerly classified as strategic and were even allowed to import formerly prohibited commodities such as military goods, with the approval of the deputy minister in charge.[41]

In a more recent amendment of purchasing regulations and tendering procedures, proposed by the Ministry of Finance, public sector purchasing committees were allowed much greater flexibility in the choice of methods employed for the import of commodities. Meanwhile the system of imports was greatly liberalized and made favourable to the private sector's greater participation. The following were the major innovations in the proposed bill:

1. Public sector purchasing committees importing goods for a given project may have the freedom of selecting the most efficient method of purchase from among the following: public tendering, negotiations, or direct contracting (previously only public tenders were allowed and negotiations with special permissions).

2. The amount of money involved in any given deal shall not influence or limit the choice of purchasing methods made by the committees.

3. There shall be no discrimination between public and private sector importers, suppliers and tenderers competing over offers in all domains. This will create healthy competition between both sectors which will not only encourage the private sector to join the competition, but will also force the public sector to increase its efficiency.

4. Deals should be made with importers and contractors having a good reputation and whose names are formally registered.[42]

The Union of Importers

The Union is yet another semi-official organization under the auspices of the Union of Chambers and functions as a typical pressure group. In the last few years the Union of Importers has been actively pressuring various responsible government authorities to postpone the execution of recent customs regulations requiring that importers pay their customs duties in foreign currency. The outcome of their activity is still unknown.[43]

The Merchants' Syndicate

Like all other professions in Egypt, merchants and traders also have a syndicate to represent their interests and protect their rights. President Sadat, it was reported, met with this syndicate as well as that of teachers and lawyers in order to discuss Egypt's future national plan.[44]

In all four of the above-mentioned associations and organizations, commercial agents are represented and are politically influential as a group. There are, however, other formal, semi-formal, and informal associations in areas not directly relevant to commercial representation where individual members of the business group under study occupy influential positions. The following are examples and do not constitute an exhaustive listing.

The Egyptian–American Business Council

The Council held its inaugural meeting in Cairo in October 1975 and was attended by 40 American business executives, 20 Egyptian businessmen and six Egyptian ministers. The meeting focused on the impediments to foreign investment in Egypt. The purpose of the Council is to facilitate foreign investment and foster cooperation between the American and Egyptian private sector entrepreneurs. The Council meets on a bi-annual basis to discuss prospects for joint American and Egyptian private sector productive participation in the various economic sectors, and to examine, analyse and study all impediments to foreign investment.

The first President of the Council, an American, was Chairman of the US giant Allis Chalmers, and the second nominated Investment Development Officer was also from Allis Chalmers. The Vice-President of the Council is the Egyptian commercial agent of Allis Chalmers and one of the most prominent commercial agents in Egypt belonging to the group of 'insiders' and also involved in contracting, export of ornamental plants and perfumes as well as fruit production and export.[45]

Although the Council's suggestions are not legally binding, it does appear to have acquired great political influence both in legislative changes and project selection. With regard to legislative changes, the Council played a very major role in reshaping the 1974 investment law no. 43 in its amended form which gave foreign investors and Egyptian businessmen greater privileges. In 1976 the Council presented to the Egyptian Government a report highlighting the critical problem areas in the former investment law and recommendations for amendments in order to attract greater numbers of foreign investors. The new amended law no. 77 took heed of most of the Council's recommendations, most important of which were:

1. improved and more advantageous conditions for the repatriation of profits in foreign exchange;
2. the reduction of the prejudice against import substitution projects;
3. the increase in tax and duty exemption rates;
4. the increase in foreign exchange availabilities for approved projects by

allowing foreign investors to fund their foreign currency accounts through purchases from local banks or selling to the local market against foreign currency;

5. the expansion of the ability of foreign investors to divest; and
6. the expansion of areas and opportunities of investment.[46]

Meanwhile with regard to project selection, in 1975 the Council established a development projects review team. The team studied 265 projects of which it selected 35 by April 1976 and 24 within the next few months, as those which were to be given official approval.[47]

The Committee for Pharmaceutical Imports
The Committee was recently (1977/78) set up at the demand of the Ministry of Health, Industry and Trade as a result of the excessive influx of 'over the counter' drugs such as vitamins and antibiotics, which Egypt has so far very successfully produced. The Committee is a semi-official organ attached to the Ministry of Trade and Health. Its function is to regulate the imports of all 40 commercial agents and importers involved in the field of pharmaceuticals and medicine, i.e. the Committee is responsible for determining which commodities shall be prohibited imports, as well as regulations concerned with their marketing and prices. The present Chairman of the Committee is a commercial agent who in fact is Egypt's largest and most famous. The Chairman, the son of a former pasha, began his business during the Egyptianization movement and thus is part of the 'insiders' group. At the time of writing he represents some of the world's most famous multinational firms for drugs, pharmaceuticals, foodstuffs, medical, laboratory and hospital equipment. His firm employs some 300 people and owns the largest delivery van fleet in Egypt to service his 1,400 customers and retailers. The firm also has subsidiaries in Port Said, Tanta and Assiout. The Chairman himself specializes in the import of pharmaceuticals, both 'over the counter drugs' as well as prescription drugs. In addition he is involved in two joint venture projects for the local production of drugs under licence. He supports government views on certain import restrictions for drugs since he himself wishes to produce a number of them locally. However, he encourages unrestricted private sector imports in most other fields, which this researcher took to mean those not directly competing with his productive plans.[48]

The Chamber of Engineering Industries
The Chamber is also a semi-public official organization including both private and public sector industries in the specialized field of engineering, as well as commercial agents supplying the factories in the above-mentioned field with the necessary equipment and raw material. It has both supervisory and counselling responsibilities. With regard to supervision it must make sure that commercial firms supplying various factories (1) have qualified technicians and staff, (2) have a large enough stock of spare parts and (3) are capable of servicing and repairing the goods they promote. With regard to its advisory capacities, the

Chamber co-operates with the Ministry of Industry in devising their industrial plan. The Chamber also gives technical advice and renders contracting services for its members. Five of the members in the Chamber are nominated by the Ministry of Industry, while ten are elected from both the public and private sectors. The manager of the Chamber, who was interviewed, is an engineer owning a commercial agency firm specializing in machine tools and air-conditioning equipment. He had assumed his managerial responsibility in the Chamber in 1970, and decided to maintain the position even after he began his own business in 1973, for in his own words, 'It was very useful for the establishment of contacts and the enhancement of the business.'[49]

The Economic Committee
The Committee is an integral part of the People's Assembly and has the function of advising, preparing and giving opinions on legislative enactments, innovations and reforms regarding all economic matters. During the course of a visit and interview with the owner of a commercial agency firm it was discovered that he was a member of the Committee through his membership of the Misr Majority Party. He generally supported the political regime in power and its recent economic policies, and he had been actively involved in the Committee's meetings and activities and had suggested ways of improving the regulations concerning commercial agency representation. One of his suggestions made early in 1977 had been approved by the Committee. He had pointed out that the competition between the private and public sector commercial firms was unfair, since the public sector had not been required to register formally before it could participate in public tenders, which not only gave it an advantage over the private sector since it appeared to be far less restricted, but also deprived the public sector purchasing committees of guarantees the suppliers normally gave to registered firms as an indication of their seriousness in meeting import demands and deadlines.[50]

The participation of the businessmen in the various executive and counselling organs studied in this chapter is an indication of the new political power they enjoy under *infitah* and its political system. In addition the examples given above constitute concrete evidence of the actual political influence they are able to exert in blocking restrictive legislative measures, enforcing favourable ones, curbing regulations and affecting policy decisions. At times they exercise influence as members of a broader ascending bourgeoisie with broader class interests cutting across territorial boundaries and coinciding with the interest of the bourgeoisies of Western capitalism. The coincidence of interests is reflected in pressure for the liberalization of foreign trade and for improving the position of foreign investors and their local partners.

The strongest opponents to this new class of businessmen, their lifestyles and consumption patterns are Muslim fundamentalist groups. These groups have expressed, through their publications, their weariness with the corrupt Western style of living which the rich indulge in. They have denounced the fact that the rich are getting richer and the poor poorer. They expressed their very strong distaste of President Sadat's lifestyle, personality and political ideology and were often overtly critical of his wife Djehan El Sadat. Among other opponents to the new class are, of course, the leftist groups. Their arguments have, however, been far more sophisticated and structurally founded than those of the Muslim fundamentalists. Which of the two groups has proved more effective in opposition remains to be seen.

The working classes continue to be very repressed, although there have been instances when they have expressed their grievances along with leftist intellectuals. Most laws made under the 'open door' economic policy have, however, been totally unfavourable to both. Suffice it here to mention the law of *Eib*, created by Sadat to enable him to incarcerate or otherwise punish any dissident behaviour. *Eib* literally means the prohibition of undesirable social behaviour. The real target was political behaviour, particularly criticism of the regime, in published or verbal forms.

Notes

1.   George Lenczowski, *Political Elites in the Middle East.*

2.   The selection of the research sample was quite heavily biased towards the core group.

3.   The above kinship networks are limited to the sample studied and were discovered essentially through the help of two key informants in the business, as well as numerous chats with knowledgeable businessmen, persons personally acquainted with members of the group, in addition to the researcher's personal knowledge. The above are merely examples of crucial kinship relations. Other forms of political connections and influence are discussed in another section.

4.   The information on the mobility and change of names on the formal registry was obtained from the officials responsible at the Ministry of Trade Registration Office.

5.   In the formal listing at the Ministry of Trade Registration Office such well-known family names as the Badrawi and Sarag El Din families appeared on four occasions. The two families had been amongst Egypt's largest landowners prior to the 1952 revolution and subsequent agrarian reform.

6.   Also in the formal listing such family names as Allouba, Al Qollali, Nakhla, Kahil, Haraki and Shoushah were listed, the latter three being of Syrio-Lebanese origins. These very same families had been involved in industrial and other trading and business activity during the post-World War Two period.

7.   Raymond A. Hinnebusch, 'From Nasir to Sadat: Elite Transformation in Egypt', pp. 28, 33.

8.   James Petras and Thomas Cook, 'Politics in a Non-democratic State: The Argentine Industrial Elite', p. 178.

9.   By externally induced I essentially mean that modernization primarily entails the import of foreign technology, capital and policy counselling.

10. By representatives I essentially mean agents who perform the 'function' of global capital, thus included are not only owners of the means of production but also those who perform the social function of capital, such as managers, sales managers and administrators of the multinationals, whose position lies within the bourgeoisie and has not been 'proletarianized' by the capitalist process. See G. Carchedi, 'Reproduction of Social Classes at the Level of Production Relations', pp. 361–407.

11. See p. XXX.

12. The businessman's income was discovered through a chat with his nephew who had worked with his uncle for some time before deciding to go into business independently.

13.   Abd El Basset Abd El Moeti, *The Distribution of Poverty in the Egyptian Village*, p. 76.

14.   Ibrahim El Issawy, 'Interconnections between Income Distribution and Economic Growth in the Context of Egypt's Economic Development', a paper for discussion by the World Bank, in the Princeton–Egypt Income Distribution Project Conference, Lisbon, 31 October–3 November, 1979.

15.   Ibrahim H. El Issawy, *Employment Inadequacy in Egypt*, ILO, Geneva.

16. World Bank *Annual Report*, 1984.

17.   Interview with a commercial agent on July 27, 1977. The interviewee is the owner of the firm upon which the in-depth case study was made.

18.   See Philip McMichael, James Petras and Robert Rhodes, 'Imperialism and the Contradictions of Development', p. 177.

19.   Susan George, *How the Other Half Dies*, pp. 69–88, and pp. 71, 72.

20.   James Petras, 'Class and Politics in the Periphery and the Transition to Socialism', pp. 24–5.

21. There are undoubtedly many more directly connected to prominent political actors through kinship and friendship networks. In most of the cases the names are carefully camouflaged and only through numerous chats with members of this business circle is one able to trace such connections. However, since one cannot technically trace the connections of all members, I shall limit myself to those names which are clearly and directly identifiable.

22. Visits to the registration office on Monday December 12, 1977 and Tuesday December 13, 1977.

23. Interview with a commercial agent on January 9, 1978. The information was cross-checked with other businessmen.

24. Interview with former President of the Chamber of Commerce and present President of the Union of Chambers on Thursday March 9, 1978.

25. Interview with former President of the Chamber of Commerce and present President of the Union of Chambers on Thursday March 9, 1978.

26. Interview with a commercial agent on December 14, 1977 and visits to the office on December 12 and 7, 1977.

27. See reported cases of corruption in the press mentioned in the previous chapter as well as a number of other cases reported in Salah Hafez, 'Watergate in Egypt', p. 10, and Essam Abou Assem 'Rose El Youssef openly discusses . . .', p. 28. Other reports were made in the press regarding the inflated prices of unnecessarily imported medical drugs due to the commissions obtained by private sector importers and commercial agents competing with the public sector, the latter having performed very successfully in this area in the past. See Souad El Zoheir, 'The Medicine War', pp. 28–30.

28. Interview with a commercial agent on Thursday March 28, 1978. It must be added that the businessman interviewed is a personal acquaintance of this researcher, which partly explains the liberty with which the story was recounted in addition to promised anonymity. Meanwhile the fact that this ex-minister's son felt free to recount such 'normal' patterns of problem-solving is indicative of their currency and partial institutionalization.

29. Law no. 189 of 1951 concerning the chambers of commerce as amended by law no. 303 in 1952, 313 in 1954, 85 in 1956, 153 in 1958 and 12 in 1956. The law was obtained in printed form from the Cairo Chamber of Commerce.

30. Council of Ministers' decree issued in March 16, 1955 for the establishment of the General Union for the Egyptian Chambers of Commerce. Obtained in printed form from the Union's headquarters in Cairo.

31. Interview with the President of the Union on March 9, 1978.

32. Mahmoud El Maraghy, 'Merchants Declare War on the Government', pp. 7–10; Salah Hafez, 'Merchants' Nationalism', p. 11; Essam Rifaat, 'The Invisible Hand which Rules the Egyptian Market', pp. 8–11; and Farouk Awad Rizk, 'The Debate of the Week', p. 38.

33. Discovered through a visit to the ministry and also see Mahmoud El Maraghy, 'Retreat in the Application of Decree 119', p. 8.

34. See *Al Ahram al Iqtissadi*, 'Some Coordination', no. 564, February 15, 1979, p. 11, where reference is made to recent ministerial changes.

35. Interview with former President of the Cairo Chamber of Commerce (Ghaydan), on March 9, 1978.

36. Ibid.

37. Meeting with recently elected president of the Cairo Chamber of Commerce, on March 2, 1978.

38. Interview with former president of the Cairo Chamber and President of the Union on March 9, 1978.

39. Ibid.

40. Interview with a commercial agent on January 2, 1978 and printed report presented to the President of the Association on the occasion of its meeting on October 1, 1977.

41. See p. XXX.

42. *Al Ahram*, August 16, 1979, p. 8.

43. *Al Akhbar*, no. 1814, August 11, 1979, p. 1.

44. *Al Akhbar*, no. 1814, August 11, 1979, p. 1.

45. Interview with a commercial agent on December 14, 1977.

46. David William Carr, *Foreign Investment and Development in Egypt*, pp. 46–50.

47. Ibid., p. 68.

48. Interviews with a commercial agent on Monday January 23, 1978, and Friday April 14, 1978, as well as numerous chats with members of this business circle well acquainted with this respondent.

49. Interview with a commercial agent on Monday February 6, 1978, in the Chamber's Office, where it was also possible to look at some of the publications on the Chamber's functions and organization.

50. Interview with a commercial agent on Saturday March 18, 1978. In the course of visits to the Ministry of Trade office of registration, on December 12 and 13, 1977 the responsible officials confirmed the fact that the public sector

was now required to register in a manner similar to the private sector firms and proceeded to show me some of the application forms presented by public sector firms wishing to participate in public tenders.

9 Conclusion

Egypt's overall internal evolution and history, coupled with global constraints, have together given the country a completely new orientation. The once proclaimed socialist ideology has now turned into its opposite; we have an 'open door' economic policy and a return of the private sector. The one-party system has been replaced by a semblance of democracy and we have returned to a multiparty system. The anti-imperialist, non-aligned foreign policy has been replaced by a Western alliance, especially with the United States, and animosity to the Soviet Union and Eastern bloc has developed. Concern with the Palestinian issue and anti-Zionism has suddenly turned into peace with Israel and the Camp David Agreement. Arabism has been replaced by a narrow sense of nationalist Egyptian identity coupled with strong antagonism to most Arab people. In short, Egypt now fits into the category of moderate Middle Eastern states, striving for peace in the area and guarding the interests of its Western allies. The new cultural and social heroes are businessmen notorious for the illegal ways by which they have made huge amounts of money rapidly and with little effort. The Arabic language has been quickly modified to make room for terminology perfectly suited for the materialistic society ours has become. 'Rabbit' is the new term for a million dollars, indicating the ease with which money can reproduce itself.

Meanwhile the conjuncture of internal and external factors has given rise to the emergence of an extremely distorted and parasitical capitalist class. This class has led the whole of Egyptian society into a compradorial position. Most sectors have been engrossed in heavy consumerism. The society itself has been fragmented, but not in ways that make class sense. The major class contradictions have not necessarily been between the bourgeois ruling classes and the working classes, but among the various fractions of the bourgeoisie itself, with segments of the working class allying with one or the other, depending on the situation. Working-class consciousness and class consciousness in general have not been very sharp. In the most recent elections, in 1984, workers and landless peasants frequently voted for right-wing parties such as the Neo Wafd.

The basic contradictions have been between the nationalist bourgeoisie, as represented by local private industrial capital and the state public sector, and the new modernizing bourgeoisie as represented by foreign capital and compradorial capitalism. The Amereya debacle reported earlier on in the introduction, is a good illustration of all the class fractions represented in the state; the most parasitical fractions of the new bourgeoisie appear to have attained a hegemonic position.

Commercial agents and other fractions of the capitalist classes have penetrated the state apparatus through kinship and business ties and have allied themselves to its members, thus rendering the state under Sadat highly permeable and vulnerable to Western domination.

The new alliance of class fractions within and outside of the state has aggravated Egypt's dependence on the Western industrialized capitalist countries. The new ruling alliance has clearly failed to bring about independent development, the kind of development that brings about national sovereignty and freedom of decision-making, social justice, increased production, self-reliance, cultural identity and creativity, technological advancement and progress. The economy is now largely dependent upon foreign loans.

In order to establish how the transition from one situation of dependency to another occurs or how situations of dependency can be dominated, we need to identify the classes and groups which, in the struggle for control or for the reformulation of the existing order (through parties, movements,ideologies, the state, etc.), are making a given structure of domination historically viable.

Moreover it is also important to ask which strategy of development the ruling classes have chosen and on which level they have succeeded. It should be fairly obvious by now that the Egyptian state, which has largely been dominated by parasitical groups, has been unable to control consumerism, and consequently 'dis-savings' have resulted. Parasitical groups have in addition eaten up large proportions of the country's already existing savings in foreign currency through their corrupt practices and the huge commissions extorted from the state. Moreover under the Sadat regime and the rule of the commercial classes, production has slumped, unemployment has appeared as a potential threat to the Egyptian economy and debt-servicing has weighed heavily on it.

One model of development allowing for growth is what Cardoso has termed 'associated dependent development',[1] a model that has prevailed in Latin America, Brazil in particular. The model operates under the rule of an authoritarian bourgeoisie. It allows for some growth and some negotiating power. The state is dominant. The ruling alliance is normally composed of a very strong military establishment in partnership with a large local productive bourgeoisie, linked to foreign capital and multinationals. Under this model, the military is extremely powerful and is able to supervise production and guarantee a certain amount of savings and growth. It is also partly able to control consumption. It is, however, not particularly concerned with independent, self-reliant development, nor with social justice or the securing of basic needs for all. This model is essentially run on capitalist profit-making lines.[2]

The Sadat regime was not even able to bring about this form of 'associated dependent development'. Internal conflicts obstructed the evolution of such a model. The military as an institution had weakened; the state sector was ideologically inflexible. Thus an alliance between the state sector and Western capital, of the sort found in Latin America, failed to take place in a satisfactory fashion. With regard to the bureaucracy as a social category, while the senior bureaucrats and civil servants are very cooperative and collaborate with both private and foreign capital, the lower civil servants, ideologically oriented towards 'Nasserism', have been opposed to the new ascending bourgeoisie and have often created problems for foreign investors as well as private capital.[3] Thus the only potential allies for foreign capital and the future managers of the foreign sector were the new commercial classes.

Nationalist capital has also been very wary of the country's compradorization and has come into direct conflict with the new classes. Moreover religious fundamentalism, which has had a genuine history of national struggle in Egypt, has also obstructed Egypt's Westernization, and has in a sense obstructed both socialist and capitalist developments, opting for an Islamic political economy. The Islamic opposition is quite pervasive and is a real force to contend with, particularly in the countryside.[4]

Given all the above contradictions the Sadat regime was faced by completely blocked development. The working classes were alienated, the national bourgeoisie dissatisfied, the military weakened, the state taking on a compradorial role, while the Arab leaders and masses became antagonistic to Egypt's new go-it-alone policies. Most sectors of the society were left with a bitter taste in their mouths, save for the parasitical commercial classes. In the end, it was the Islamic groups who physically ended the Sadat regime in 1981 – a paradoxical situation, since Sadat had greatly hoped for a reconciliation between the state and the Muslim fundamentalist groups and had on several occasions tried to win them over.[5]

Notes

1.   F. H. Cardoso, 'Associated Dependent Development', pp. 142–76.
2.   Mostapha Kamel El Sayyid, 'The Various Faces of the Semi-peripheral Capitalist State', pp. 132–5.
3.   David William Carr, *Foreign Investment and Development in Egypt*, pp. 115, 116.
4.   Saad Eddin Ibrahim, 'Egypt's Islamic Militants', pp. 5–14.
5.   See Hassanein Haykal, *The Autumn of Fury* (In Arabic).

Postscript

In the 1980s the Egyptian economy still faces an impasse. The accession to power of the new regime coincided with the beginnings of a new stage in both international capitalist development and its relationship to the semi-peripheral Egyptian formation. It is clear that tighter control of the economy is being attempted under the guise of 'productive' rather than 'consumption oriented' open door policies. Control of the economy can but guide the 'open door' policy towards the stage where it will be able to enhance the internationalization or delocalization of capital. A number of purges have been carried out and corruption has been relatively circumvented. Imports have also been restricted and the commercial representatives placed under tighter control.[1]

Despite all the above signals of change, the new bourgeois class fractions continue to be politically powerful. They are still able to obstruct legal changes which would threaten their privileged position. In January 1985 a series of economic measures and decrees were promulgated by Mustapha Al Said, then the Minister of Economy. The measures, which were only very moderate and liberal in nature, attempted to control black market dealings in foreign currency and to control prices and receipts of foreign exchange. They also attempted to reintroduce some degree of economic national planning by controlling and centralizing banking activity. No sooner had the measures been announced, than businessmen, importers, exporters and bankers all allied and launched a powerful campaign opposing them. As a result of the new bourgeoisie's systematic pressures upon government, in April of the same year the new economic decrees were annulled and replaced by ones that once again asserted the predominance of the market, the rule of supply and demand, and the private sector. Private banks were once again the major decision-makers in questions pertaining to foreign exchange. Private businessmen won the day and the Minister of Economy subsequently resigned.[2]

In more recent times, decree 119 for 1977, which had been the subject of great national debate,[3] was finally cancelled and replaced by decree no. 121. The 1977 decree, which had been issued through the Ministry of Supply, had aimed at placing a 30 per cent ceiling on the profits made by importers. The decree met with great opposition from all the pressure groups representing the interests of importers, businessmen and commercial agents. For a while the law was made ineffective, i.e. it was frozen and its proponent, Sayyid Al Masri, was removed to another department of the Ministry. Finally in 1986 the decree was cancelled by the Minister of Supply and replaced by decree 121 which not only removed the profit ceiling but also for the first time allowed the private sector to import food at official foreign exchange rates.[4]

In addition to having continued political power, the members of the new bourgeoisie involved in parasitical activity are increasing in number. In 1983, according to the Ministry of Foreign Trade records, commercial agents totalled 2,241, as opposed to 1,164 in 1977, and 1,170 in 1978/79. Meanwhile the activity is now spreading rapidly among different groups, namely technocrats and new university graduates, particularly young engineers.[5] The class origins of this group involved in parasitical activity appear to be rapidly changing, which might broaden the power basis of the new bourgeois classes involved in parasitical activity. Alternatively it might create inner contradictions of a different nature.

The nature of the next internal and external power struggle remains to be seen. How will the interplay of power manifest itself among the social forces now existing on the Egyptian scene? The military has gained renewed power, various overtures have been made to the Arab states and the Eastern bloc,[6] while America continues to hold an unquestionably important position. The position of businessmen remains strong, while workers lack class consciousness, solidarity and power.[7] Meanwhile Muslim fundamentalist groups are still a very real force to be contended with. Given all the above, what are the chances that the country might slowly embark on 'associated dependent models of development', achieving growth and resembling a number of Latin American societies? Time alone will tell.

Notes

1.   See law no. 120 for the year 1982, which organizes commercial agency activity.
2.   Ibrahim El Issawy, 'The Results and Important Implications of the New Economic Decisions'.
3.   See p. XXX.
4.   Amany Kandil, 'Decree 119 and the Plight of Economic Policy Making', pp. 16–17.
5.   Interview with the former employee responsible for the registration of agents, now employed at the Ministry of Foreign Trade, August 1984.
6.   Judith Tucker and Joe Stork, 'In the Footsteps of Sadat', in *MERIP Reports*, July–August 1982, pp. 3–6, and Joe Stork, 'Egypt's Military', in ibid., p. 17.
7.   Amany Kandil, 'Interest Groups and the Evolution of the Egyptian Political System' (unpublished).

Bibliography

Abd El Azim, Loutfy, 'The Real Face of Tourism', in *Al Ahram al Iqtissadi*, no. 533, November 1, 1977.

Abd El Moeti, Abd El Basset, *The Distribution of Poverty in the Egyptian Village*, Cairo, 1979.

Abdallah, Ismail Sabri, *The Organisation of the Public Sector: Theoretical Bases and Major Political Problems*, Cairo, 1961.

———— 'The Round Table Discussion on the Nature of Power in Egypt', *Qadaya Fikriya*, July 1985.

Abdel Fadil, Mahmoud, *Development, Income Distribution and Social Change in Rural Egypt (1952–1970), A Study in the Political Economy of Agrarian Transition*, Cambridge, 1975.

———— *The Political Economy of Nasserism: A Study in Employment and Income Distribution in Urban Egypt 1952–1972*, Cambridge, 1980.

———— *Reflections upon the Economic Matter in Egypt*, Cairo, 1983.

———— 'Mesures et composants de l'économie cachée, et mouvements des capitaux noirs dans l'économie Egyptienne, 1974–84, dans le cadre d'un système développé de comptabilisation nationale', *L'Egypte contemporaine*, April 1985, 76th year, no. 400.

———— 'Critical Comments around the Concept of a Parasitical Capitalist Class in the Egyptian Context', *Al Taliah*, January–March 1985, no. 1.

Abdel Malek, Anouar, *Egypt Military Society*, New York, 1968.

Abou Assem, Essam, 'Rose El Youssef openly discusses with the new public prosecutor – no investigations are made outside the parquet and courts – cases dealing with public money and supply are observed in special sessions of the ordinary courts', *Rose El Youssef*, no. 2634, December 4, 1978.

Ahmed, Ahmed Youssef, 'The Arab Policy of the July Revolution and the Formula of Priority Setting: Independence versus Social Revolution', in Ali El Din Hilal (ed.), *National Independence*, Cairo, 1982.

Ahmed, J. Youssef, *La Capacité d'absorption de l'économie égyptienne: une analyse des problèmes et perspective*, Paris, 1976.

Al Ahram al Iqtissadi, no. 533, November 1, 1977, p. 13.

———— 'What is Happening in Al Amereya: The *Ahram Iqtissadi* Presents a Complete File on the Case', no. 557, November 1, 1978.

———— 'The Amereya Battle in the People's Assembly, a Full Report of the Specialised Committee's Report', no. 564, February 15, 1979.

———— 'Some Coordination', no. 564, February 15, 1979.

———— no. 572, June 15, 1979.

Al Taliah editorial board, 'Glances at the Critical Internal Situation', *Al Taliah*, no. 11, November 1967.

Al Alwi, Mostafa, 'International Behavior from the Viewpoint of National Independence', Ali El Din Hilal (ed.), *National Independence*, Cairo, 1982.

Alavi, Hamza, and Khusro, Amir, 'Pakistan: The Burden of United States AID', Rhodes (ed.) *Imperialism and Underdevelopment*, New York, 1970.

Ali, Shafiq Ahmed, 'Top Secret, Those who Received Commissions for al Amereya', *Rose El Youssef*, no. 2636, December 18, 1978.

Amin, Samir, *Accumulation on a World Scale: A Critique of Underdevelopment*, vol. 1 (1974).

———— 'Some Thoughts on the Nature of Capitalism in Egypt', *Al Taliah*, June 1985.

Amr, Ibrahim, 'At Last the Boeing Case before Criminal Court', *Al Ahram al Iqtissadi*, no. 560, December 15, 1978.

Anderson, J. H. D., 'Law Reform in Egypt: 1850–1950', in P. M. Holt (ed.), *Political and Social Change in Modern Egypt*, London, 1968.

Annan, Fatma, 'The Egyptian Banks are in Difficulty', *Rose El Youssef*, Monday March 20, 1978, no. 2597.

Arab Centre for Political and Economic Studies, *The Problems and Bases for the Establishment of the Contracting Sector: Preliminary Studies*, Al Ahram, 1968.

Aulas, M. C., 'Egypt Confronts Peace', *MERIP Reports* no. 72, 1978, vol. 8, no. 9.

Awad, Louis, *The History of Egyptian Thought: from the Period of Ismail till the 1919 Revolution*, Part 1, Cairo, 1980.

Baker, Raymond, *Egypt's Uncertain Revolution under Nasser and Sadat*, Cambridge, Massachusetts, and London, 1978.

Baran, Paul and Paul Sweezy, *Monopoly Capital: An Essay on the American Economical and Social Order*, Great Britain, 1966.

Barawy, Rashed El, *Economic Development in the UAR (Egypt)*, Cairo, 1972.

Bradon, Russell, *Suez, the Splitting of a Nation*, London, 1973.

Bukharin, N., 'World Economy and National Economy', in Hugo Radice (ed.) *Authoritarian Brazil*, New Haven, 1973.

———— *International Firms and Modern Imperialism*, Middlesex, 1975.

Carchedi, G., 'Reproduction of Social Classes at the Level of Production Relations', *Economy and Society*, vol. 4, no. 4, November 1975.

Cardoso, F. H., and Faletto, F., *Dependency and Development in Latin America*, USA, 1977.

———— 'Associated Dependent Development', in A. Stephan (ed.) *Authoritarian Brazil*, New Haven, 1973.

Carr, David William, *Foreign Investment and Development in Egypt*, New York, 1979.

Carrée, Olivier, 'Pouvoir et idéologie dans L'Egypte de Nasser et de Sadate (1952–1975)', *L'Egypte d'aujourd'hui: permanence et changements 1805–1976*, Paris, 1977.

Chenery, H. and others, *Redistribution with Growth: Policies to Improve Income Distribution in Development Countries within the Context of Economic Growth*. A joint study by the World Bank's Development Research Centre and the Institute of Development Studies at the University of Sussex, London, 1974.

Clawson, Patrick, 'Egypt's Industrialisation: a Critique of Dependency Theory', *MERIP Reports* (Middle East Research and Information Project Inc.), November 1978, vol. 8, no. 9.

Doweidar, Mohamed, *The Egyptian Economy between Underdevelopment and Development*, Alexandria, 1978.

El Emary, El Gritly and Handoussa, The Ministry of Economy, Foreign Trade and Economic Cooperation, The Economic Studies Unit, *A Study on Law 43 Investment Policies* (Cairo, December 1979).

El Issawy, Ibrahim H., *Employment Inadequacy in Egypt*, no. 3, ILO, 1980.

———— *Egypt's Future, A Study in the Development of the Social System and the Future of Economic Development in Egypt* Cairo, 1983.

———— 'The Results and Important Implications of the New Economic Decisions', *Al Ahaly*, April 17, 1985.

El Issawy, Ibrahim and Mohamed Nassar, 'Some Indicators of the War Costs', *The Third National Conference for Egyptian Economists*, Cairo, March 1978.

El Zohier, Souad, 'The Medicine War', *Rose El Youssef*, no. 2599, April 2, 1978.

Ernst, V., *Impérialisme au Moyen-Orient*, Paris, 1970.

Evans, Peter, 'Multinationals, State Owned Corporations, and the Transformation of Imperialism: A Brazilian Case Study', *Economic Developments and Cultural Change* 26, October 1, 1977.

Farsoun, Samih and Walter F. Carroll, 'State Capitalism and Counterrevolution in the Middle East: A Thesis', in Barbara H. Kaplan (ed.), *Social Change in the Capitalist World Economy*, London, 1978.

General Spinning and Weaving Workers' Syndicate, 'The Truth and Scandals behind the 1,300 Million Dollar Project', *Rose El Youssef*, no. 2641, Monday January 22, 1979.

George, Susan, *How the Other Half Dies*, England, 1976.

Ghoneim, Adel, 'Around the Issue of the New Class in Egypt', *Al Taliah*, no. 2, February 1968, 4th year.

———— 'Some Light on the Tendencies of Nationalist Capitalism', *Al Taliah*, June 1966, no. 6, 2nd year.

Glavanis, Pandeli, 'Peripheral State and Economy in the International Division of Labour: The Sadat Era in Historical Perspective', *Journal of the Social Sciences* (Kuwait University), special issue, spring 1983.

Gritly, Ali El, *Twenty-Five Years: An Analytical Study of Economic Policies in Egypt*, Cairo, 1977.

Hafez, Saad, 'The Reflection of the Ruling Class upon the Structure and Direction of Industry in Egypt', *Qadaya Fikreya*, 1985.

Hafez, Salah, 'Merchants' Nationalism', *Rose El Youssef*, no. 2566, August 15, 1977.

———— 'Watergate in Egypt', *Rose El Youssef*, no. 2634, Monday December 4, 1978.

Halliday, Fred, *Arabia without Sultans*, Middlesex, 1975.

Hamdan, Gamal, *The Strategy of Imperialism and Liberation*, Cairo, 1983.

———— *Egypt's Personality: A Study in the Genius of its Location*, Cairo, 1984.

Hanafi, Assem, 'The Legal Immunity of Ministers and the Accusations of the General Prosecutor', *Rose El Youssef*, no. 2551, May 2, 1977.

———— 'The Boeing File', *Rose El Youssef*, no. 2587, January 1, 1978.

Hanna, Milad, *I Want a House Problem which has a Solution*, Cairo, 1978.

Hansen, Bent, and Girgis Marzouk, *Development and Economic Policy in the UAR (Egypt)*, Amsterdam, 1965.

Hassan, Abdel Razek, 'The National Economic Map – Between the Public Sector and Private Sector', *Al Taliah*, no. 6, June 1966.

Hassanein, Midhat, 'Our Foreign Debt – What is the Reality?', *Al Ahram al Iqtissadi*, no. 870, September 1985.

Haykal, Hassanein, *The Autumn of Fury* (in Arabic), Beirut, 1983.

Hilal, Ali El Din, 'National Independence as Strategic Premiss for the 1952 Revolution' in Ali El Din Hilal (ed.), *National Independence*, Cairo, 1982.

Hiltermann, Joost, 'Egypt and America, an Uneasy Embrace', in *The Middle East*, no. 131, September 1985.

Hinnebusch, Raymond A., 'From Nasir to Sadat: Elite Transformation in Egypt', *Journal of South Asian and Middle Eastern Studies*, vol. 7, no. 1, Fall 1983.

———— *Egyptian Politics under Sadat, The Post-populist Development of an Authoritarian–Modernizing State*, Cambridge, 1985.

Hussein, Adel, *The Egyptian Economy from Independence to Dependency 1974–1979*, Part I, Beirut, 1981.

Hussein, Mahmoud, *Class Conflict in Egypt (1945–71)* (New York: Monthly Review Press, 1978).

Ibrahim, Saad Eddin, 'Egypt's Islamic Militants' in *MERIP Reports*, no. 103, vol. 12, no. 2, February 1982.

Ikram, Khalid, *Egypt: Economic Management in a Period of Transition*, a World Bank Country Economic Report, Baltimore and London, 1980.

Imam, Abdallah, *Al Nasseriya* (Beirut: The Arab Nation, 1977).

Imam, Mostafa, 'The Consultancy Market and the Trap of Middle Men', *Al Ahram al Iqtissadi*, no. 635, March 16, 1981.

Issa, Hossam, *Capitalisme et sociétés anonymes en Egypte: Essai sur le rapport entre structure sociale et droit*, Paris, 1970.

Issawi, Charles, 'The Entrepreneur Class', in S. N. Fisher (ed.), *Social Forces in the Middle East*, New York, 1955.

Kaissouny, Abdel Moneim, 'Some Aspects of Foreign Trade in the Southern Region within Half a Century', in *Studies in Honour of the Fiftieth Anniversary of the Egyptian Society for Political Economy Statistics and Legislation*, Cairo, 1960.

Kandil, Amany, 'Decree 119 and the Plight of Economic Policy Making', *Al Ahram al Iqtissadi*, no. 900, April 14, 1986.

Kay, Geoffrey, *Development and Underdevelopment: A Marxist Analysis* London, 1975.

Laclau, Ernesto, *Politics and Ideology in Marxist Theory*, London, 1977.

Lenczowski, George, *Political Elites in the Middle East*, Washington, 1975.

Mabro, Robert, and Radwan, Samir, *The Industrialisation of Egypt 1939–1973*, London, 1976.

McMichael, Philip, Petras, J., and Rhodes, R., 'Imperialism and the Contradictions of Development', *New Left Review*, no. 85, May–June 1974.

Magdoff, Harry, 'The American Empire and the United States Economy', in R. Rhodes (ed.), *Imperialism and Underdevelopment*, 1970.

Mahfouz, Madame El Kosheiry, *Socialisme et pouvoir en Egypte*, Paris, 1972.

Malash, Kamel Amin, *The Encyclopaedia of Companies*, Cairo, 1980.

Maraghy, Mahmoud El, 'Retreat in the Application of Decree 119', *Rose El*

Youssef, no. 2601, April 17, 1978.
———— 'Merchants Declare War on the Government', *Rose El Youssef*, no. 2566, August 15, 1977.
Mead, D. C., *Growth and Structural Change in the Egyptian Economy*, Illinois, 1967.
Messiha, Wahib, 'The Evolution of Egyptian Industry within the Past Fifty Years', in *Studies in Honour of the Fiftieth Anniversary of the Egyptian Society for Political Economy Statistics and Legislation*, Cairo, 1960.
Michalet, Charles Albert, *Le Capitalisme Mondial*, Paris, 1976.
Miliband, Ralph, *The State in Capitalist Society, The Analysis of the Western System of Power*, London, 1973.
Mishriqi, Anis, *The Customs Guide*, Ahram Distribution Department, 1977.
Mitwalli, Mahmoud, *The Historical Origins of Egyptian Capitalism and its Development*, Cairo, 1974.
Montasser, Essam, 'The Housing Sector as a Component in Egypt's Development Planning', in Cairo University/Massachusetts Institute of Technology Seminar: Proceedings seminar on development of new approaches to housing policy and production in Egypt, January, 1973.
Morawetz, David, 'Twenty-Five Years of Economic Development', *Finance and Development* (World Bank/IMF), September, 1977.
Morsi, Fouad, *This Economic Opening*, Cairo, 1976.
———— 'Specific Socialism and Scientific Socialism', in Anouar Abdel Malek, *Contemporary Arab Political Thought*, London, 1982.
O'Brien, Patrick, *The Revolution in Egypt's Economic System, from Private Enterprise to Socialism 1952–1962*, London, 1966.
Othman, Abdel Moneim, 'From the Statistics of the Central Bank: The Real Picture of the New Banks in Egypt', *Al Ahram al Iqtissadi*, no. 545, May 1, 1978.
Petras, James, and Cook, Thomas, 'Politics in a Non-democratic State: The Argentine Industrial Elite', in Petras and Cook (eds.), *Latin America: From Dependence to Revolution*, USA, 1973.
———— 'Class and Politics in the Periphery and the Transition to Socialism', *Review of Radical Political Economics*, 8 (2), 1976.
Poulantzas, Nicos, *Classes in Contemporary Capitalism*, London, 1978.
———— 'The Problem of the Capitalist State', in Robin Blackburn (ed.), *Ideology in Social Science: Readings in Critical Social Theory*, Britain, 1973.
———— *Pouvoir politique et classes sociales*, Paris, 1978.
Radice, H. (ed.), *International Firms and Modern Imperialism*, Middlesex, 1975.
Rey, Pierre Philipe, *Les Alliances de classes*, Paris, 1973.
Rhodes, Robert (ed.), *Imperialism and Underdevelopment*, New York, 1970.
Riad, Hassan, *L'Egypte Nassérienne*, Paris, 1964.
Rifaat, Essam, 'The Mafia in the Real Estate Market', *Al Ahram al Iqtissadi*, no. 584, December 15, 1979.
———— 'The Invisible Hand which Rules the Egyptian Market', *Al Ahram al Iqtissadi*, no. 531, October 1, 1977.
Rifaat, Kamal, 'The Internal Front is the Key to the Situation', *Al Taliah*, no. 1, January 1968.
Rizq, Farouk Awad, 'The Debate of the Week', *Rose El Youssef*, no. 2596, March 1, 1978.
Rose El Youssef, no. 2646, February 22, 1979.

Roushdy, Mohamed, *Economic Development in Egypt*, vol. 2, Cairo, 1972.

Roxborough, Ian, *Theories of Underdevelopment*, London, 1979.

Rudra, Ashok, 'In Search of the Capitalist Farmer', *Economic and Political Weekly*, vol. 7, no. 13, March 31, 1973.

Saad El Din, Ibrahim, 'Parasitical Capitalism – Is it the Essence of the Economic System in the Analyses of the Left in Egypt?', *Al Taliah*, no. 1, January–March 1985.

Sabri, Ali, *The Years of Socialist Transformation and the Evolution of the Five-Year Plan*, Cairo, 1961.

Samad, Abdel, *The Field Marshal's Last Supper*, Cairo, 1979.

Sampson, Anthony, *The Sovereign State of ITT*, Connecticut, 1973.

Sayyid, Mustafa Kamel El, 'The Various Faces of the Semi-Peripheral Capitalist State', *Qadaya Fikriya*, no. 1, July 1985.

Sharkas, Ibrahim Mahmoud, 'The Amereya Project and the Dangerous Effects upon the Egyptian Economy', *Al Ahram al Iqtissadi*, no. 5672, January 15, 1979.

Sharqawi, Gamal, 'A Preliminary Investigation on the Issue of Millionaires', *Qadaya Fikriya*, no. 1, July 1985.

Sirfy, Atteya El, *Seasonal Workers*, Cairo 1975.

Stork, Joe, 'Egypt's Military' in *MERIP Reports*, July–August 1982.

Sutcliffe, B. and Roger Owen (eds.), *Studies in the Theory of Imperialism*, London, 1972.

Tignor, Robert, 'Nationalism, Economic Planning and Development Projects in Interwar Egypt', *The International Journal of African Historical Studies*, X,2 (1977).

———— 'Bank Misr and Foreign Capitalism', *International Journal of Middle East Studies*, 8 (1977).

Tucker, Judith, 'Economic Decay, Political Ferment in Egypt', *MERIP Reports*, no. 65, March 1978, vol. 8, no. 2.

Tucker, Judith and Stork, Joe, 'In the Footsteps of Sadat', *MERIP Reports*, July–August 1982.

Vatikiotis, P. J., 'Some Political Consequences of the 1952 Revolution in Egypt', in P. M. Holt (ed.), *Political and Social Change in Modern Egypt*, London, 1968.

Wassef, Wissa Ceres, 'Problèmes économiques et sociaux', in *L'Egypte d'aujourd'hui: permanence et changements, 1905–1976*, Paris, 1977.

Waterbury, John, 'The Opening: Part I: Egypt's New Look', *American Universities Field Staff Reports*, North Coast African Series, vol. XX, no. 2, June 1975.

———— 'The Opening: Part II: Luring Foreign Capital', ibid., no. 3, June 1975.

———— 'Egypt 1976', ibid., vol. XXI, no. 3 (Arab Republic of Egypt), June 1976.

———— 'Public versus Private in the Egyptian Economy', ibid., vol. XXI, no. 5, June 1976.

World Bank Report no. 931b, *Egyptian Agricultural Development Problems, Constraints and Alternatives* (March 18, 1976. Projects Department, Europe, Middle East and North African regional office).

———— Report no. 1815, *Egypt, Arab Republic of Egypt: Economic Management in a Period of Transition* (6 vols.), vol. 1, November 1977.

———— Report no. 1818, *Egypt, A Survey of a Small Scale Industry*, December 2, 1977.

———— 'Recent Growth Trends in Developing Countries', *Finance and Development*, March 1978.

———— Report no. 3123 EGT, Arab Republic of Egypt, *Domestic Resource Mobilisation and Growth Prospects for the 1980s*, November 3, 1980.

———— Report no. 4136-EGT, 'Arab Republic of Egypt: Issues of Trade Strategy and Investment Planning', January 14, 1983. Document of the World Bank.

Zaki, Ramzi, *The Crises of Foreign Loans: A View from the Third World*, Cairo, 1978.

Zaytoun, Mohaya, 'Towards an Objective Basis for the Determination of the Role of Tourism in the Development of the Egyptian Economy', in *The Strategy of Development in Egypt: The Second Annual Scientific Conference for Egyptian Economists*, Cairo, 1978.

———— 'The Housing Problem in Egypt and Trends for its Further Development', a paper presented to *The Fifth Conference for Egyptian Economists*, Cairo, March 1980.

Unpublished Works

Abdallah, Ismail Sabri, 'Some Socio-economic Changes appearing upon the Egyptian Economy (1974–1984)' (report presented to the research committee of the Tagam'oo Party).

Abdel Khaliq, Goudah, 'The Most Significant Indices of Structural Transformations in the Egyptian Economy with the Open Door Economic Policy: 1971–1977', a paper presented to *The Third Scientific Conference for Egyptian Economists*, sponsored by the Egyptian Society for Political Economy, Statistics and Legislation, March 23–25, 1978.

———— 'Development, Self Reliance and Social Justice', a paper presented to the *Fifth Scientific Conference for Egyptian Economists*, sponsored by the Egyptian Society for Political Economy, Statistics and Legislation, 1980.

Amin, Galal, 'The Economic Opening in Egypt', a paper presented to *The Third Scientific Conference for Egyptian Economists*, Cairo, March 23–25, 1978.

El Issawi, Ibrahim, 'Interconnections between Income Distribution and Economic Growth in the Context of Egypt's Economic Development', a paper discussed by the World Bank, in the Princeton–Egypt Income Distribution Project Conference, Lisbon October 31 to November 3, 1979.

El Sheikh, Fatma, *Housing in Egypt: Some Economic and Technical Aspects*, Institute of National Planning, 1980 Diploma, no. 1935.

Ibrahim, A. Hassan, 'Agricultural Capital Project Analysis Course', in *The Institute of National Planning (U.S.D.A.)* December 15, 1979 to January 31, 1980.

———— 'The Impact of Certain Agricultural Policies on Income Distribution in the Rural Areas' (soon to appear in published form).

Kandil, Amany, 'Interest Groups and the Evolution of the Egyptian Political System', paper delivered to the Symposium on the Egyptian Political System, April 2–3, 1986.

Newspapers

Al Ahram, May 1, 1978.
———— 13 July, 1977.
———— August 22, 1978.
———— October 16, 1978.
———— October 22, 1978.
———— October 23, 1978.
———— October 24, 1978.
———— February 6, 1980.
Al Akhbar, August 11, 1979.
———— August 13, 1979.
———— September 2, 1978.
———— October 15, 1978.
———— October 21,1978.
———— October 22, 1978.
———— October 24, 1978.
———— October 29, 1978.
Guardian, November 24, 1978.

Documents

Al Ahram al Iqtissadi, supplement, September 15, 1978.
———— supplement, January 1, 1980, The Fiscal and Economic Policy of 1980.
AID, 'Congressional Presentation, by FY 1980 Commodity Import Program' (unpublished handout obtained from the American Embassy in Cairo).
————/controller, 'Summary of Economic Assistance to Egypt FY 1975 to 03/31/79' (unpublished Xerox copy obtained from the American Embassy in Cairo).
———— 'Security Supporting Assistance Loan Activity Data, FY' 1977 (unpublished handout obtained from the American Embassy in Cairo).
———— 'Congressional Presentation FY 1980: Egypt' (unpublished handouts obtained from the American Embassy in Cairo).
———— 'CIP Information Sheet', June 30, 1979 (unpublished material obtained from the American Embassy in Cairo).
————/project, 'Egypt Agricultural Mechanisation Project' 263–003 (unpublished material obtained from the Ministry of Agriculture).
———— Regulation I, *Rules and Procedures applicable to Commodity Transactions* (AID Department of State, Washington DC 205 23, 1971).
CIP, *Monthly Summary*, April 30, 1978 (unpublished Xerox sheet obtained from the American Embassy in Cairo).
Central Bank of Egypt, *Annual Report 1976*, p. 26, and *Annual Report 1977*.
Council of Ministers' decree issued on 16 March 1955 for the establishment of the General Union for the Egyptian Chambers of Commerce.
Egypt 1978: The plan and fiscal policy in *Al Ahram al Iqtissadi*, Supplement, January 1978.
Egyptian Central Bank, *Annual Report 1976*, Cairo, 1977.

Egyptian Federation of Industries and Chambers, *The Industrial Directory* (1974), pp. 46–66.

Egyptian National Bank, *The Economic Bulletin*, vol. 33, no. 1, 1980.

General Authority for Investment and Free Zones, *Law no. 43 of 1974*.

Investment and Free Zones Authority, *Facts and Figures* (July 1979).

Law no. 189 (1951) concerning the chambers of commerce as amended by Law no. 303 in 1952, 313 in 1954, 85 in 1956, 153 in 1958 and 12 in 1956.

Law no. 24 (1957) regulating commercial activity obtained from the Ministry of Trade legal publications.

Law no. 43 (1974) concerning the investment of Arab and foreign funds and the free zones as amended by Law no. 32 of 1977, articles 3,6 (General Authority for Investment and Frèe Zones).

Legal publications, *Legislations for 1979, Including Laws Ministerial and Presidential Decrees* (Part II), Cairo, 1979.

Licensing Committee, *Statistics of the Total Value of Imports without Currency Transfers during 1976 and 1977*.

Ministerial decree no. 247 for 1976, *Al Jarida Al Rasmeya, (The Official Journal)*, no. 275, December 5, 1976.

Ministry of Agriculture, Department of Agricultural Foreign Relations – the American branch, 'A Listing of the Research Projects under the U.S. AID PL480' (unpublished material).

Ministry of Agriculture, the Agency of Aqua Culture, 'A Report presented to the Minister on the Achievements made with regard to Fish Farming till August 1979' (unpublished material).

Ministry of Agriculture, 'The Joint Projects between the Egyptian Ministry of Agriculture and the United States Agency for International Development' (unpublished material).

Ministry of Economy and Economic Cooperation, 'Statistics of imports permits for 1977 out of the 1978 budget in free currencies at official rates and a report of the allotted parcels of foreign currency transfers to meet the payment of consumer, investment and intermediate imported commodities for 1977' (unpublished material obtained from the Central Bank of Egypt files).

Ministry of Economy and Economic Cooperation; General Department for Finance, 'Total transfers and letters of credit through banks for the payment of commodity imports 1977' (the report was obtained from the Central Bank of Egypt).

Ministry of Economy and Economic Cooperation –The general administration for the financial budget, 'Financial instalments for the import of intermediate investment and consumer commodities according to the 1977 budget and agreements of the purchasing committees issued from 1/1/1977 to 31/12/77' (unpublished material obtained from the Central Bank Foreign Affairs Department).

Ministry of Economy, Foreign Trade, and Economic Cooperation, Economic Studies Unit, *A Study on Law 43 Investment Policies* (Cairo, December 1979), p. 21 and table 5 in the statistical appendix.

Ministry of Finance circular no. 8, 1978, 'United States Commodity loan funds allocated to the private sector' (unpublished material obtained from the American Embassy in Egypt).

Ministry of Industry and Mineral Resources, *Total private sector exports from*

1/1/1977 to 31/12/1978 (printed statistical handout obtained from the Federation of Egyptian Industries).

Ministry of Information – State Information Service, *The October Working Paper presented by president Mohamed Anouar Al Sadat*, Cairo, April 1974.

Ministry of Trade, the Supreme Council for Foreign Trade, *A Report on the Activities of Foreign Trade Companies in the Field of Imports during 1977 compared with 1976*.

Ministry of Trade and Anis Mishriqi, *The Customs Guide*, Cairo, 1977.

Official Journal, vol. 30 (Bis) A, July 29, 1974.

United Nations Commodity Indexes for the Standard International Trade Classification in its Revised Form (ISIC–UN, New York, 1963).

Unified Decree for Imports and Exports, *Al Ahram al Iqtissadi*, supplement, September 15, 1978.

Index